American Nonviolence

American Nonviolence

The History of an Idea

Ira Chernus

ORBIS BOOKS

Maryknoll, New York 10545

Founded in 1970, Orbis Books endeavors to publish works that enlighten the mind, nourish the spirit, and challenge the conscience. The publishing arm of the Maryknoll Fathers and Brothers, Orbis seeks to explore the global dimensions of the Christian faith and mission, to invite dialogue with diverse cultures and religious traditions, and to serve the cause of reconciliation and peace. The books published reflect the views of their authors and do not represent the official position of the Maryknoll Society. To learn more about Maryknoll and Orbis Books, please visit our website at www.maryknoll.org.

Manufactured in the United States of America.
Manuscript editing and typesetting by Joan Weber Laflamme.

Library of Congress Cataloging-in-Publication Data

Chernus, Ira, 1946–
  American nonviolence : the history of an idea / Ira Chernus.
    p. cm.
  ⌐┌ ┌┌ ┌┌┐┌ ┐ ┌ ┌   ┐ ┌x.
                                    ates—History. I. Title.

For Ann

Contents

Introduction

People commit themselves to nonviolence for many reasons. Some have no objection to violence in principle. They just believe that violence will not succeed in gaining their goals. They may be too few, too poor, or too poorly armed to win a victory by violent means. Some avoid violence for tactical reasons, because they want to embarrass their opponents and get public sympathy for their cause. Some are afraid of getting hurt, or they are too squeamish to see others hurt. Some reject violence because it takes too much energy, or because they do not know how to persuade others to join them in violence. All these people would do violence, if circumstances were different. Their nonviolence may be called the nonviolence of convenience or pragmatic nonviolence. Mahatma Gandhi called it the nonviolence of the weak.

This book is not about those people. It is about people who have committed themselves to principled nonviolence. These are people who might have had the reason, the means, the courage, and the physical and emotional strength to do violence. Yet they freely decided not to do violence under any circumstances. Gandhi called this the nonviolence of the strong.

People commit themselves to principled nonviolence of the strong for many reasons, too. They may be inspired by the courageous example of others. If those others are their friends, the effect is even stronger. If someone is part of a group that commits to nonviolence, group support and the emotional satisfaction it brings can play a big role. Emotions are always part of nonviolence. Sometimes intuition is part of it, too. Some people cannot explain why they are strictly nonviolent; it just feels right to them. Some people just seem naturally inclined to nonviolence.

Then there are people who commit themselves to nonviolence because they think it is reasonable. They consider all sides of the issue, analyze all the alternatives, and conclude that the logical arguments for principled nonviolence are persuasive. This book is about those logical arguments. It is about the most prominent ideas advanced by nonviolence adherents throughout U.S. history.

It would be a mistake to classify people's motives as solely social, or emotional, or intuitive, or rational. All these factors play a part in every person who commits to nonviolence. Perhaps no one can ever say for sure which is predominant. Ideas always play some part, even for those who do not come to nonviolence primarily through logical thought. Everyone in the U.S. nonviolence movement partakes of a rich intellectual tradition. This book offers an introduction to that tradition.

The ideas and ideals of nonviolence cannot be understood as timeless disembodied abstractions. Ideas are products of their time and place. As the following chapters show, ideas of nonviolence are always embedded in a very concrete historical context, and they must be studied in their context. However, since these chapters focus on ideas, they do not give a full picture of the practical impact nonviolence movements have had on U.S. history.

Nonviolence runs, like a thread of alternative thinking and acting, through the fabric of U.S. history. It played a significant role in the Abolitionist movement, the struggle for women's rights, the debates about imperialism and about entering the two world wars, the rise of unions and the struggles for workers' rights, the civil rights movements of African Americans and other minority groups, the antiwar movement of the Vietnam era, the antinuclear movement, the environmental movement, and other historical episodes. From the 1820s to the 1950s, scarcely a decade went by in which a nonviolence movement did not play some significant role in the practical outcome of political, social, and economic events. Since the 1960s, scarcely a day has gone by in which a nonviolence movement did not play a significant role.

The heritage of U.S. nonviolence thought is actually a heritage for the whole world. Its roots go back to the Anabaptist Protestants in central Europe (beginning in the sixteenth century) and to the Quakers in England. But the United States can claim credit for leading the world to a new idea: society can be permanently improved when people band together in organized groups to work actively and nonviolently for social change. Nonviolent social and political movements emerged first among the Quakers in colonial North America and then among the Abolitionists before the Civil War. The idea gradually spread around the world. The great novelist and Christian nonviolence writer Leo Tolstoy was inspired by the writings of the Abolitionists. So was the greatest of all nonviolent activists, Gandhi. The ideas of Tolstoy and Gandhi came back here to the United States, where they inspired many others, who often did not know that ideas they ascribed to Tolstoy and Gandhi had their origin in this country.

Nonviolence movements in the United States have helped to spawn similar movements around the world. From Northern Ireland to Eastern Europe to Burma to the Philippines to Central and South America, people have not only studied but implemented the concepts and techniques of nonviolence pioneered by Americans. Often, they have achieved major improvements in their conditions of life. In the long view of history, the United States is at the center of an ongoing global process of nonviolent social and political change.

This outstanding contribution to world culture is too little honored in its home country. Apart from Henry David Thoreau and Martin Luther King, Jr., few of the great names of the nonviolence tradition are known even to well-educated Americans. How many of us today know anything about the Americans who kept alive the tradition that has inspired activists around the world: men like John Woolman, William Lloyd Garrison, A. J. Muste, and Norman Thomas; women like Elizabeth Cady Stanton, Lucretia Mott, Sojourner Truth, Jane Addams, Barbara Deming, and Dorothy Day?

Nonviolence leaders are easily forgotten, perhaps because their contributions rarely have been recorded in headlines in the mainstream press. Headlines are devoted to the most vivid, immediately arresting deeds of the day. These are often the most bloody deeds. (Journalism students still learn: "If it bleeds, it leads.") Headlines are devoted to the most obviously powerful leaders, those who most visibly shape events. These leaders are usually willing to shed blood to achieve their purposes. Headlines shape our view of the world. They tell us what seems worth remembering. They subtly define what counts as history. In recent years, historians have paid increasing attention to the social history of ordinary people's lives. When it comes to political events and relations among nations, though, historians still tend to focus on the people and events that made headlines. Thus we know and remember the great presidents and generals but not the great peacemakers.

The nonviolence tradition runs quietly, like an underground stream, through U.S. history. Its effects have been less visible than the tradition of war and violence. But its effects may some day prove to be more lasting. A Chinese leader was once asked to assess the effects of the French Revolution. Though it was nearly two hundred years after the event, he wisely replied: "It is too soon to tell." The same may be true of the men and women who led America's nonviolence movements.

The important role of women in the history of nonviolence raises a troubling issue. Nearly all the major figures discussed in this book are men. Women have made huge contributions to the history of nonviolence. The most outstanding among them are mentioned in the following chapters but not discussed in any detail, with the exception of Dorothy Day and Barbara Deming. This reflects the book's focus on the intellectual tradition. Throughout most of the history surveyed here, women were very actively organizing, supporting, and encouraging nonviolence movements and groups in all sorts of ways. However, they were often discouraged from, and sometimes actually barred from, making major contributions to public intellectual life. This is tragic, of course; had women been encouraged they surely could have enriched the tradition greatly. But the sad fact is that women's intellectual efforts were done largely outside of the public limelight. In almost every case, it was men who publicly taught and promoted the leading ideas of nonviolence. Future research may show that these men were benefiting from, though not crediting, ideas developed by women. At present, though, the historical record indicates that women fostered the movement in many different ways but only occasionally played a decisive role in shaping the intellectual tradition.

That situation is changing rapidly. Women are increasingly sharing equally in every role within the nonviolence movement, including an intellectual role. As the idea of nonviolence continues to develop and grow, women are participating fully in fostering that growth. Feminist thought has enriched the idea of nonviolence already and surely will enrich it even more. Recognizing the limits placed on women's influence in the past should challenge men to be more open to and appreciative of the important contributions women are making today and will continue to make in the future.

Most of the great nonviolence leaders in the United States, both men and women, were people of deep religious and moral faith. Most of them came to nonviolence first through their faith, not cerebral analysis. They were preachers more than philosophers. They exhorted people, hoping to sway them by a combination of spiritual conviction, logical ideas, and passionate enthusiasm. They were generally not intellectual theorists who relied strictly on the power of logical ideas. So they usually presented their thinking in rather fragmentary and unsystematic ways, often containing sizeable amounts of contradiction. Their legacy of words allows for many different concepts and interpretations. That is why, in the history of the idea of nonviolence, no single theory has ever dominated. The history has been a process of endless debate and innovation. It has been, in Gandhi's phrase, a continuing experiment with truth.

Even though these leaders did not rely primarily on ideas to lead them to nonviolence, they did have very complex ideas. Far from being fanatics or impulsive extremists (as popular imagination sometimes pictures them), they were people who thought deeply, carefully, and soberly about all the important issues of human life. They could explain patiently why nonviolence was the most reasonable, and perhaps the only, conclusion to be drawn from the facts of life as they understood those facts. To see the full logic behind their ideas of nonviolence, it is necessary to understand their thinking and their view of life in all its complexity.

Therefore, the following chapters reconstruct the logical arguments expressed or implied in each individual's or movement's words. Each chapter explains the individual's or group's basic world view and values and then shows how they led logically to a commitment to nonviolence. Often this means explaining the logic in ways that were never written down or fully articulated. Sometimes it means putting the ideas together in ways that the individual or group never quite achieved, or even attempted. This effort is worthwhile because it shows how the commitment to nonviolence grew from many different intellectual seeds, but always out of a deep soil of ideas. It shows the full richness of the intellectual tradition of nonviolence in the United States.

Although the practice of nonviolence involves far more than logically reasoned ideas, the study of ideas is always valuable. Its value depends on what the reader brings to it. This book is addressed to three kinds of readers. First, it is addressed to those who have no personal commitment to nonviolence and no interest in considering it. This study can broaden and deepen their knowledge of the American cultural heritage. They can also find it a useful intellectual exercise, a way to test and clarify their own ideas, not only about violence but about many other aspects of life. Studying ideas from the past can help us sharpen our thinking, reflect on the nature and bases of our commitments, and refine our goals, our means to them, and the links between means and ends.

This book is also addressed to people who already participate fully in the nonviolence movement. A better understanding of ideas in historical context can support, enhance, and deepen their practice of nonviolence. A focus on the intellectual side of the tradition can serve as a check upon excessive emotion that may lead us astray. It can help us understand and communicate with others. And it can help us discover new ideas. If the nonviolence movement is to move forward vigorously, it must have (among many other qualities) a sophisticated and durable intellectual foundation. No doubt, the idea of nonviolence in the future will be different from anything it has been in the past. But the thinking of the past is a valuable reservoir of ideas, some of which may prove surprisingly relevant in the present and the future. As we try to clarify our views about violence and nonviolence, it is worth going back to those who have pondered the same issues before us. Reinventing the wheel is always wasted effort. Although our predecessors never faced exactly the same problems we or our descendants will face, the problems of the past were often surprisingly similar to those of the present and future. If none of our predecessors failed to come up with formulations that are fully satisfying to us, at least they have seen virtually all the problems that nonviolence thinking must deal with. They have left us a legacy of vigorous mental wrestling with those problems and some insightful, even inspired, solutions to those problems.

Finally, this book is addressed to readers who are not yet committed to nonviolence but are considering it and exploring the role it might play in their lives. They may find that logical reasoning, intellectual exploration, and historical understanding enhance the appeal of nonviolence. At least, it will help them to clarify their own thinking and reach a better informed judgment about it. But reading *about* the great thinkers of nonviolence is no substitute for reading their own words. Most of the following chapters quote extensively from generally available collections of writings. I hope this book will encourage readers to go to the original sources, to read the quotations in their original contexts, and to gain a fuller understanding of their meaning.

In years to come, as in years gone by, a commitment to nonviolence will mean participating in the experiment with truth, carrying on the tradition by exploring and acting upon new ideas, no matter how unsystematic or even contradictory they may be. Those new ideas will be tested, and some will prove themselves worthy, in the lived reality of feeling and action. Although nonviolence needs ideas, it can never thrive on ideas alone. It needs example, community, emotion, and perhaps something more. To appreciate fully and to evaluate the nonviolence tradition, one must get involved in groups and actions promoting social change by nonviolent means. That is the lived reality of the movement. So I also hope this book will encourage readers to go out and meet the nonviolence tradition, not only its original words, but in the flesh and blood of the people who live it from day to day.

I want to acknowledge help I received in writing this book from many students at the University of Colorado at Boulder who took my course in religion and nonviolence. I also had the help of two fine student assistants, Brian Keady and Alexs Thompson. My colleague Robert Lester offered copious helpful comments on the chapter on Gandhi. Robert Ellsberg was a supportive and perceptive editor. I dedicate this book to Ann, who taught me that the heart of nonviolence is love.

1.

The Anabaptists

The idea of nonviolence in the United States has deep roots in Christianity. Before the twentieth century, virtually everyone in the United States who chose the path of nonviolence was a Christian. Such individuals chose that path because they understood it as the truly Christian way of life. Throughout the twentieth century, Christianity continued to be the foundation for most nonviolent individuals and organizations. Although it is certainly possible to live a life of principled nonviolence without being a Christian, it is not possible to understand nonviolence in the United States without understanding its Christian origins.

Christian nonviolence began with the beginnings of Christianity. According to the book of Matthew in the New Testament, Jesus of Nazareth preached nonviolence. In a sermon that Christians call the Sermon on the Mount (chap. 5), he told his followers that good behavior is not enough. They must have perfect love in their hearts, for everyone: "Do not resist an evildoer. If someone strikes you on the right cheek, turn and offer him your left. . . . Love your enemies and pray for those who persecute you. . . . You shall be perfect, as your heavenly Father is perfect." There is no way to know for sure whether Jesus actually said these words. But since the early Middle Ages, the Christian tradition has been unanimous in affirming that he said them and in considering them Sacred Scripture.

Yet that hardly settled the question of the proper Christian attitude toward violence. The question was debated from the religion's earliest days. Some Christians served in the Roman army, for example, whereas others refused on religious grounds. Once Christianity became the official religion of the Roman Empire, most European Christians came to consider violence quite compatible with their religion. After all, the empire was not likely to disband its army. The great theologian Augustine of Hippo, writing in the early fifth century, gave the Roman Catholic Church its classic justifications for violence, which was permitted only under the stringent conditions he laid out. Of course, practice did not always follow theory. Christians committed plenty of violent acts that did not conform to Augustine's rules. But Roman Catholics had no theological basis for ruling out violence completely.

Occasionally, however, small groups arose that did commit themselves to strict nonviolence. Their idea of true Christianity was to return to "primitive Christianity," the religion of Jesus and his disciples. So they tried to live according to Jesus' literal words, as they understood them. That included perfect love and nonviolence. These groups remained rather marginal and had relatively little influence until the great turning point of modern Christianity, the Protestant Reformation.

The Reformation began with the teachings of Martin Luther. In 1517, Luther announced that true Christians do not need to gain God's grace through rituals administered by priests. Many priests had abused their authority, so people were quite ready to listen to Luther's ideas. But he did not base his complaint on the abuses; he did not say priests should behave better and then regain their authority. Rather, he rejected the theoretical basis for the priesthood. Grace comes through faith, he proclaimed. Faith is a direct relationship between the individual Christian and God. Actions or "works," including actions of priests, have nothing to do with it. Therefore, there is no need for priests at all. God's word as recorded in the Bible is the only necessary link between the Christian and God. The Bible alone is sufficient to create and maintain that link, as long as an individual can read the Bible and learn how to interpret it. By understanding the Bible through faith, and living in God's grace, every Christian can know what Christ wants and live a Christlike life.

Luther's teachings set off a storm of new religious ideas and religious movements throughout northern Europe. The 1520s was a decade of immense religious creativity. Among the most radical of the reform movements (that is, those that departed most from Roman Catholicism) were the groups that came to be known as Anabaptists. They initiated a tradition of Christian principled nonviolence that continues to this day. In a very broad sense, the Anabaptists were the source of virtually all Christian nonviolence in Europe and the United States since the sixteenth century. More specifically, the Anabaptists are still the source of particular churches known as the historic peace churches. The best known of these in the United States include the Mennonites, the Hutterites, and the Amish. These churches continue in their commitment to nonviolence, rooted in Anabaptist principles.

Anabaptist Religion

Anabaptism began in Switzerland in 1523. Historians have traced many sources for this movement. But it seems that they all centered on one main issue: a radical commitment to Luther's idea that the Bible is the only source of religious truth. Even more than Luther and other Reformation leaders, the Anabaptists reject any kind of clergy or official religious authority. They believe that every individual reading the Bible is, and should be, free to find the truth. They turn especially to the New Testament to find truth. Unlike some other early Protestant groups, they count the Bible even more important than logical reasoning or direct inspiration from the Holy Spirit. However, they do allow some role for the Spirit (and, to a lesser degree, reason) in finding the correct interpretation of the Bible.

Bible interpretation is the central form of religious experience for Anabaptists. They believe that the truth of the Bible emerges from a process of active cooperation between God and the individual Christian. This idea solves two problems at one time: What is the true way to relate to God? What is the correct source and form of religious authority? For Anabaptists, the answer to both is found in radical individualism. They are convinced that a right relationship with God gives them a new kind of life, free from the authority of priests and traditional institutions. Their radical individualism naturally engenders many disputes about the particulars of belief and practice. Historically, these disputes often led groups to splinter off and create new churches. So it is difficult to make many valid generalizations about Anabaptism. But from the earliest days, Anabaptists seem to have agreed on certain general points.

Anabaptists do not reject every aspect of Roman Catholic tradition. For example, they accept the doctrine of original sin. But they do not believe that the stain of sin can be absolved by a priest's sacramental rituals. It takes a spiritual transformation in the individual, which only God can bring about. When offered God's grace, the person can accept it by confessing his or her sin and receiving the Spirit. But this must be a free and voluntary choice. The Anabaptists teach that all true faith comes from the combination of God's free gift and the individual's free choice. Therefore, it is always wrong—and foolish—to try to coerce others into true faith, because it cannot be done anyway. It is right to combat false religion through preaching and example, but never through force.

For the same reason, Anabaptists argue, it is wrong to baptize an infant, as Roman Catholics do. An infant can make no conscious choice. Since the infant's receiving of the Spirit is not a voluntary act, it cannot be a source of true faith. Only an adult has the full freedom and consciousness to choose to become a genuine Christian. To show their staunch commitment to this belief, the first Anabaptists (who had been baptized in infancy as Catholics) rebaptized one another. Hence their name, Anabaptists, which literally means "rebaptizers," that is, people who are baptized again. For the Anabaptists it is necessary to choose, as an adult, to be reborn. Yet they see baptism not as a sacrament to obtain God's grace but rather as a symbol that they have already received grace.

For Anabaptists, the true Christian church is a community of individuals who have chosen to accept grace, which means accepting Jesus Christ as their savior. Each member is equal to all others, because each is in direct contact with God. Each church is independent of all others, too. Each elects its own leaders. There is no professional clergy and no church hierarchy. In this way they see themselves imitating the original disciples of Jesus, witnessing for their faith and preaching it to others with no formal organization. They believe, as the book of Revelation promises, that Christ will come again to redeem the world. (The earliest Anabaptists generally believed that the Second Coming would be very soon.) But that belief is not as central for most of them as for other radical Reformation movements. Instead, they usually stress their desire to re-create, in their own lives, the primitive church of Jesus and the apostles. Whether they emphasize the future or the past, however, Anabaptists agree on the need for a radical break with the present, a life totally different from the way most people live today.

The first Anabaptists intended to re-create all of Christianity according to their model. Within a very short time, they saw that this was not going to happen. They rapidly changed their focus and began trying to bring individual Christians into their fold. They created what they called gathered churches, meaning that they gather together outside of the mainstream Christian churches. Like most Protestants, Anabaptists reject the idea of having monasteries, where the most devoutly religious people live apart from the ordinary world. But they all commit themselves to being devoutly religious; they try to bring the intense spirituality of the monastery into their daily lives in the world. While some Protestants view the church primarily as an invisible, spiritual entity, Anabaptists stress the visible church, a collection of specific people in a specific place and time. So they are concerned about creating a better social structure in the real history of this world. They aim to create an alternative to the mainstream Protestant religion and to the dominant society, to show in their lives what a better society would look like.

The question is how to do so. The Anabaptists agree with other Protestants that all people are sinners, that the only antidote to sin is God's grace, and that grace can be attained only through faith, not through works. But Anabaptists put special stress on the power of faith to produce good works and a more moral life. Although they agree that no one can ever be perfect, they are guided by the concluding injunction of the Sermon on the Mount: "You shall be perfect, as your heavenly Father is perfect." They strive for perfection; they view their church as the visible body of Christ, which must be, and can be, a "spotless congregation." As one of their greatest early leaders, Meno Simmons, said: "The reborn willfully here sin no more."

Anabaptists claim that, because they have voluntarily chosen to follow Christ as their only authority, they can attain a higher moral level than others. Their ideal is to obey God's commands out of love, not fear of the law or human authorities. Their moral code is based on Christ's commandment to follow his example by showing love and sacrificing for one another. As Anabaptists understand it, that means sacrificing their own selfish desires in favor of serving others. Because they feel called upon always to serve others, they also feel called upon always to be willing to suffer for others. Christ's example of self-sacrifice is their model. So their goal is to choose always to treat other people lovingly. They base their ethics on this ideal of freely choosing the way of love rather than on obedience to an external authority. Their church is intended to be a community based on love relationships, in which harmony is to be the general rule, not the exception.

Anabaptist churches are not free of conflict. In fact, their individualism ensures that they will always have to deal with considerable internal dissension. Because they want their church to be pure, they feel it necessary to impose discipline in their own community. But they must observe the principle that religion cannot be a matter of compulsion or externally imposed authority. So they cannot force anyone to act differently. Therefore, discipline is carried out first through warnings and then through the ban (ostracism). Critics have said that Anabaptists actually use the ban to act out their aggressions indirectly. But in principle, at least, the ban is never supposed to mean withdrawing love. And the community should always be ready to take back banned persons, if they repent.

Anabaptist Nonviolence

This brief sketch has already suggested why Anabaptists are committed to strict nonviolence. There was some debate about this among the earliest Anabaptists. But after a short time, most of them agreed to principled nonviolence, which became the fundamental stand and hallmark of the movement. Taking the New Testament as the source of all truth, they had to accept all of its teachings, including the injunction not to resist evildoers. Trying to imitate the life of Christ, they had to strive to love everyone, including their enemies. Believing that they were living in a state of grace, they felt themselves capable of attaining such a high moral standard. Their ideal was to overcome all traces of sin and selfishness. Since violence is always an effort to impose one's own self and selfish desires on others, it had to be rejected. These are the obvious sources of Anabaptist nonviolence, the ones that adherents to the movement are quick to explain.

Some historians suggest that the sources of nonviolence were more complicated. In 1527, Anabaptist leaders met in the Swiss town of Schleitheim to agree on a statement of principles for their movement, known as the Schleitheim Confession. When it comes to nonviolence, the Schleitheim Confession certainly mentions their desire to imitate Christ's perfect love. But this is a relatively minor theme. The text explains the commitment to nonviolence in the context of a larger principle: separation from the world.[1]

The Confession explains that all of reality is divided into two mutually exclusive categories: "For truly all creatures are in but two classes, good and bad, believing and unbelieving, darkness and light, the world and those who have come out of the world." According to the Confession, the world is mired in sin; therefore it is dark and impure. That is why Anabaptists must reject participation in everything worldly and gather in their own separated, pure communities. Only the believers, who have separated themselves from the world, can "walk in the obedience of faith" and do God's will. God's will is for a life of perfect love.

After explaining all this, the Confession continues that "therefore" Anabaptists must have nothing to do with the state and/or government, because they are manifestations of the sinful world. The principal mark of the state is its constant use of "the sword"—violence—to enforce its laws. Since an Anabaptist may not participate in the state or anything worldly, an Anabaptist may not use the sword or any "unchristian devilish weapons of force." The Confession generalizes from this principle to forbid all forms of violence.

So it seems that the early Anabaptists rejected violence not only in order to live a Christlike life but also to manifest their total rejection of the world and its status quo. They were intent on making everything different in the world, overturning all existing norms. Since the worldly people hated their enemies, the Anabaptists would imitate Christ and love their enemies. Since the worldly people used violence, the Anabaptists would take the opposite route and observe strict nonviolence. Nonviolence and rejection of "the world" were two sides of the same coin; each required the other.

At the same time, of course, they were also signaling their rejection of all external authority. They would not allow any official, whether of church or state, to enforce religious truth. They would accept only the truth that God would give to them through their interpretation of the Bible. In a larger sense, the Anabaptists were rejecting the essence of state authority: its use of violence to impose control over the populace. Their commitment to non-violence reflected their willingness to renounce all efforts at control of others. In rejecting the world, they were rejecting all hierarchical structures of authority in favor of a more egalitarian way of life.

The Schleitheim Confession goes on to say something that may seem contradictory at first: "The sword is ordained by God." In other words, God wants the "magistrates"—the government officials—to use violence. God has appointed the magistrates to "guard and protect the good" people from violence and to punish criminals. He approves of the magistrates' violence, if they use it for these righteous purposes. This is not a contradiction, however, when understood from the Anabaptist point of view. The full text reads: "The sword is ordained by God outside the perfection of Christ." In other words, the world is full of sin, and it will be until the Second Coming of Christ. There is nothing anyone can do to change that. So God, in his mercy, has made sure that some sinners, the magistrates, will use their sin to control the worst excesses of other sinners. But the magistrates are still in the world, the realm of darkness and sin, outside "the perfection of Christ." Thus they are far from where the Anabaptists dwell. The magistrates' "houses and dwellings remain in this world, but the Christians' citizenship is in heaven."

The Confession stresses that Anabaptists, who live "inside the perfection of Christ," must withdraw totally from all sin. This is how Anabaptists interpret the words of Jesus in the New Testament: "Render unto Caesar what is Caesar's and unto God what is God's." There is an absolute opposition between God's will and the worldly government. One must choose between them. The Anabaptist choice is to be gathered out of the world, to have nothing to do with sin, the government, or violence. They also stress that, since true religion must be a totally voluntary matter, the state can neither establish nor enforce rules pertaining to religion.

Although this attitude toward violence is logically consistent, historians suggest that it was actually the product of a complicated historical situation in early Anabaptism. When the movement began, it generally attracted poor peasants and craftspeople. Most of them rarely had any positive experiences with magistrates, so they saw no value in them. Occasionally, though, some were treated well by local officials. In some instances, for a short time, it looked as if their movement might become powerful enough to take over local governments. For these reasons, they were led to say that it was permissible, perhaps even desirable, to obey the government. Some made a compromise and said that it was permissible to be involved with government as long as they did not have to use violence. Yet the Schleitheim Confession shows that the movement as a whole rejected this compromise, because it assumed that anyone involved with government would inevitably end up using, supporting, or at least tolerating violence.

One more factor profoundly affected Anabaptism and its attitude toward violence: massive persecution. When Anabaptism began, governments and upholders of the status quo saw the movement as a serious threat. Perhaps Anabaptists were a threat, for a very short time, when they hoped to get all Christians to accept their radical views. But they very quickly gave up trying to change their society. Their absolute dualism meant that they had no hope of improving society as a whole. They wanted nothing more than to be left alone and to be allowed to preach their message. Once they made this clear, it would seem that there would be no reason to fear or persecute them.

But the early Anabaptists lived in an era of radical social change. There were serious revolutionary movements brewing among the lower classes. Since most Anabaptists came from the lower classes, and they were clearly independent thinkers given to unorthodox views, it was easy enough to suspect them of being somehow associated with revolution. In fact, some of them may have been involved in the 1525 Peasants' Revolt. But once the movement opted for nonviolence, the link between them and revolution was broken. (A few skeptical historians suggest that the Schleitheim Confession's rejection of violence may have been intended as a message to the governments: since Anabaptists would not use violence, they should not be suspected of involvement in revolution, and so should not be victims of antirevolutionary repression.)

The Anabaptists did continue to represent a threat, however, in a more subtle way. European society assumed that a strong state, linked to a single unifying religion, was necessary for social order. The Protestant Reformation challenged the precise nature of state and religion, but few Protestants questioned the basic premise that state and religion had to work together to keep society intact. The Anabaptists did question this premise. They wanted to separate religion from the state and create total freedom of religious choice. In this sense they threatened the foundations of the existing order. So it is understandable that they were persecuted.

Apparently the supporters of the status quo felt extremely threatened, because they subjected the Anabaptists to amazingly fierce persecution. In the movement's early years, every Anabaptist knew that he or she might well be the victim of torture and murder. New Anabaptists understood that they would not, in fact, withdraw physically from the world and its risks. They would join a gathered community that understood itself to be spiritually separated. But they would be expected to go out into the world, to witness, to preach, and thus to risk more persecution. Many Anabaptists ended up as martyrs to their faith. Martyrdom became a major theme in Anabaptism. For a movement dedicated to the imitation of Christ, it was easy to accept and sometimes even glorify martyrdom as the fullest evidence of faith. Martyrdom could be the strongest statement of rejecting the status quo at any cost. It was the ultimate way of withdrawing from the world.

Persecution confirmed the Anabaptists' belief that the world is inherently immoral, that all worldly people act upon their selfish desires and therefore are prone to violence. Since most of the persecutions were organized and carried out by government officials, they also confirmed the belief that magistrates would inevitably use the sword. In the long run, persecution intensified the dualism of the Anabaptists. They translated the moral dualism of good versus evil behavior into the religious dualism of the godly versus the ungodly and faith versus sin. To the Anabaptists, the magistrates and the worldly were not merely people who did evil acts; they were evil in their essence, embodiments of a cosmic principle of evil. This reinforced the Anabaptists' determination to withdraw from everything having to do with the world and its prevailing status quo. The further they withdrew, the more they were persecuted, confirming their dualistic view. This cycle created a physically dangerous but spiritually meaningful and comforting structure for Anabaptist life.

This cycle also confirmed the Anabaptists' commitment to renounce the violence of the world. Necessity—the fact that Anabaptists were powerless and could not fight back effectively—became a virtue. Anabaptists became even more convinced that, although they might have to die for their faith, they could and would never kill, or use any kind of force, even for the sake of God. As thousands died without fighting back, the commitment to nonviolence gave spiritual meaning to persecution and martyrdom.

The powerful example of martyrs dying for their faith may have helped to bring others to Anabaptism. No doubt the example made it easier for others to continue in their faith, despite the risk that they too would become martyrs. But the positive value placed on martyrdom can hardly be the whole explanation for the movement's survival and success amid such dangerous conditions. Its success seems to show that there are always people willing to die for the sake of the truth, people to whom truth matters infinitely. What is most impressive about the Anabaptists is their commitment to die for truth, but never to kill for truth. They made that commitment because they were true to their original impulse of freedom from authority. If all people should be free to find God's truth in their own way, and if that freedom is worth dying for, then all forms of compulsion and coercion must be rejected as contrary to God's will.

The Anabaptists in History

The persecution of the Anabaptists gradually diminished. Their descendants spread around the world and formed the various historic peace churches. Wherever they went, however, they remained socially marginal; they were unconventional people and were treated as such. That hardly surprised them. Their beliefs prepared them to assume that they would be outsiders and to want that status. Why should anyone want to be inside a society that is thoroughly sinful and pervaded by violence? The historic peace churches also assumed that the larger society would remain sinful and violent. Therefore it made no sense to work actively to improve the larger society. In that sense they were politically passive, and many have remained so (though some became more active in the twentieth century). Some interpreters have concluded that Anabaptism is inherently nonpolitical.

Others, though, challenge this view. They say that Anabaptism is essentially a movement of revolt against the status quo and therefore always has a political dimension. Anabaptists are always preaching their message to the world at large, even at the risk of persecution. So they are not fleeing the world. On the contrary, they are challenging the world to look at itself from a new, perhaps more objective perspective. And they are insisting that every individual is free to discover truth and to choose a new path in life. They are making a powerful social and political statement about the nature of authority and the need to take responsibility for one's own truth, regardless of consequences. They are also modeling a way of life that wholly rejects violence. In these ways Anabaptists may be demonstrating a new form of social action. Yet it remains true that the history of nonviolence in the modern Western world began with people who saw little, if any, hope for changing the world through direct political action.

Anabaptists first came to North America in the late seventeenth century. The largest number of early immigrants were Mennonites, who settled in Pennsylvania. The Amish in Pennsylvania were another important group of Anabaptists arrivals. In the nineteenth century other waves of Mennonites came from Switzerland and Russia and settled in the Midwest, along with another Anabaptist group know as the Hutterites. These groups were joined by others that were similar in form, though not technically Anabaptist: the Church of the Brethren (known as Dunkers), the Church of the United Brethren (Moravians), the Schwenckfelders, the Shakers, and others. All of these groups have been called, collectively, the historic peace churches. Until the twentieth century, they generally stayed out of political involvement or movements for social change. Some of them still maintain that strictly apolitical stance today.

All of the historic peace churches held it against their Christian principles to serve as combatants in the armed forces. Until World War I, virtually every recorded act of conscientious objection was grounded in some version of Christianity. The objection was almost always to war in any form. The idea of a "selective" conscientious objector (CO), one refusing to fight in a particular war because it is immoral, was almost unknown. Before the twentieth century, it was always possible for men who were drafted to serve as noncombatants or to hire a substitute. Many chose one of those options. If their conscience did not permit either route, they were typically fined. If they refused to pay, their property was seized instead. Only those already drafted into the service who refused to obey orders were likely to face prison.

In the years through the Civil War the fate of each CO depended much more on the individual whim of people in authority (though the COs would have called it divine Providence) than on the dispassionate application of systemic rules. Indeed, there were few efforts to develop systemic rules until the Civil War, when both sides legislated some relief for COs (more in the North than in the South). During the two world wars, most COs were still members of historic peace churches. By then, there were more formal rules in place to offer them alternative service. But significant numbers served time in prison.

The need to make concrete decisions in wartime raised a virtually endless series of theoretical questions: Can Christians hire someone else to do their killing for them? Can Christians train with the militia, though they would not actually engage in battle? Can they do nonlethal service for the military (building forts, driving wagons, and so forth)? Can they refuse all service but willingly pay the required fine? Can they refuse to pay the fine but willingly give the state their property in place of the fine? Can Christians pay taxes used to support military activities? Can they refuse service to the state but use lethal weapons for immediate self-defense? Can they violate their own conscience and conform to the majority will of their fellow-religionists for the sake of congregational unity?

Such questions were debated widely and thoughtfully in the historic peace churches. Few of the members were religious fanatics who read in their Bible "turn the other cheek" and let it go at that. They were much more likely to explore all the nuances of the issues and come up with every imaginable answer to the questions. Some were quite narrow-minded. But most tended to think the issues through carefully, thoroughly, and independently. Many could see opposing views as equally valid. Sometimes they even recorded their own doubts and changes of opinion.

Because peace churches generally kept a distance from the rest of society, their witness of nonviolence had little effect on the larger society through the early twentieth century. That began to change during the two world wars, when those who were imprisoned came into contact with other jailed COs who were not members of the peace churches. Through this contact, the peace church tradition influenced the other traditions of nonviolence thinking and activism that will be described in this book. By the late twentieth century, many peace church members were actively engaged in using nonviolent means to pursue social change. They became full participants in the broader stream of the nonviolence movement. However, some still kept apart from society and held to nonviolence strictly as a matter of personal spiritual purity.

2.

The Quakers

During the seventeenth century the nonviolence movement developed in new ways, creating a new path that combined the rejection of violence with more active efforts to engage with the larger society and move it in more moral directions, working through the political process. The first people to walk on that new path were members of the Society of Friends, better known as the Quakers. Although the early Quakers had much in common with Anabaptist movements, they were not Anabaptists. One of the things that made them different was precisely their willingness to get involved in social and political issues.

The Quakers began with the preaching and organizing work of George Fox (1624–91). Fox was born in England. At the age of nineteen, he felt a divine call to wander about the country, Bible in hand, preaching a new religious message. The "friends" he gathered about him formed organized communities throughout England. By the time Fox died, the Society of Friends was well known as a somewhat radical but generally highly respected addition to the English religious scene.

The Quakers were not Puritans. However, their movement emerged from the much larger Puritan movement, which was affecting England deeply during Fox's youth. Puritans stressed that religious truth would be found by looking inside oneself and changing one's spiritual state, rather than by obeying external authorities or depending on external behavior. Since Puritans believed that everyone could have access to God's truth, they were more egalitarian than other English Protestants. They believed that God called them to bring God's kingdom on earth by spreading their own religious truth. They hoped to organize all social, cultural, and political forces to advance God's plan for human history. Therefore, they hoped to get control of their nation's political institutions to serve their mission.

The Puritans were strongly opposed by the more conservative religious elements who grouped around the Church of England. In Fox's youth, the

Puritans were suppressed by the church and the government until the Puritans deposed the king and a civil war broke out. Fox agreed with the many Puritans who viewed the political civil war as a manifestation of an eternal cosmic civil war between the forces of God and the forces of the devil. In this dualistic view, the godly forces (manifest in Jesus Christ and the Holy Spirit) represent a cosmic unity that exists beyond all time. The devil's forces are all those fragmented and conflicting aspects of life that exist only within time and history.

Fox's great innovation, which he discovered in his own religious meditations, was the claim that this spiritual civil war is raging within every human being. Good and evil are primarily inner states, he preached. We all have evil within us, which is the source of all our selfish and unloving actions. But everyone also has an "infinite ocean of light and love, which flow over the ocean of darkness."[1] Fox felt he had experienced this inner light and love directly in moments of religious exaltation, and he was trying to lead others to the same experience.

On the basis of this direct experience (which some would call mystical), Fox developed a moral teaching. He said that the only way to overcome the external evils of the world is to overcome inner evil, particularly the tendency to be proud and to follow one's own selfish desires. He called the battle between inner good and evil "the Lamb's War." According to Fox, the way to win the Lamb's War is to follow the inner Light, which is God's Light, and to act in loving ways. God's Light, which is the divine will within oneself, is "a cross to one's own will."[2] True Christians crucify their individual will and let the will of Christ replace it. This is certainly not easy. It requires a long struggle with one's own inner darkness. Those who win this struggle experience a spiritual rebirth. They are still tempted to do evil, but now they find that they can always resist temptation. So they can obey the divine Light perfectly, and this brings them inner peace.

Fox taught that everyone has the inner Light, which reveals itself progressively within each individual. Each of us is at a different stage of moving toward its full truth. Each of us has some truth to guide us in life. Therefore, no one is permanently damned. Anyone and everyone can be a source of truth. If all people have this Light available to them as part of their human nature, then the way to find the truth is not to look outward, not even to read the Bible; although the Bible can be a helpful guide, the ultimate source of all truth, and therefore of all authority, is the inner Light. Truth is found by looking within oneself, where one can always find "that of God in every one."

This all adds up to a radical doctrine of following one's own conscience, which always contains at least a seed of God's truth. Since everyone has "that of God" within, there is no cause for pride or lording it over others.

Everyone should be treated as an equal and a friend. In religious terms, this means doing away with the familiar church hierarchy, the authority of tradition, and the elaborate rituals based on hierarchy and tradition.

In political terms, it means that there can never be any grounds for coercing others. Government officials are fighting the Lamb's War just like everyone else, doing evil but gradually working toward the good. Though they inevitably do sin, they are also capable of doing moral good and justice. But the government should never force people to act against their own conscience. On this basis, Quakers are willing to be loyal citizens as long as the government does not try to force them to violate their consciences.

But their real sense of belonging comes in their own communities, which they call the Meetings of Friends. There, no coercion is allowed. When differences of opinion arise, individuals are expected to test their own conviction of the truth against the "sense of the Meeting." All members of the Meeting wait quietly for an "opening" or "leading" of the Light; that is, they wait until an individual expresses a new thought or feeling that has just arisen within him or her, one which may move the discussion toward some kind of resolution. No votes are taken; all decisions are made by consensus. People who still disagree with the majority may decide to stand aside, to let the decision go forward anyway, so that they will not block consensus. In this way, decisions are made, yet everyone's right to differ is respected. Sometimes the dissidents will not stand aside, and no decision is reached. When there is a resolution of the debate, it is viewed as guidance from the divine Light. Thus the Meeting is a model for the way all differences may be resolved nonviolently.[3]

The earliest Quakers felt compelled to bring their new spiritual path to the wider world. Here is perhaps the greatest difference between Quakers and Anabaptists: the Quakers set out to improve their society. They combined elements of Anabaptist theological belief with elements of the Puritan drive to save the world through political and social change. Like the Puritans, they saw themselves as Christ's army, conquering the world for love and peace and thereby fulfilling God's plan for history. They claimed that when God's plan is fulfilled, at the end of history, all social and political relations will follow the will of God. The early Quakers' turn to politics grew partly from their social makeup. They came from all classes, but their leaders were mostly from the working class. So they were drawn toward the larger movement of socioeconomic leveling that was being supported in many quarters. But the turn to politics was also a logical deduction from their basic beliefs. Since every person has "that of God" within and is on the way to being saved as an individual, it is clear that every society can be saved, which means becoming perfectly free from sin. So it makes sense to apply the spiritual dynamics of individual life to whole societies.

Quakers, therefore, combine their religious beliefs with humanistic ideas of social progress through rational enlightenment. They expect everyone to learn to follow the promptings of conscience and to become progressively more moral. Therefore they bring religion into politics and apply utopian moral standards to political life. But the premise of their political work is that the constantly changing material world can be reshaped by the unchanging values of the spirit. The way to reshape the world is by patient Christian suffering, which means crucifying one's own will to serve the needs of others, in love.

It was not immediately clear to George Fox that his new religious insights demanded strict nonviolence. He developed his new religious community in the midst of the very violent civil war between the Puritans and their foes. Some of the earliest Quakers were strict pacifists (perhaps influenced by Anabaptists). But some, including Fox himself, were more ambiguous on the subject. While the Puritans ruled, the Quakers were not persecuted. So they could have a relatively positive view of government and believe that the government's "sword" can serve justice.

The first theory of Quaker nonviolence was developed by James Naylor in his book *The Lamb's War* (1657). Naylor approached the issue psychologically. He argued that pride, the fundamental sin, leads to anger, which in turn leads to violence. People who succumb to pride are avoiding a basic truth: all evil in the world stems from the evil we each have within ourselves. The way to salvation is to face that truth directly and, through suffering, purge ourselves of pride. Then there will be no reason for, nor possibility of, doing violence to others. But the early Quakers who followed the teaching of nonviolence did not make it a strict principle for all their fellow Quakers. The more basic principle was that every person has some truth. Therefore, those who still use violence must be accepted, as long as they are sincerely following their own conscience. They may be imperfect Christians, but more perfect Christians would rather suffer than impose their will on others who see the Light differently.

Yet in 1661, George Fox and other Quaker leaders wrote a declaration in which they made strict nonviolence a fundamental principle for the entire Society of Friends. Scholars have advanced several theories to explain this change. All relate to the great event of the preceding year: the victory of the traditional Protestants over the Puritans, which brought an end to the brief Puritan rule and restored the English monarchy. Perhaps the Quakers realized that they no longer had any chance to gain political power, and thus they felt free to renounce the violence that government officials must sometimes use. Perhaps they decided that the Puritans' violent revolt had failed to make a lasting change, so they decided that spiritual means were more effective than violence to oppose governments and work for political change. Along with this, they may have been disappointed with the nature of the Puritan government and so turned away from political life. Perhaps (more cynically) they were just trying to avoid repression; they embraced nonviolence to show that the Quaker movement posed no threat to the government. They may even have claimed that they had always been committed to nonviolence, trying to escape charges that they had fought alongside the Puritans in the civil war.

Whatever the reason, after 1661 nonviolence became an article of faith among Quakers. Soon their writers were arguing that violence is always a carnal weapon, motivated by carnal desire. Because Quakers want to bring the world under the rule of spirit, they would use only spiritual weapons. "Fighting in the gospel is turned inward against the lusts, and not outward against the creatures," one of their leaders wrote.[4] The teachings of George Fox made it easy to believe that all outward fighting is an expression of selfish desire and therefore a turning away from the Light, the will of God. Yet this did not send the Quakers out of the political arena, in Anabaptist fashion. They continued to criticize the government when its actions violated their consciences and their sense of truth as revealed by the inner Light.

Quakers in America

Quakers began coming to the New World in 1681, when William Penn (1644–1718), a Quaker aristocrat, received a royal grant of land in the British colonies. Penn was one of the great Quaker peace visionaries. Like some other Quakers of his day, he combined Bible-based belief with rational arguments for a more humane way of life and government. He argued that peace always brings a better life for everyone, materially as well as spiritually. War always costs more than it is worth; good ends can never be gained by bad means. So, in 1693, he offered a famous plan for bringing peace through a parliament of nations *(An Essay toward the Present and Future Peace of Europe)*. He wanted all governments to use kindness, goodness, and charity rather than coercion. Penn believed that it was perfectly realistic to implement such seemingly idealistic political plans, especially if Quakers ran the government. So he established his new colony of Pennsylvania as a "holy experiment" in order to test his belief.

Through the middle of the eighteenth century, the experiment seemed to be a resounding success. Quakers were widely respected for their honesty and efficiency, and many prospered. Within a few decades, economic success became as much a mark of Quaker identity as the nonviolent "peace testimony." Because of their wealth, Quakers were able to keep effective control of Pennsylvania's political life, even when non-Quakers became a majority of the population. The Quakers also followed Penn's injunction to "live together as neighbors and friends" with the Native American people. Pennsylvania had less conflict between natives and immigrant settlers than other colonies.

As subjects of the English king, the Pennsylvania Quakers had some hard decisions to make. Would they pay the taxes the king imposed to finance his wars, which violated the Quaker conscience? Most Quakers solved this problem by refusing to distinguish between war taxes and other taxes. They paid all their taxes in one lump sum. If the king wanted to use some of it for war, that was his responsibility, not theirs. Would they follow the king's command to impose capital punishment, which violated their conscience? Their compromise was to allow capital punishment, but for fewer crimes than was the rule in England; thus they avoided direct conflict with the king. By making such compromises, the Quakers in Pennsylvania were able to go on flourishing. On one issue, though, they were increasingly firm. In the 1680s, Quakers began to oppose slavery, because they recognized that it could continue only through violence. By 1754, the Quaker community was officially opposed to slavery.

Compromise became harder in 1756, when the Seven Years (or French and Indian) War broke out. For the first time, the king demanded direct support for a war through a specific war tax. The Pennsylvania legislature agreed to impose the tax on the people. (This may have been a complex political ploy to strengthen the legislature's power and weaken the English proprietors.) A minority among the Quakers were outraged. They refused to pay the war tax and accepted punishment, hoping that their suffering would prompt the legislators to change their minds.

These dissidents were mostly rural folk, who saw themselves leading a reform movement. Under the influence of the first Great Awakening (a wave of spiritual revivals that swept through all the colonies in the 1730s and 1740s), they stressed individual inner experience as the essence of religion, and they held to a rigid morality. They wanted all Quakers to return to the original simplicity of Quaker life, with stricter obedience to the group's principles and customs, which they were sure reflected God's will. They opposed war because they saw it as a quest for this-worldly goals. There can be no "good" side, they argued, because taking sides in war always means attachment to the things of this world. True Christians desire only to do the will of God. They follow the gospel injunction to love their enemies and therefore refuse to fight.

However, the reformers were not particularly tolerant. The allowed no differences of opinion on fundamental moral issues like war and war taxes. They began to oppose marriage with non-Quakers, which led toward making the Quakers a closed sect. But they did not want to lead Quakers away from social involvements. On the contrary, they still wanted to improve their whole society, which in their view meant bringing religion into every aspect of life.

Yet their methods for improvement no longer included direct political activity. They had seen how easily politics can lead to compromise, which they firmly opposed. So they urged people to trust God, not government. By keeping a critical distance, they expected to do more to improve society. They argued that they could analyze social problems more objectively if they stayed outside of the mainstream. For example, they recognized that the upsurge in violence by Native Americans was caused by oppressive government policies and by clever schemes that whites developed to cheat the Indians. They also saw that poor whites who fought with the Indians on the frontier had been forced there because they could not afford the high rents charged by rich landlords in eastern Pennsylvania.

The reformers' demands became central issues in every Quaker Meeting and soon polarized the Quaker community. Although they were strongly opposed in some quarters, they rapidly gained a dominant voice. They demonstrated their ascendancy during the Revolutionary War, when the community confirmed its strict peace testimony and refused to fight. (In fact, the conservative bent of most Quakers kept them loyal to Britain, fearing that revolution would change the social order too much.) From then on, Quakers tried to avoid conflict by staying out of political life completely. Under the growing influence of the reformers, they moved increasingly out of the social mainstream of the new nation, too. The Quaker community as a whole would not return to political activism until the twentieth century.

John Woolman

The most famous of the eighteenth-century Quaker reformers was John Woolman (1720–72). He attained his greatest fame after he died, when his *Journal* was published and became a minor classic of U.S. literature. During his life, though, he was widely known and influential not because of his writing, but because he set a powerful example of a simple, sincere moral life. He seems to have followed his own dictum: "In the real substance of religion practice doth harmonize with principle."[5] Although Woolman was not a philosopher, his *Journal* and his conversations during his lifetime revealed a fairly consistent underlying religious world view, which combined ideas from Quaker tradition, the Great Awakening religiosity, and Enlightenment humanism. In other words, he took individual conscience, the Bible, and reason as valid and complementary sources of truth.

From these sources, Woolman developed a dualistic understanding of the world similar to that of George Fox. But his focus was somewhat different from Fox's. He was not an innovator offering a new kind of religious experience and truth. Rather, he was a reformer, pained by what he saw as moral lapses in a community that should know better, because it already had the religious experience and truth necessary for a moral life. So he emphasized the need to reshape society in a more moral direction. Woolman held that God has created a moral order in the world, parallel to its natural order. Therefore order, along with unity and eternity, is a mark of the divine. Whatever reflects disorder, multiplicity, and change is of this world and opposed to the divine. Following the inner Light means finding God's truth, conforming to the divine order in the world, and living a life of love. The key to Woolman's thought is the idea that truth and love necessarily imply and evoke each other.

Woolman developed this key idea in ways that were both ancient and modern. The basics of his moral philosophy would have been familiar to almost any Christian thinker of the Middle Ages. Those who follow the spirit of truth care only about inner life, not the outer world. They know the truth: nothing but God is of any value. So they set aside all desire for anything but God. Their "eyes being single to the Lord" (that is, caring about nothing but the Lord), they crucify their own will to obey the inner "Divine Fountain of truth." They suppress their own desires in order to conform to God's moral order. "All the cravings of sense must be governed by a divine principle"; there is an "appearance of right order in their temper and conduct whose passions are fully regulated."[6]

Not all desires are bad, however, in Woolman's view: "Desires arising from a spirit of Truth are pure desires." The goal of life is to have only pure desires: "To labor for an establishment in divine love where the mind is disentangled from the power of darkness is the great business of man's life." Those who act only on pure desires attain an innocence and intellectual happiness that are more satisfying than any sense pleasure. "The true felicity of man in this life, and that which is to come, is in being inwardly united to the fountain of universal love and bliss." "Nothing is more precious than the mind of Truth inwardly manifested." People whose only motive is to obey God have no desire for wealth or personal gain. Because there is a moral order in the universe, goodness is rewarded, but only if done for its own sake, not from a selfish desire to gain the reward.[7]

Once selfishness is overcome, it is possible to love. To love God rather than self is also, necessarily, to love God's created order, "to love him in all his manifestations in the Visible world."[8] Since each of us is part of that single order, it makes no sense to love ourselves more than any other part of creation. True happiness comes from loving God by loving every part of creation equally. Those who truly understand God and human life will devote themselves to universal love. And the more lovingly they act, the more they reinforce their awareness of the world as a single divine order. Just as truth leads to love, so love leads back to truth.

Woolman's *Journal* records his struggle to live this pious kind of life. He wanted to crucify his self, to suffer for all creatures as Christ did: "Every trial was a fresh incitement to give myself up wholly to the service of God." He claimed to discover that selfless love of God leads to a love of all creatures: "As the mind was moved by an inward Principle to Love God as an invisible, Incomprehensible Being, by the same principle it was moved to love him in all his manifestations in the Visible world. . . . A universal love to my fellow creatures increased in me." The less we are caught up in our own selfish desires, the more we can "get a feeling sense of the condition of others." One way Woolman manifested this was in wanting to spend more time among the Native Americans, to "bring me into a nearer sympathy with them."[9]

For Woolman, truth and love combine to shape action. When one follows the "opening of the Light," which is the "power of Truth" manifest in personal conscience, one's actions are motivated by God's will, not one's own will. Therefore, one feels compelled to act in obedience to conscience. Those who care about self will fear others' reactions and therefore refuse to do what they know is right and true. But a selfless person who knows what is right will necessarily do the right. The crucial first step is to search very carefully within oneself for the truth. Woolman lived a life of intense introspection. He felt that he had to justify every act. Once he had a subjective feeling of certainty, which he took to be the voice of conscience, he felt confident that his course was moral, even if it was quite radical (as it often was). He was willing to follow his conscience even when it meant going against the majority of Quakers and destroying the community's unity.

On the basis of this rather traditional moral philosophy, Woolman developed a strikingly modern critique of Quaker society in Pennsylvania (and his native New Jersey). This critique amounted to a rather sophisticated theory of political economy. Wealth, like desire, is not a problem in itself, he argued. In fact, the material improvement that wealth can buy may be good if it is used for moral improvement: "To turn all the treasures we possess into the channel of universal love becomes the business of our lives." "All we possess are the gifts of God. Now in distributing it to others we act as his steward."[10]

At the base of Woolman's economic theory there is a utopian vision. Because there is a divinely created order in the world, he argued, everyone has enough, if everyone takes only what he or she needs. If everyone were motivated by universal love, not love of wealth, all could "live comfortably on honest employments." "Were all superfluities and the desire of outward greatness laid aside and the right use of things universally attended to, such a number of people might be employed in things useful that moderate labour with the blessing of heaven would answer all good purposes . . . and a sufficient number have leisure to attend on proper affairs of civil society."[11] The obvious problem is that too many people take more than they need.

But Woolman went beyond this to see a less obvious problem: "Too small a number of people are employed in things useful; and therefore they, or some of them, are necessitated to labour too hard, while others would want [that is, lack] business to earn their bread were not employments invented which, having no real use, serve only to please the vain mind [of the rich]."[12] He pointed out the direct links between the unjust distribution of labor and resources, and the two social problems that pained him most: slavery and war.

Although Woolman was surely moved by the suffering of the slaves, his attack on slavery was based primarily on what it did to the slaveowner. He asserted that slavery would be morally permissible if there were no selfish motive involve—if it could be done only from a sense of a moral duty and if the slaves were treated with love. In fact, though, he was sure that people owned slaves because they loved wealth, which really meant they loved self and wanted to get more wealth while doing less work. Woolman spoke out loudly against slavery and refused to get any gain from it. Often this meant that he refused the hospitality of slaveowners as he journeyed through the colonies. On some occasions he did seek a compromise to avoid insulting his hosts; he left money with them to be given to the slaves who had served him during his stay. (He never said whether he had any way to know that the money reached the slaves.)

As a Quaker moralist, Woolman opposed the injustice of slavery, but even more he opposed its violence. He argued against the institution not only because it led to violence but because it was coercive, and therefore itself a form of violence. In his political-economic analysis, slavery was part of a larger pattern. Unjust distribution of labor and resources also forced many whites into poverty. Some of them felt compelled to move to the frontier, where land was still free. The pressures they put upon the native people there inevitably led to conflict. Once again, injustice was both a cause and a form of violence.

Woolman's view of violence combined his sharp political-economic insights with an equally sharp and modern psychological analysis. Wealth and property always bring with them a fear of losing that wealth and property, he noted. It seems only logical that one must defend what one has accumulated. This means accumulating the power and the weapons needed for defense. But this concern for defense and power only breeds more anxiety.

The inevitable result of this spiral is conflict and violence. "This is like a Chain, where the end of one link encloses the end of another. . . . Wealth is attended by Power, by which bargains and proceedings contrary to Universal Righteousness are Supported, and here Oppression, carried on with worldly policy and order, clothes itself with the name of Justice, and becomes like a seed of Discord in the soyl. . . . So the seed of War Swells & Sprouts and grows & becomes Strong, till much fruit are ripened."[13] The whole chain begins with selfish desire and the injustice it breeds. But to oppose that injustice with violence only creates more injustice and therefore more violence. There is no way to break the chain as long as one is ensnared in it.

The only way to break the chain, Woolman argued, is by a strict commitment to nonviolence. For him, nonviolence is above all a method for and fruit of self-denial. Those who have renounced worldly desires will have no reason to fight. They do not create ill will in others, so they never provoke conflict. Nor do they have any psychological urge to fight. Living simply, having no wants, they have nothing to lose and therefore nothing to fear. They trust in God under all circumstances. So they are not afraid of anything. Therefore, they feel no need to fight back against the world or anyone in it. If suffering comes, they accept it as God's will, a chance to grow in self-denial and to create more justice and peace.

Perhaps the deepest source of nonviolence, for Woolman, is the peace of mind that comes from following the inner Light. This means having only one desire: to do God's will. When this is the only motive for all actions, the mind is not being pulled in conflicting directions. The result is an "inward unity of heart and spirit." Inward unity gives a sense of a solid, unchanging foundation amid a constantly changing world. So one can be content and enjoy life, no matter what it brings: "Many were the afflictions which attended me, and in great abasement with many tears, my cries were to the Almighty for his gracious and fatherly assistance. . . . Being thus helped to sink down into resignation, I felt a deliverance from that tempest in which I had been sorely exercised, and in calmness of mind went forward, trusting that the Lord, as I faithfully attended to him, would be a counsellor to me in all difficulties." A person who is so calm and contented has no reason to use violence, because violence is always an effort to change the situation for selfish gain. Nonviolence, on the other hand, stems from acceptance of one's own lot (though not of the lot of others who are oppressed). And it reinforces that acceptance: "Heavenly peace is the reward of our labors."[14]

When the Quaker reformers emerged in opposition to the Seven Years War, they based their opposition mainly on the gospel's command to love your enemies. Woolman did not rely heavily on this line of argument. Yet it was certainly implicit in everything he said. Emptying oneself of selfish desire and self-love makes it more possible to love others. The inner Light is the Light of love. Still, Woolman's persistent stress on moral reform led him to use the language of self-denial more than the language of love.

Although Woolman was an energetic social crusader, he never sought to improve society directly through the political system. He spoke to individuals and focused on changing society one person at a time, not on changing social institutions. His main response to institutions was to withdraw from the evil ones, not to use the political system to create new and better ones. When he refused to pay the war tax, he hoped that it might "put men athinking about their own public conduct."[15] But he did not organize an antiwar political party. He merely saw to it that he himself was not directly contributing to the war.

In a remarkable dialogue with a friend in 1758, Woolman anticipated the fundamental issues involved in such an act of civil disobedience. His friend argued that "civil government is an agreement of free men by which they oblige themselves to abide by certain laws as a standard, and to refuse to obey in that case is of like nature as to refuse to do any particular at which we had covenanted [that is, agreed] to do." Woolman clearly understood the force of this argument, but he replied: "If I should unwarily promise to obey the orders of a certain man, or number of men, without any proviso, and he or they command me to assist in doing some great wickedness, I may then see my error in making such promise, and an active obedience in that case would be adding one evil to another; that though by such promise I should be liable to punishment for disobedience, yet to suffer rather than act to me appears most virtuous."[16]

Woolman's primary concern was not political change, but religious virtue. He engaged social and political issues because he wanted to overcome sin, and he defined sin primarily in social and political terms. Institutions like slavery, war, and the unjust economic system were the essence of sin for him. They were also the prevailing forms and principal causes of violence. So he concluded that nonviolence and social reform are necessary to overcome sin. But the ultimate goal is for each individual to overcome the power of sin in order to attain personal salvation. He never claimed that any one religion is the only path to salvation. Since all people have "that of God" within them, there must be truth in all religions: "Sincere upright-hearted people, in Every society that truly love God are accepted of HIM." But love of God means conquering love of self. Only those who prefer "the real good of Mankind universally" to their own selfish good can be saved. Only they can be nonviolent. They must, and inevitably will, be nonviolent.[17]

The *Journal* and the other writings of John Woolman stand out for their literary grace as well as their probing intellect and moral strength. But Woolman could not have developed all of these ideas alone. He is merely

the best-known representative of the whole community of Quaker reformers. His writings show how deeply and subtly this community explored all
the issues related to nonviolence. Even before there was a United States, the
Quaker reformers bequeathed to the nation-to-be a rich legacy of thinking
about nonviolence. After several decades, that legacy would spread beyond
the bounds of the Society of Friends and have a profound impact upon the
entire nation.

3

William Lloyd Garrison
and the Abolitionists

The Quakers' commitment to nonviolence was a well-known, though rather marginal, feature of the U.S. cultural scene in the early nineteenth century. Anabaptist groups were also well established as historic peace churches, though they were smaller and less widely recognized. During the 1820s, a number of factors converged to create, for the first time, a nonviolent movement for social change that was not based in the historic peace churches. Those factors came together around the issue that would soon tear the nation apart: the movement to abolish slavery. Abolitionism was the spark for the first broad-based nonviolence movement in U.S. history. The leader of that movement, and the greatest figure in U.S. nonviolence in the nineteenth century, was William Lloyd Garrison (1805–79).

What was the situation in which Garrison and the Abolitionists emerged? In many ways, it was a crisis of authority. During colonial times, the social elites of each colony had expected, and usually received, deference from their "inferiors." The political rulers had come largely from the social elites. The churches were supported by those elites. And, in most cases, the churches had been officially sanctioned by the political structures of the states. Social, political, and religious authority had been tightly interwoven in the same small group of elite leaders.

The first two decades of the new nation's life saw a slow but steady erosion of that compact authority structure. In the years after 1815, its last vestiges seemed to be rapidly disappearing. The last states that still had official state churches gave up those links. There was a rising movement to extend the vote to more white men (though certainly not to women or people of color). That movement would soon be symbolized by Andrew Jackson, who won the popular vote for president in 1824 and took office after winning the electoral vote in 1828. In economic life, more and more people were gaining wealth by their own efforts rather than by inheriting it. So it was harder and harder to recognize the old, established, "better" families.

This crisis of authority hit hardest in Massachusetts. That state had the strongest tradition of a clearly defined elite wielding political and social control. It also had the strongest tradition of an official state-sponsored church supported by that elite group. Because Massachusetts combined religious, political, and social authority so tightly, it felt most intensely the rising challenges to that traditional structure. It epitomized the cultural change that the whole nation was experiencing and the confusion that it caused for many people. Naturally, it also saw the sharpest responses to that change and confusion.

The Era of Moral Reform

One of the most important responses was a wave of moral reform movements centered in New England and especially in Massachusetts. By the 1820s, devout Christians throughout the nation were following the lead of that state's reformers. Some focused on using the political system to regulate individual behavior by prohibiting alcoholic drink, banning gambling, and imposing stricter laws on sexual behavior. Others bent their energy to improving social institutions like schools, prisons, and mental hospitals, so that they could reform wayward individuals. Some looked at the whole world and worked for peace among nations. All agreed, though, that the way to make people more moral—which meant, to the reformers, more obedient to God's will—was to work for political and social change. Conversely, however, they also agreed that the way to bring political and social change was to make people adopt an inward spirit of morality.

The reformers saw themselves primarily as agents of God trying to overcome the power of sin. Because they focused on sin acted out in antisocial behavior, they also interpreted all social problems as religious problems. They did not see misbehavior as a result of social, political, or economic structures and processes. Those processes were merely the ways in which the misbehavior caused by sin was manifest. So they set out to change society by religiously converting individuals. From this perspective, issues of individual and group behavior were interchangeable. They applied the same moral rules to groups and institutions as to individuals. All had to make the same fundamental choice between God and sin.

The reformers drew on several religious and cultural traditions. Many were descendants of Puritans, who had come to the New World to create a perfect society, one in which each individual worked out his or her own relationship with God, while all agreed to be ruled by God's law. Some were also influenced by the Quaker tradition of reforming society by improving the individual conscience. Yet all had lived through the Second Great Awakening, when a highly evangelical millennialism had swept the nation. Evangelical religion called on every individual to have an intense religious experience that generated voluntary efforts to improve both self and society. Millennialism was the belief that humans should strive to bring about the millennium—to create a society perfectly ordered under God's will. Churches became, more than anything else, voluntary groups to promote evangelical religion, support reform, and thereby bring the kingdom of God on earth.

The reform movements also betrayed secular influences. The increasingly popular Romantic movement stressed a universal feeling of sympathy and love. Even more important was Enlightenment rationalism, which was an old movement that was firmly established by the 1820s. It was a strong basis for the Jacksonian trend toward political and social equality, which bred suspicion of all forms of authority. Although the Christian reformers were influenced by rationalism, they were not always champions of democracy. Many feared that democracy would make "the people" the source of truth. Then truth would constantly change as "the people" changed, and there would always be conflicting truths, which would create social chaos. The reformers were sure that there was an absolute, unchanging truth determined by God. For them, God's truth was the only firm basis for social order.

The ultimate goal of the reform movements was to eradicate sin by making society conform to the will and truth of God (as they were understood by the reformers, of course). When they spoke of God, they imagined a loving but stern father in heaven, far transcending all of creation and demanding perfect obedience from all creatures, an ultimate and all-powerful moral ruler who has provided the moral rules needed to create a perfect social order. Drawing on the Enlightenment, the reformers taught that God's rules are rational. People have the freedom to either obey or disobey God's rules. Any rational, enlightened person will choose obedience.

But, under the influence of the Second Great Awakening, the reformers taught that people are usually quite irrational. All are sinners and need something more than educated minds to make the right choice. They need a direct relationship with God, which was the goal of the many Christian revivals then taking place. Since all the reformers were Christians, and they lived among people who were virtually all Christians, they usually assumed that Christianity defined the only legitimate ways to relate to God. For most of them, being Christian was virtually synonymous with being religious.

So the Enlightenment and the Second Great Awakening combined to persuade the reformers that all people could and would choose to obey God perfectly. As more and more people were led to perfection, the whole society would come under the rule of God and therefore become more orderly. The United States would gradually move toward the perfect order of the millennium. The task they took upon themselves was to turn this ideal into reality.

The moral reform movements that emerged after 1815 were perhaps the most energetic response to the nation's crisis of authority. Although they assumed the freedom of every individual to make moral choices, their teachings implied that true freedom comes from rejecting every human authority and submitting only to the authority of God. Unfettered human freedom would create not only individual sin but social chaos, they argued. Freedom and social order are perfectly compatible, if both are defined as obedience to God. So they adopted an ambiguous attitude toward social and political institutions. On the one hand, they were saying that those institutions compel obedience and therefore limit freedom; real freedom means escaping from their control. On the other hand, they were saying that social and political institutions should be thoroughly reformed. They should be the agencies by which the whole society is brought to true freedom, which means rule by God, the only true authority.

The Abolitionists

For the history of nonviolence and for the history of the United States, the most important of all these reform movements was the movement to abolish slavery. The Abolitionists were certainly moved by sympathy for the slaves' plight. But their overriding motive was to answer the question of authority. Though some might take slavery to be a political question, the Abolitionists addressed it in religious terms. For them, political analysis and true theology were inseparable. Politics and religion were simply two ways of talking about the same reality. Slavery was wrong and had to be abolished, they insisted, because no human being can be lord of another. The only permissible lord of any person is the divine Lord. All of the Abolitionists' words and ideas were based on this foundation.

The most famous of the Abolitionists was the great writer, journalist, and orator William Lloyd Garrison. From the late 1820s to the outbreak of the Civil War in 1861, in an unending stream of articles and speeches, Garrison articulated the creed by which he and his followers lived. Their views on specific issues changed somewhat as time went on, in response to changing historical circumstances. But the underlying foundation of beliefs, articulated most famously by Garrison, remained constant. God is the only legitimate ruler, he declared, and all human life should be a direct response to God. In the founding statement of his famous Abolitionist journal, *The Liberator* (1837), he wrote that it would promote "universal emancipation . . . from the dominion of man, from the thraldom of self, from the government of brute force, from the bondage of sin—and bringing [all people] under the dominion of God, the control of an inward spirit, the government of the law of love, and into the obedience and liberty of Christ." One of Garrison's most influential colleagues, Henry C. Wright, stated the ruling principle even more clearly: "God, and God alone, has a right of dominion over man; and he has never delegated this right to another. . . . Men, women or children never should be subjected, in any kind or degree, to the will of man. . . . A desire to hold dominion over man is rebellion against God."[1]

Human institutions violate this principle, Garrison argued, because they create hierarchies. They set privileged individuals between the ordinary person and God. So the ordinary person is compelled to respond not to the laws of God, but to orders given by some other, more powerful human. The only way to be free of all humanly made rules is to abolish all human government. Moreover, institutions and hierarchies always create boundaries that divide people from one another and prevent universal love. Some divisions and diversity in humanity are good and necessary. "But whenever they are made the boundaries of [that is, whenever they limit] human disinterestedness, friendship, sympathy, honor, patriotism, and love, they are as execrable and destructive as, otherwise, they are beautiful and preservative."[2] For Garrison, there was only one basic boundary that had always to be maintained: the boundary between virtuous faith, which comes from obeying God, and sinful disobedience.

Garrison did not shrink from the logical conclusion to this line of thinking. No group of persons should ever govern or make rules for others. Anarchy is the only way to be free of all humanly made rules and thus the only legitimate political mode for true Christians. Yet this need not lead to social disorder if, once all human rules are swept away, God becomes the ruler of all. In fact, according to Garrison, that is the only path to true order. Once people are committed to obeying God's will, they free themselves from the control of human institutions and their rules. The only control comes from their own free conscience, which ascertains God's will and freely chooses to obey it. That choice allows them to control their own sinful impulses and thus to act in a socially orderly way.

Good Christians rule themselves perfectly. They follow the injunction of the Sermon on the Mount literally; they are perfect as their Father in heaven is perfect. They have perfect freedom to change their behavior, root out all sin, and act with perfect love, as Christ did. So they can be perfectly just and kind in all relationships. True Christians will spontaneously cooperate with one another to create the perfect social order of the millennium. Their society will therefore be anarchic yet perfectly orderly and peaceful.

Was this a realistic vision? Many reformers did not think so. They still accepted the doctrine of original sin, which teaches that sin can be controlled but never fully eliminated in any person. So they spoke only of making things better by increasing self-control, not making things perfect. Garrison rejected this view. He feared that if people believed sin was inevitable, they would make compromises with sin. He argued that if human beings cannot be perfect, then inevitably they must sin. If sin is inevitable, it is no one's fault and no one is responsible for his or her sins. Then efforts at moral reform, including the abolition of slavery, are not only useless but unjustified. So Garrison demanded an uncompromising, absolute moral virtue. He was convinced that his vision and his demands were realistic.

His perfectionism went hand in hand with his absolutism. If perfection is always possible, there is never any reason to compromise on issues of moral truth or to delay doing perfect good until tomorrow. Perfect morality can come as suddenly as the spiritual perfection of a conversion experience in a revival. Moreover, he believed that the ideal of perfection would motivate people to confess their sins and "put on the whole armor of God, that we may be able to stand against the wiles of the devil."[3] Conversely, he contended, the argument that perfection is impossible all too often becomes an excuse for passive acceptance of the evil status quo.

Beyond these logical arguments, Garrison also appealed to his own experience: "I have sacrificed all my national, complexional and local prejudices upon the altar of Christian love, and, breaking down the narrow boundaries of a selfish patriotism, inscribed upon my banner this motto: My country is the world; my countrymen are all mankind." He assumed that if he could do this, so could everyone else. All had to make the same choice between submitting to God as ruler and submitting to some other ruler. So the differences among various groups were ultimately irrelevant. Since all groups, like all individuals, could choose moral perfection, all could learn to cooperate with each other to bring the kingdom of God on earth.[4]

Of course, Garrison recognized that few people were following his example. Most were still "slaves to their own lusts," not to the will of God.[5] Although it was not a theme he spoke of at length, the battle between submission to God and selfish desire underlay much of his thought and language. Indeed, some interpreters have suggested that the most vigorous moral reformers feared their own desires and therefore labeled them sinful. Most reformers recorded some kind of personal religious crisis, which was quite common and socially encouraged in their day. The crisis was typically understood as a battle between the inner forces of God and the devil. One way to resolve that crisis was to feel a divine calling to work for immediate and total abolition of slavery.

Perhaps these "immediatist" Abolitionists were so uncompromising because they were trying to prove to themselves that they had sided with God, that they could be perfectly self-controlled. They seemed to be very concerned about personal sin. Even after joining the movement, they generally continued to be extremely self-observant and self-critical. Perhaps only by demanding immediate perfection could they feel morally fit and worthy to be on the side of God, not the devil. If so, then immediatism was a sign of their particularly strong tendency to see sin in themselves, and therefore in social institutions as well.

Whatever the psychological facts, it is clear that Garrison and the immediatists always focused on issues of social concern. And they always interpreted social and psychological, as well as political, issues in the language of religion. They always linked individual sin to the sin evident in all social institutions. The freedom they expected to gain was, above all, freedom from sin. They were trying to conquer sin in themselves by detaching themselves totally from sinful institutions. As they conquered their own sin in this way, they expected to conquer sin in the world.

Yet it may be that they were seeking another kind of freedom, too. Some historians point out that the reform movements generally appealed to people uncertain about maintaining their social status in the emerging market economy. They tended to support the new pattern, in which all white people were theoretically free to sell their labor to the highest bidder in the open market. Their ideal of self-improvement included the social and economic mobility that was supposed to be available to the self-made individual. Few doubted that individual economic efforts would somehow combine to create social harmony—as long as all maintained strict obedience to God's moral laws. But many of them may have been uncertain about their own ability to succeed economically, or to maintain their sense of self-worth if they did not succeed. Perhaps some took up Abolitionism so fervently to free themselves from doubts about their self-worth and their value to society.

Whatever their underlying socioeconomic motives, they always interpreted these issues in the language of religion. By combining individual religiosity with social processes, Garrison and his followers were following the precedent of the Bible, which they revered as the highest written source of truth. Like the biblical writers, they viewed history as a religious drama, a contest between the godly and the ungodly. They were sure that God was guiding God's people toward the ultimate goal of history, a perfect society. Since they were sure that they were among God's people, they saw themselves as agents of God's plan. And, like so many Christians in the United States, they were sure that their own nation was leading the world toward millennial fulfillment: "Our responsibility is awful, our ability to do good to the whole world unequalled, our influence commanding and prevalent." So they represented themselves as the truest American patriots. In this sense they were trying to redefine the meaning of American identity (though they never made that an explicit goal of their efforts). Garrison praised his followers as the most exemplary Americans: "It is by the victorious power of such examples as they have set . . . that the dominion under the whole heaven is ultimately to be transferred from human authority . . . to Him who is King of kings and Lord of lords."[6]

For Garrison and the movement he led, one evil, towering above all others, blocked the path to God's kingdom in the United States: the enslavement of African Americans. The abolition of slavery was their great passion, the issue that gave concrete meaning and urgency to all of their general principles. Their attack on slavery combined the Quakers' outraged conscience with the emotional intensity of evangelical millennialism. But it was not just the slaveowners who were guilty, according to the Abolitionists. All U.S. whites were guilty, because they tolerated the evil in their midst. Moreover, nearly all whites were guilty of another sin inherent in slavery: racism. Racism is a sin, Abolitionists said, because it places humans in a hierarchy of separate categories, denying the fact of universal brotherhood. The Abolitionists intended to promote a Christian moral revival that would end racism as well as slavery. The immediatists among them were a radical fringe group, not least because they were willing to include blacks as equals in U.S. society—though they wanted blacks to merit inclusion by "improving" themselves, which meant adopting the cultural values of upright white New Englanders.

For Garrison and the immediatists, slavery was the test case that would decide the future of the United States. The choice was apocalyptic. They believed that ending slavery would solve all the nation's problems, including the problem of authority. If slavery could be ended, so could all the institutions blocking the path to the millennium. On the other hand, if slavery continued, it was bound to end in a total slave revolt that would destroy the entire society. So they warned their fellow citizens that they must either repent or be destroyed. This sense of urgency reinforced the message of their perfectionism: abolition must be total and immediate.

Nonviolence

People who became Abolitionists were generally extremists. They believed in an absolute truth that must be rigidly followed. They were not likely to be compromisers. Moreover, since they refused to accord any human being authority over another, they had to allow maximum freedom for the individual conscience: no individual would or should allow another to say how the Bible or true religion should be interpreted. Therefore (like the Anabaptists) their movement was often split by internal disagreements. Some male Abolitionists believed that women should have an equal role in the movement. They pointed to the tremendous contribution made to their movement by women like Elizabeth Cady Stanton, Lucretia Mott, Sojourner Truth, and sisters Angeline and Sarah Grimke. Other men refused to accept such a radical threat to the patriarchal culture. Some Abolitionists were convinced that the only practical way to end slavery was through a slow, gradual program. Others were immediatists, insisting that something as evil as slavery had to be abolished immediately. Because they were the most rigid and extreme in their views, the immediatists were perhaps most likely to fight rather than compromise with other Abolitionists.

One of the issues they split on most divisively was how to fight. Some of them were willing to countenance physical violence in extreme situations. Some rejected violence only because it would alienate potential recruits for their cause. Others, though, rejected violence completely and on principle. They created the first non-Quaker movement for nonviolent social change. They were certainly influenced by the Quakers. Some among them were, in fact, members of a Meeting of Friends. But the nonviolent Abolitionist movement as a whole was separate from the Society of Friends.

Garrison and his followers viewed slavery as the paradigm of all violence. The source of all violence is the desire to rule over others, they argued. That desire leads to coercion, which means violating the rights of another human being. This is a sin, because those rights are God-given. More fundamentally, though, coercion is a sin because any effort to rule over another is an attempt to play God and "usurp the prerogative of Jehovah." Slavery is the epitome of all coercion, they claimed, because it requires humans to play God, to rule over other humans and treat them as objects. "The moment a man claims a right to control the will of a fellow being by physical force, he is at heart a slaveholder," said Henry C. Wright. "All slaveholders do this. They are then hardened invaders of God's prerogative." Under the rule of God, every individual is entitled to be, and must be treated as, a free moral agent. Slavery clearly denies this freedom.[7]

The link between slavery and all forms of coercion means that slavery is intrinsically linked to all other societal institutions. Every effort to usurp God's authority leads to more social disorder; thus it poses a danger to every member of society. When people depend on violence rather than trusting in God, they reinforce the habit of depending on violence and therefore perpetuate the cycle of violence, which perpetuates slavery. On the other hand, if slavery could be ended, then every form of coercion could be ended, and the millennium would soon arrive.

If the goal was to end all forms of coercion, it was obvious that Abolitionists themselves should be the first to renounce coercion. This soon became a central plank in Garrison's moral and social platform. He emphasized that there is no way to achieve a good end by bad means, especially if the goal is moral purity. Since the "wickedness of man" is most evident in coercive deeds, physical violence and coercion can never end that wickedness. It can be overcome only by spiritual weapons: moral suasion and the power of faith and love. That means following the biblical injunction not to resist evil. Because nonresistors accept God as the only ruler, they reject all human efforts at coercion. Their nonresistance shows that they refuse to give others any power over them, neither the power to command nor the power to provoke retaliation: "Non-resistance makes man self-governed. The kingdom of God is within them." In other words, they no longer live by the rules of conventional society, where people behave in an orderly way because they are following commands given by other people. Rather, they control their own impulses only because they are following God's commands, given through the voice of conscience.[8]

Nor are they constrained by the fear of human punishments. Garrison read the Bible to mean that even if threatened, we should not defend ourselves, but rather trust in God to provide safety, "giving ourselves no anxiety as to what may befall us, and resolving, in the strength of the Lord God, calmly and meekly to abide the issue [that is, accept the outcome]." If God is in charge of everything, then God alone must be allowed to determine how things turn out. Nonresistors fear only God, "Him who says—Vengeance is MINE—I will repay."[9]

With no fear or revenge in their hearts, they can love and forgive their enemies. If their love is not returned, and they suffer at the hands of their enemies, they will not use violence "even if their enemies are determined to nail them to the cross with Jesus." Indeed, "they rejoice, inasmuch as they are partakers of Christ's sufferings." By imitating the purifying sufferings of Christ, they can more easily overcome sin: "If we suffer with him, we know that we shall reign with him." Unfortunately, Garrison had more than one chance to put his creed to the test, when he was attacked by angry anti-Abolition mobs. He saw these attacks as chances to help redeem the nation through his own sacrificial efforts. So he did not resist. (He was usually hustled away to safety by his supporters.[10])

Garrison sometimes used rational and humanistic arguments to support nonresistance. He offered historical examples to show that nonresistance could succeed and even keep people safer. He claimed that everyone could understand his very practical message: slavery must be enforced by violence, and violence always creates more violence. Eventually, slavery would provoke the violence of a slave rebellion. That would be God's way of punishing a slaveholding and slavery-tolerating nation. He explained the mob attacks on himself and other Abolitionists as a symbol of the apocalyptic judgment awaiting the whole nation. He also used these attacks as evidence that violence was simply not a practical way to bring about abolition. He hoped that this pragmatic approach would appeal to common people; he wanted his movement to be anti-elitist. As his career progressed, he relied increasingly on rational arguments. He drew heavily on the Enlightenment faith in progress through reason. By 1845, he was saying that reason, as well as the life of Christ, was a more certain source of truth than the literal meaning of the Bible; nonresistance was simply "true in the nature of things."[11]

But reason never provided Garrison's main arguments for nonresistance. He doubted that rational moral persuasion would ever be decisive. The crux of the issue was always faith and sin, the acceptance or rejection of God as the sole authority. The fact that Garrison always used the term *nonresistance*, not *nonviolence*, shows that his central concern was not the violence itself, but authority. Anyone who resists others and tries to coerce them is clearly trying to exercise human authority, and thus refusing God's authority. Anyone who accepts God as the sole authority must renounce all resistance to others and all efforts to coerce them.

Not all Abolitionists agreed on the necessary link between their cause and nonresistance. As they were attacked more often and grew more frustrated, some were willing to resort to violence. The most famous of these was an Illinois newspaper publisher, Elijah Lovejoy. He was fired on by a mob, eventually shot back, and died in the battle. This incident split the Abolitionist movement. Many accepted and even endorsed his action. Among them were members of the American Peace Society, who were dedicated to the elimination of all war. They argued that individual violence in self-defense is a different matter, and therefore acceptable. Others, including Garrison, lamented his death but condemned his use of violence. Garrison suggested that Lovejoy had provoked his fate: "It was not until he forsook this [nonviolent] course, and resorted to carnal weapons . . . that he became a victim to his mistaken sense of duty."[12]

To oppose what he saw as the immoral compromise of the American Peace Society, Garrison formed the New England Nonresistance Society (1838). The NENS, composed of immediatist Abolitionists, brought the same absolutism to the question of violence. It rejected both war and individual violence for the same reasons. It made nonresistance a symbol of the total transformation of society that it hoped to instigate. As Garrison was forced to defend nonresistance even among Abolitionists, he placed increasing stress on it. In his rhetoric it became central to the Abolitionist idea and the basis of all other reforms. (At the same time, though, he still wanted to stay allied with Abolitionists who would use violence. So he usually spoke of nonresistance as if it were a reform separate from the abolition of slavery, in order to minimize his conflicts with other Abolitionists.)

Although he called himself a "nonresistant," Garrison was not at all passive. He was tireless and bitter in opposing slavery, and he urged his followers to use all their energy to do the same. The question was how to fight this righteous battle without any violence. Here he found himself in something of a quandary. He wanted to live a perfectly pure moral life. He viewed his society as steeped in sin. And, like all reformers, he assumed that sin begins within individual hearts, not in the structure of social institutions. The logical thing might be to withdraw from society completely.

But he could not withdraw. Because he focused on sin as it was manifest in social problems, he needed to work for social change and find social solutions. He could not be one of the "come-outers" of his day, who came entirely out of society, like the Anabaptists. Nor could he be a sectarian, like the Quakers. He had to engage with society. And he had to organize an Abolitionist movement if he was to succeed in ending slavery. Ultimately, he was organizing people to conquer sin in the world, as well as in themselves, and thereby to bring the millennium. This required new institutions, as his formation of the NENS showed. In theory, then, he had to reject all institutions; in practice, he had to accept them and work with them.

Government and Politics

This dilemma was most evident in Garrison's views about government and politics. This issue has received more attention than any other from historians and scholars of Abolitionism. It is no wonder that they offer quite different assessments, because Garrison and all the Abolitionists held very complex and sometimes changing opinions. They all saw clearly the problem raised by Anabaptist and Quaker thinkers: Can a Christian ever be involved in government processes at all? Many Abolitionists, generally seen by historians as conservatives, answered yes. They recognized that politics often involves compromise. They were willing to make compromises because they believed that original sin still made moral perfection impossible; gradual improvement was the best one could hope for. They feared that Garrisonian perfectionism, aiming to bring the kingdom of God on earth, would distract people from the political campaign to abolish slavery. To win that campaign, they planned to use the ordinary processes of electoral politics, either by gaining control of one of the existing parties or by founding a new party dedicated to Abolitionism.

Garrison's very different answer was clearly stated in the NENS "Declaration of Sentiments": "We cannot acknowledge allegiance to any human government. . . . We are bound by the laws of a kingdom which is not of this world."[13] Garrison was convinced that government must always be hierarchical, use coercive force, and therefore be unjust. Moreover, politics always involves compromise, which means being imperfect and doing some evil. No nations or power elites "are guided by the example of Christ, in the treatment of enemies: therefore they cannot be agreeable to the will of God," he declared flatly. Governments "are all anti-Christ."[14]

His own government certainly appeared no different to him. The United States was "a fruitless attempt at self-government, totally distinct from the government of God in Jesus Christ." Because the United States was affronting and attacking not only human rights but the will of God, Garrison warned, the nation was preparing its own downfall. By 1844, he had decided that the Constitution was sinful and should not be obeyed, even though this meant the dissolution of the Union. He called for the overthrow of the U.S. government because he was a patriot and believed in America's divinely appointed mission. The millennium was destined to begin here, but the sinful government was blocking its coming. His goal remained the kingdom of God, where there is no sin because "laws are not written upon parchment, but upon the hearts of its subjects."[15]

Yet at times Garrison said that he was not totally opposed to government. He rejected the popular description of his movement as the "no government men." He *did* want government, he insisted—government by God, carried out through God's righteous agents on earth. Always plagued with charges of being an anarchist, he insisted that he did not want to destroy social order but to promote a higher order. He argued that human government, as presently constituted, actually promotes anarchy because it is based on domination and violence. The dominated will always use violence in return to resist domination, so no harmonious order can ever be attained. Nonresistants have the only real antidote to anarchy.

In fact, the Garrisonians feared the specter of anarchy. Therefore, they accepted the need for human government, at least in the present. Like the Anabaptists, they argued that government is a temporary necessity, to punish evil and thereby keep order, until all people learn to obey God alone. In that sense government is God's punishment when "people turn the grace of God into lasciviousness, or make their liberty an occasion for anarchy."[16] Until the perfection of the millennium is attained, government is preferable to anarchy. Garrison hoped that people would increasingly reject the authority of government in order to become perfect. But he advised those who were not yet perfect to obey the government and its laws.

He also insisted that he and his followers would "obey all the requirements of government, except such as we deem contrary to the commands of the gospel; and in no wise resist the operation of law, except by meekly submitting to the penalty of disobedience." Their submission to human law would allay public fear of these radicals and show that "it is impossible for us to be disorderly."[17] Sometimes, he took an even more indulgent view of government. He could call it a preparation for the voluntary moral institutions of the millennial future. He could even say, on occasion, that the spiritually perfected should obey the government because God had created it.

Overall, though, Garrison's writings leave no doubt that human government is a poor substitute for the only truly legitimate government, one run by true Christians in strict obedience to God's rules: "It is better that men should be sober than drunken, and more desirable that they should have even an arbitrary government than that they should live in a state of anarchy. But, to be in a sober condition is not spiritual redemption; neither is any government of man's device to be compared with the government of Christ."[18] Since he was convinced that the governments of his day had nothing to do with redemption, he urged people to have nothing to do with them. They should not hold office, or even vote, to make it clear that no one in government office truly represented them. (He never took definite positions on several other practical issues, such as whether people should pay taxes, register for the draft, or testify in courts.)

How, then, should the Abolitionists work for their goal of ending slavery, which would obviously require new laws and government enforcement? And how should they get governments to cease fighting wars and using violence? They would transform the moral and spiritual conscience of the individual. This had to be done outside the political party structure, Garrison argued. The parties were steeped in sin; they tried to replace individual free will with unthinking party loyalty. No party would have any reason to change its platform unless the moral convictions of the public had changed first. It was only logical, then, to work outside the party structure.

Therefore, instead of party platforms, Garrisonians used independent magazines, speeches, and sermons: "We expect to prevail through the foolishness of preaching. From the press, we shall promulgate our sentiments as widely as practicable. . . . We shall employ lecturers, circulate tracts and publications, form societies and petition our state and national governments."[19] In other words, they planned to use all of the traditional techniques of political lobbies and pressure groups to persuade governments to do the right thing. Yet Garrison did not consider this to be participating in the process of government. He would do his best to change the minds of government officials, but he would not himself be an official. He would do his best to persuade voters to agree with him, but he would not himself cast a vote.

Some historians see Garrison trying to walk a fine but logically consistent line at the very edge of the political process, both inside and outside at the same time. He wanted to remain outside of society's values and language yet be sufficiently inside to use those values and language to change society. Maybe he thought that the millennium was coming so soon that the specific problems of political theory and practice were irrelevant. Maybe his "no government" slogan was only a way of symbolizing the ideal of perfection and criticizing the status quo, not meant to be taken literally as a plan for action. Garrison's many words on the subject make it difficult to come to any firm conclusion. Some historians suggest that he could never quite decide whether all governments are intrinsically sinful and irredeemable, or whether it was just the particular governments he lived under that were run by sinners and therefore should be reformed.

The conservatives of Garrison's day charged that he was caught in a fatal contradiction. He rejected government because of its inherent sinfulness. Did he not admit, then, that the world was steeped in sin? If so, didn't his rejection of all human authority encourage everyone to reject the law, the only thing that held sin in check? Perhaps Garrison himself was stymied by this problem. He saw his own society as immersed in sin, so he had to say that government and law were a necessary solution. But they were a solution to a temporary problem, if, as he believed, U.S. society was traveling the path to millennial perfection. In that case, government and law were barriers in the path; in the long run, they were more the problem than the solution. This was a dilemma that Garrison never fully resolved.

Government was not the only issue on which he was ambiguous. He warned of the danger of control by powerful elites, but he also warned that democracy would become controlled by the mob. He was a religious enthusiast promoting a spiritual revival, but he was clearly influenced by the Enlightenment's rational humanism. Therefore he based his message on both the text of the Bible and the dictates of human reason. He called for a moral reform that depended on individual conversions, but he also campaigned to change basic social structures. He wanted society to make progress through reason, but he also wanted faith that God would soon bring the perfection of the millennium. He wanted to be both separated from and engaged in the historical process of social change.

On most of these issues Garrison tried to find a delicate balance, but often he seems to have ended up confused, or even contradictory. That was not necessarily a weakness in his efforts. He was a journalist, publicist, orator, and organizer, not a philosopher or theologian. He was willing to use whatever arguments worked to promote a particular cause at a particular time. And he was never ambiguous about the cause or about its moral righteousness.

Adin Ballou

Among Garrison's followers and associates, Adin Ballou (1803–90) stands out as the most systematic thinker of the nonviolent Abolitionist movement. His writings analyzed the ideas and practices of nonviolence more philosophically than any other writer of the nineteenth century (which may explain why they were not nearly as widely read as Garrison's). Ballou's argument for nonviolence began with a simple point: everyone must choose either to practice or to abstain from violence. "They who will not be obedient to the law of love, shall bow down under the law of physical force." Among those who practice violence, the more violent will always rule over the others; hierarchy is inevitable. Therefore, "if men will not be governed by God, it is their doom to be enslaved by one another." Yet the enslaved will always resist violently. In the way of violence, there can be no end to the violence, nor can there be any real freedom.[20]

If enough people choose to be governed by God, Ballou contended, their efforts will produce the perfect peace of the kingdom of God on earth. No miraculous divine intervention is needed. Nonresistants are already practicing the virtues of the kingdom. They have the millennium within them: "Let us have the spirit of the millennium, and do the works of the millennium. Then the millennium will have already come." He asked, "Ought not each true Christian's heart be a germ of the millennium? Is not the Kingdom of heaven 'within' and 'among' men?" (Years later the great Russian writer Leo Tolstoy, after reading Ballou's works, would title his most famous book on nonviolence *The Kingdom of God Is within You*.) Ballou reasoned that, if the millennium has to begin within each individual, each person in the present should act as if the era of perfect peace and nonviolence were already here. The means of reaching the millennium cannot contradict the end to be attained.[21]

There is no hope of reaching the millennium, Ballou insisted, as long as the existing system of government prevails in the United States. Violence is woven into the most basic fabric of government. The Constitution requires preparation for war. The government uses violence to enforce the laws. To participate in government in order to reform it is hypocritical, because it means participating in a violent system while professing nonviolence.

Ballou took the "no government" philosophy to its logical extreme by founding a utopian community, separated from society, where people could live out their ideals. At his community, Hopedale, he taught that violence is a learned habit, not a necessary part of human nature. He warned his followers not to assume that something cannot exist, simply because they had never seen it before. Should Africans deny that ice exists, he asked, just because they have never seen it? Is it any more logical to deny that moral perfection is possible, just because we have never seen it? Using arguments like these, Ballou was the first to show that nonviolence could be supported on purely rational grounds, with no religious basis. However, his own commitment was always staunchly rooted in Christianity.

Of course, Ballou recognized that the elimination of all violence would be a long, slow process. That was why he founded Hopedale. He wanted a community where moral purity could flourish. As soon as life was in any way touched by the existing political and social institutions, it would be tainted by their immorality. So he and his followers withdrew, following the logic of the Anabaptists and the historic peace churches. And, like the Anabaptists, they looked to the past and the future. They aimed to re-create the original model of all Christian nonviolence: the early Christian community of New Testament times. At the same time, they saw their community prefiguring the perfectly peaceful society of the millennium.

Yet Ballou was realistic enough to realize that no community in the present could really attain that perfection. A certain amount of social control was necessary even among the best of people. So he offered the members of Hopedale only as much freedom "as is conducive to the general good." Leaders of the community would offer the others "Christian nurture," enforcing rules to guide them gradually toward perfection. There were even moral police, "official servants," who would use "noninjurious force" to persuade misbehaving residents to follow the rules.[22]

The differing emphases of Garrison and Ballou reflect the complexity and diversity of the nonresistant Abolitionists. They failed to achieve harmony, in part, because their ideals appealed to such uncompromising personalities. But there was also a political motive involved. They were consciously trying to avoid making hard choices that might split their movement. One lesson they never learned, yet perhaps taught later generations, is that avoiding hard choices only perpetuates internal tensions that may eventually split the movement even more. The Abolitionist movement was certainly weakened by the schisms that broke out, most notably over violence and over women's rights. The latter issue was perhaps the most damaging of all to the movement's unity.

These schisms weakened Abolitionism in the 1840s, when many factors began converging to move the nation toward a violent resolution of the slavery question. It is useless to speculate whether a strong, united Abolitionist movement might have headed off the Civil War. But it is true that as

Abolitionism weakened, from both internal and external stresses, the idea of a nonviolent end to slavery began to slip away. The numbers of staunchly nonresistant Abolitionists began to dwindle. Still, the movement remained a visible, if weakening, presence on the national scene until war broke out in 1861. Then the movement suffered its greatest defection. William Lloyd Garrison himself, the nation's greatest advocate of nonviolence, declared his support for the Union war effort. With the guns of war raging, he declared, it was time for the voice of nonresistance to be silent, because it could no longer be heard anyway. Most of his followers followed him once more (though some, like Adin Ballou, stuck to their nonresistant commitment).

Why did such uncompromising people finally compromise? When war broke out, it seemed to most of them that violence had become the only way to end slavery. Abolitionism had been their great passion before they committed to strict nonviolence. Now they felt they had to choose between ending slavery and remaining nonviolent. Most made ending slavery their higher priority. Some had committed to nonviolence only because they were persuaded by historical examples that it could achieve their goals. With war raging, that seemed obviously untrue, so they were easily persuaded to endorse violence.

Others acted out of principle—the principle of apocalyptic holy war. They had always seen their Abolitionist efforts as an apocalyptic battle of virtue against sin. They were generally comfortable with the language of holy war. That language was very common on all sides in the Civil War, which further encouraged the Abolitionists to use it too. Since holy warriors see themselves fighting in the service of an absolutely good goal, they tend to permit any means that will help them achieve that goal. For a long time, Garrison and his nonresistants had strictly limited their means. But once war broke out, many could not resist the pressure to allow any violent means that would achieve what they viewed as the final victory of good over evil. Moreover, the nonresistant Abolitionists had never considered the possibility of a limited war, so they had never thought about norms to govern violence in war. Those who decided to permit violence did it, as they did everything else, to the extreme. So they had no basis on which to criticize the unbridled violence of the Civil War. Instead, they accepted the war as God's judgment on a sinful nation.

Perhaps many Abolitionists felt relief when they abandoned their commitment to nonviolence. No doubt they had been frustrated by their lack of success. They were always a socially marginal group. By participating in the war effort, they could end their alienation and feel part of a righteous national community whose "truth was marching on." At times, perhaps out of frustration, Garrison had predicted that God would eventually have to coerce the sinners to end slavery. Now he and others like him could easily believe that the Union armies were doing God's work.

Was Garrison's movement therefore a failure? Although it failed to transform U.S. society as it hoped, it still left an important mark. Some nonresistants stuck to their commitment during and after the Civil War. This remnant continued to keep the ideals alive. The writings of Garrison and Ballou spread around the world, eventually inspiring Tolstoy and Gandhi.

Most important, perhaps, nonresistant Abolitionism served as a sort of laboratory for experimenting with modern nonviolent social change. It was the first movement in U.S. history that combined principled nonviolence with a primary commitment to improving society by resisting a specific social injustice. Perhaps inevitably, it was the first movement to encounter all of the basic problems that later nonviolence movements for social change would encounter. The Garrisonians could never achieve consensus on all of these problems. But in their debates they discovered virtually all the possibilities of nonviolent theory and practice that their heirs would explore. If they could not agree on the answers to the questions that arose, at least they showed later generations what the essential questions were. And perhaps their failure to find consensus was more honest to the complexities of nonviolence than easy answers reached by compromise. Rather than simplifying the issues, they persisted in what Gandhi would later call experimenting with truth. In that sense their movement can be counted a success.

4.

Henry David Thoreau

Henry David Thoreau (1817–62) was one of the great U.S. writers of the nineteenth century and perhaps the greatest of all U.S. nature writers. He is best known as the man who fled from civilization to live alone, with nature, at Walden Pond. His masterpiece, *Walden*, recounts that experience. In the nonviolence tradition, Thoreau is best remembered as the author of the essay "Civil Disobedience." This was the first great declaration of the right and duty to commit civil disobedience, to set the demands of conscience above the demands of the law and the ruling authorities.

At first glance, *Walden* and "Civil Disobedience" seem to be written by two different people: one who wants to escape human society, including its political strife; and one who thinks deeply about political issues and takes strong political stands. This raises the obvious question: Was Thoreau's commitment to civil disobedience, and his political thinking in general, related in any way to his larger philosophy of nature?

Scholars who study Thoreau give different answers. Some see him as an anti-political writer, concerned only with the individual, not with society at large. They claim that he dealt with politics only peripherally, as one of the many ways he found to shape a better self. Others see Thoreau as a full-fledged political and social critic, vitally concerned with the improvement of his society. These different views of Thoreau may depend on which of his writings a scholar studies. Thoreau was a friend and, in some sense, a disciple of Emerson, who said that "a foolish consistency is the hobgoblin of little minds." Thoreau certainly took these words to heart. Even more than most writers in the nonviolence tradition, he made no effort at systematic philosophy. He did not try to fit his thoughts into a single intellectual framework that stayed the same over the years. He wrote whatever he was inspired to write at the moment. Therefore, his ideas were always changing.

Nevertheless, some scholars do find underlying principles that endured throughout Thoreau's mature writings. And some see those principles fitting together in a coherent whole, with political and social concerns an integral part of the overall structure. This approach is especially useful for understanding his commitment to civil disobedience, which was a vital contribution to the idea of nonviolence. So we shall approach Thoreau as a man and a writer who had important and philosophically consistent things to say about every aspect of human life, including the political.

The "Solid Bottom"

All of Thoreau's ideas were rooted in a somewhat vague yet very powerful set of religious convictions. He expressed them best by using Walden Pond, his home for three years, as a metaphor. The pond "was made deep and pure for a symbol," he wrote. "While men believe in the infinite some ponds will be thought to be bottomless." In fact, though, "There is a solid bottom everywhere." In other words, beneath the finite appearances of life there is an infinite, ultimate reality that is the foundation of everything. Ultimate reality is not something set apart from the world; it is the essence of the world and all that is in it.[1]

Everything changes, but the foundation of reality is eternal: "Only great and worthy things have any permanent and absolute existence. . . . Petty fears and petty desires are but the shadow of the reality." Thoreau wanted to be aware at every moment of the great and worthy things: "Time is but the stream I go a-fishing in. I drink at it; but while I drink I see the sandy bottom and detect how shallow it is. Its thin current slides away, but eternity remains."[2]

For Thoreau, the "solid bottom" of reality is actually a dynamic process of spiritual powers, which are "identified with the substance of things, they cannot be separated from them." That process is manifest most clearly in the eternal laws of nature, which were created by God: "Nearest to all things is that power which fashions their being. Next to us the grandest laws are continually being executed." "If we knew all the laws of Nature, we should need only one fact, or the description of one actual phenomenon, to infer all the particular results at that point." "As I stand over the insect crawling amid the pine needles . . . I am reminded of the greater Benefactor and Intelligence that stands over me the human insect." Nature teaches, better than anything else, the interconnectedness of all reality, the spiritual unity of the cosmos.[3]

Thoreau's religious life, which was for him the sum total of his life, was a quest for direct experience of this spiritual process of ultimate reality. He lamented that most people live by what they imagine to be true or what others say is true. That was not good enough for him. He wanted constant, intense contact with that reality. "We are enabled to apprehend at all what is sublime and noble only by the perpetual instilling and drenching of the reality that surrounds us." "A voice said to him—Why do you stay here and live this mean and moiling life, when a glorious existence is possible for you? Those same stars twinkle over other fields than these." His way of experiencing ultimate reality directly and living "a glorious existence" was to live in immediate contact with nature, directly under its laws: "I wanted to live deep and suck all the marrow out of life . . . to walk with the Builder of the universe, if I may."[4]

For Thoreau, the human mind has access to infinite reality. He urged everyone to make the mind a temple, consecrated to the service of the gods. "If I were confined to a corner of a garrett all my days, like a spider, the world would be just as large to me while I had my thoughts about me."[5] To experience reality directly is to know absolute truth. But the quest for absolute reality is not merely an intellectual exercise. It is also an act of moral improvement and purification:

> There is never an instant's truce between virtue and vice. . . . The laws of the universe are not indifferent, but are forever on the side of the most sensitive. . . . We are conscious of an animal in us, which awakens in proportion as our higher nature slumbers. . . . If I knew so wise a man as could teach me purity I would go seek him forthwith. . . . The generative energy which, when we are loose, dissipates and makes us unclean, when we are continent invigorates and inspires us. Chastity is the flowering of man; and what are called Genius, Heroism, Holiness and the like, are but various fruits which succeed it. Man flows at once to God when the channel of purity is open.[6]

Mind is the way to the absolute. This led Thoreau to a principle that was absolutely crucial for him: since every person's mind is different, every person has a unique route to the absolute. Everyone has a unique way to fit into the divine plan. "I would have each one be very careful and find out his own way, and not his father's or his mother's or his neighbor's instead." So he urged everyone to dig always deeper toward the truth: "Be a Columbus to whole new continents and worlds within you, opening new channels, not of trade, but of thought. Every man is the lord of a realm beside which the earthly empire of the Czar is but a petty state. . . . Explore the private sea, the Atlantic and Pacific Ocean of one's own being. . . . Let them wander and scrutinize the outlandish Australians. I have more of God, they more of the road."[7]

Thoreau made this notion the center of his philosophy. If each person's way to truth is different, then each person's path in life must be unique. The

goal of life is to discover and fulfill one's own destiny, not to accept it sec-
ondhand from others: "If a man does not keep pace with his companions,
perhaps it is because he hears a different drummer. Let him step to the
music which he hears, however measured or far away."[8] The only way to
discover the truth of reality is to follow one's own conscience.

The great evil of human life is conformity to the beliefs, values, and behaviors of others. Yet conformity was virtually all that Thoreau saw around
him in Boston and its environs in the 1830s and 1840s. A man expressing
his own opinion was "a phenomenon so rare that I would any day walk ten
miles to observe it."[9] He understood that every society produces social institutions and routines that confine the individual. But he saw conformity
to the rules and routines made by others as the main threat to the independent search for the truth. And he saw political life as a constant spur to
conformity, because it is always a matter of coercion. Yet Thoreau did not
blame political leaders. When they impose their will on the masses, he said,
the fault lies with the masses who let themselves be coerced.

Thoreau added economic to political analysis. He lived at a time when
industrialization and the new market economy were changing every aspect
of life. His main complaint was that the dominance of marketplace thinking
reduced all individual freedom to the economic terms of free enterprise—
the freedom to produce, sell, and buy goods. Therefore, people no longer
understood the real meaning of human freedom. He lamented the "seemingly wealthy, but most terribly impoverished class of all, who have accumulated dross, but know not how to use it, or get rid of it, and thus have
forged their own golden or silver fetters." People were fascinated by the
rapid advances in technology and the freedom it seemed to open up. But
their lives were being narrowed to fit the confines of what technology allowed and demanded: "But lo! Men have become the tools of their tools."
Most people cared only about the trivial and superficial aspects of life related to material goods.[10] Moreover, the luxuries of life were too often produced by systems that depended, somewhere along the line, on slavery or
war.

"Simplify, simplify," was Thoreau's famous prescription. A person who
does not own or use luxuries does not have to depend on the market
economy—and thus can escape its corrupting influence and superficial life.
"The only true America is that country where you are at liberty to pursue
such a mode of life as may enable you to do without these [material luxu-
ries], and where the state does not endeavor to compel you to sustain the
slavery and war and other superfluous expenses which directly or indirectly
result from the use of such things."[11] With enough simplicity, he argued, a
person can become really free, which means free to improve the self morally
and indeed to re-create the self. But he saw little of such freedom in the

people around him. Instead he saw conformity, superficiality, and enslavement to petty things.

The scholars who view Thoreau as a social and political critic say that he went into nature to get a critical distance from society, to be able to question the status quo, and to understand it better. He wanted to be a prophetic critic, to alert society to the gap between its spiritual ideals and the way people really lived. He intended to "brag as lustily as chanticleer in the morning, standing on his roost, if only to wake my neighbors up." He assumed that people are capable of waking up and raising the moral level of their society. He assumed that it is always possible to transcend or go beyond the status quo: "I know of no more encouraging fact than the unquestionable ability of man to elevate his life by conscious endeavor."[12]

The first step in that endeavor is to imagine the highest moral ideals. The second step is to change one's life to move closer to them. As a writer, Thoreau took his role to be both imagining the ideals and encouraging people to strive toward them. The second part was more important than the first. People know what is morally good, he said, but they don't do it. They need courage in order to carry out the needed reforms. They will have that courage if they get the right encouragement. That was his self-appointed task. He went to live at Walden Pond to create an example of a morally independent and responsible citizen. He wanted to prove his point more by the example of his life than by logic. In this sense his life itself became a political statement. At the same time, though, he hoped that his words about nature would provoke a radically new perspective that would lead to radical political change.

For Thoreau, nature was more than a symbol of freedom. It was the very source of freedom. Only by leaving human society, he argued, could he gain direct access to God's cosmic laws, simplify his life, and escape the pressures of conformity. Direct contact with nature made him conscious of his own unique relationship with nature, he said. He could discover processes of nature as they moved through his own self. That made him directly conscious of the spiritual unity of the cosmos. From that perspective of unity, everything has its proper role and value: "Shall I not rejoice also at the abundance of the weeds whose seeds are the granary of the birds?"[13] Nature teaches how to see from a cosmic perspective, not the petty perspective of human utility.

Thoreau felt it necessary to be in constant contact with the wilderness for personal re-creation. But he did not expect to merge into nature. He understood that he remained always a conscious human being, unable to live permanently in the wilderness. He also saw a danger of gaining too much distance from society and cutting himself off from other people. Precisely because of his human consciousness, he always had to know himself as both a part of nature and a "spectator" standing apart from nature. He was not seeking to accept his natural self but to learn from nature to improve his moral self. That meant transcending nature to move closer to the spirit:

> The spirit can for the time pervade and control every member and function of the body and transmute what in form is the grossest sensuality into purity and devotion. . . . He is blessed who is assured that the animal is dying out in him day by day, and the divine being established. . . . Nature is hard to overcome, but she must be overcome. . . . All that he could think of was to practise some new austerity, to let his mind descend into his body and redeem it, and treat himself with ever increasing respect.[14]

Thoreau's ideal was not reverting to nature but creating an ideal blend of nature and civilization. In some ways his ideal was symbolized by the frontier, the place where humans are always meeting and taming the wilderness, but running the risk of imposing too much civilization. So he looked to nature to teach, not how to live outside society, but how to live in a better society. He viewed nature as the best model for a good society. In a good society, all people would be in their natural state, equal and equally innocent. All would relate to one another organically and authentically. Each individual, and the whole society, would show that it is rooted directly in its spiritual grounding. There would be constant diversity and surprise. The eternal laws of nature offer a symbol for the eternal laws of human justice. Just as there is rebirth in nature, so there is always hope for better justice in the future.

Civil Disobedience

Thoreau was not a pure nature mystic, as he is sometimes pictured. He had a clear grasp of social and political facts. He understood that people live in groups, that every group is shaped by power relationships, and that these relationships create historical and social structures, which become the human environment. (For example, he was acutely aware of the history of white-Indian relationships as the context for all human experience in the United States.) His close contact with nature showed him all the more clearly that human institutions and human categories are artificially constructed. And his life in society showed him that humanly constructed institutions, especially law and government, always demand compliance and conformity. So any obedience to the law tends to diminish individuals' freedom to follow their own conscience.

This is especially harmful to individual integrity when the law is obviously immoral. In 1846, the law said that Thoreau had to pay taxes that would go, in part, to support the U.S. war against Mexico and, in part, to support a judicial system that countenanced slavery. Thoreau refused. He was taken to jail. The next day he was bailed out (though not at his request). But the story of his night in jail became the basis for his great political essay, "Civil Disobedience."

"Civil Disobedience" begins with an approving nod to the Garrisonian "no-government men": "That government is best which governs not at all; and when men are prepared for it, that will be the kind of government which they will have."[15] Thoreau compares the existing bases of government, the U.S. Constitution and the Bible, to ponds on a mountainside. For those who cannot go any further up the mountain, he says, it is fine to stop there, that is, to make these the guiding rules of their lives. But he encourages his readers to find the streams that feed these ponds and follow them further up to their source, that is, to seek their own direct encounter with the divine or the absolute reality from which all human laws claim to derive.

Of course, each person has a unique way to discover that source. So he ends the essay with a prophetic vision of a state that treats all people justly and allows some to "live aloof from it, not meddling with it, nor embraced by," but simply fulfilling "the duties of neighbors and fellow-men." That state would be merely a stepping stone, however, preparing the way for "a still more perfect and glorious State, which also I have imagined, but not yet anywhere seen."[16] In this "glorious" state, there would be no need for government at all. People would fall away from the state like ripe fruit falling off of a tree. Every person would be in direct contact with absolute reality and the divine laws of nature. Rather than worrying about what the arbitrary, humanly made law demands, each person would worry only about what is morally right, what God demands. The "glorious" state could safely give all individuals full freedom to follow their individual conscience and march to their own drummer. Thus the essay ends as it begins, with a clear statement of the author's political ideal: enlightened anarchy.

The way to move society toward the "glorious" state of anarchy is to begin to live freely now. That is the only way to true justice, Thoreau implies. Justice means obedience to God's eternal laws, not to the temporal laws enforced by government. A sane person will often oppose "what are deemed 'the most sacred laws of society,' through obedience to yet more sacred laws. . . . the laws of his being, which will never be one of opposition to a just government, if he should chance to meet with such."[17] He made this point especially clear in 1854, when Massachusetts courts enforced the Fugitive Slave Law and sent a runaway slave back to slavery in the South.

Slavery, he argued, was permissible under the current human laws of the United States, but never under God's laws:

> In important moral and vital questions, like this, it is just as imperti-
> nent to ask whether a law is constitutional or not, as to ask whether it
> is profitable or not. . . . The question is . . . whether you will now, for
> once and at last, serve God . . . by obeying that eternal and only just
> Constitution which He, and not any Jefferson or Adams, has written
> in your being. . . . The law will never make men free. It is men who
> have to make the law free. . . . Whoever has discerned truth has re-
> ceived his commission from a higher source than the chiefest judge in
> the world who can discern only law. He finds himself constituted judge
> of the judge.[18]

Of course, for Thoreau, no person can tell another what God's law is; individuals must discover that on their own. Justice therefore requires personal responsibility. And it leads not to uniformity or conformity but to infinite diversity. Consistent with that view, he also argues against any form of state involvement with religion. No one can make another person religious by coercion or threat of punishment. Shared religious or moral values will enhance community only if they are adopted voluntarily.

Since justice, not obedience to the state's law, is the duty that each person must fulfill, there is only one possible conclusion: "Let each inhabitant of the State dissolve his union with her, as long as she delays to do her duty."[19] Much of "Civil Disobedience" is a lament that, in the present, so few people are courageous enough to take that step, to judge the state and its laws independently. Most people think that merely by voting once a year they fulfill their responsibility to the body politic. Yet, for Thoreau, this is not an act of conscience but a way to evade the voice of conscience. The same people will accept the outcome of the election, even if it means continuing the moral horror of slavery or paying taxes to support an immoral war. The only way to be genuinely responsible, free, and human is to follow one's own conscience. That means refusing to participate in such a government, regardless of the consequences. If enough people refuse to obey a law, the government will not be able to enforce that law. Civil disobedience can "clog the machinery" of the state if enough people press against it with their whole weight. "Let your life be a counter friction to stop the machine," he urged.[20]

However, Thoreau was not primarily interested in the tactics of civil disobedience. In fact, he did not even offer a detailed, generalizable philosophy of civil disobedience. As one scholar has put it, he "was less concerned to articulate the conditions under which disobedience would be legitimate than he was to explore those conditions under which one could render one-self capable of disobedience."[21] His whole life was a search for genuine independence, so that he could find his own way to absolute reality. And only when one is capable of civil disobedience, he concluded, can one be really free. Civil disobedience is both the route to and the result of detaching oneself from subservience to the state.

So Thoreau went to jail mainly to demonstrate his moral freedom and to raise the level of his own moral being, not to change government policies or social institutions. Indeed, his night in jail was a concrete symbol of his withdrawal from the conventional political and social process. That, in turn, was a symbol of his conclusion that the system could not be changed from within. He criticized reformers who wanted to "meddle with the exposed roots of innocent institutions rather than with their own." "There are a thousand hacking at the branches of evil to one who is striking at the root."[22] He feared institutional reformers as agents of conformity, trying to tell other people how to live their lives. He urged social reformers to change them-selves rather than trying to change him. In this respect he was a typical man of his times, pursuing social change primarily through the reform of indi-vidual souls, not societal institutions.

In this, as in all other areas, Thoreau's guiding principle was fidelity to conscience: everyone should do whatever he or she really wants to do most sincerely. So he had to say that it was all right for reformers to try to change society, if that is their genuine calling in life, though he made it clear that it was not his calling. And he acknowledged that social improvements might come from following conscience. One man expressing his own opinion "amounted to the re-origination of many of the institutions of society." With these words Thoreau acknowledged that, as a writer and lecturer, he was inevitably engaged in affecting society. No doubt he knew that some writers have a powerful political impact precisely because they reject con-ventional political language and categories.[23]

Eventually he admitted that he could not totally withdraw from the po-litical and social reform process. When Massachusetts returned the run-away slave, he concluded that the state's enforcement of slavery diminished everyone's life, including his own: "I had foolishly thought that I might manage to live here, minding my private affairs, and forget [the state and its government]. It has interrupted me and every man on his onward and up-ward path. . . . Who can be serene in a country where both the rulers and the ruled are without principle? The remembrance of my country spoils my walk."[24]

But no matter how much a writer may improve society, Thoreau insisted that this should not be the goal. In fact, he thought it best to be uncon-scious of the good results that come from one's own behavior. "The true husbandman will cease from anxiety . . . and finish his labor with every day, relinquishing all claim to the produce of his fields, and sacrificing in his mind not only his first but his last fruits also." (This idea may well have been drawn from his favorite reading: "In the morning I bathe my intellect in the stupendous and cosmogonical philosophy of the Bhagvat-Geeta . . . in comparison with which our modern world and its literature seem puny and trivial.")[25]

Although he had no interest in changing institutions, Thoreau was determined not to participate in bad institutions. The same reasons that led him to withdraw from society led him, even more strongly, to withdraw from what he saw as the most evil practices of society. This is the part of his thinking that led him directly to civil disobedience, and hence into the history of nonviolence.

It is important to recognize, however, that Thoreau never actually embraced the principle of nonviolence. It is better to shed blood, he argued, than to have a bleeding conscience: "Show me a free state, and a court truly of justice, and I will fight for them, if need be." When John Brown and his men took up arms against slavery, Thoreau called their assault at Harper's Ferry "a brave and humane deed." "I shall not be forward to think him mistaken who quickest succeeds to liberate the slaves," he explained. "I do not wish to kill nor to be killed, but I can foresee circumstances in which both these things would be by me unavoidable. . . . For once the Sharps rifles and the revolver were employed in a righteous cause."[26]

It may seem ironic that, years later, nonviolent activists would make Thoreau one of their heroes. Yet it was quite logical. Once the nonviolence movement decided to move beyond the nonresistants' "foolishness of preaching" to a more active stance of resisting injustice, the movement needed a weapon that was powerful yet not violent. By developing the idea of civil disobedience, and justifying it in stunning prose, Thoreau provided that weapon.

The real irony is that Thoreau would inspire so many thousands who were fervently committed to social change, although he himself doubted the usefulness of their efforts and certainly had higher priorities on his own agenda. Yet there was a tension in his work between the self-absorbed nature mystic, with no responsibility for social change, and the politically conscious responsible citizen, committed to social change. As a writer, he wanted to use that tension wake up his neighbors and prod the whole society toward fulfilling its highest ideals.

Perhaps inadvertently, he discovered how to bridge the tension and make it a creative force for social change. Acting consistently as a mystic with no desire to change society, he refused to participate in a bad system. As he and many others after him discovered, if enough people refused to participate, they would "clog the machinery" of the system. And that itself could be the most effective way to change society for the better. Even if Thoreau despaired of his neighbors, he hoped to make their descendants better citizens, able to create a better society by freeing themselves from unquestioning obedience to the system.

5.

The Anarchists

Anarchism is not a single idea or a single movement. The word refers to a loosely related network of ideas and movements that emerged during the nineteenth and twentieth centuries. Anarchists have all agreed that humans would be better of without the rule of any state government or centralized political power. But they have never agreed on exactly how and why humans would be better off, or what should follow the overthrow of the centralized state. It is hardly surprising that the anarchist movements have no clear structure that defines them or holds them together. After all, the word *anarchy* means "without any foundational structure." Anarchists are the most radical of individualists. So they are bound to go off in many different directions.

One of the issues anarchists have disagreed about is violence. Some have espoused principled nonviolence; most have not. But anarchism has an important place in the history of the idea of nonviolence, because its views on authority, social change, and direct action for change exerted a sizeable influence on the principled nonviolence tradition in the United States. Because anarchism is such a varied and vaguely defined trend, any attempt to summarize it must be rather tentative and subjective. Every interpreter will describe the movement somewhat differently. This chapter offers one interpretation of the main ideas that most anarchists have shared, as well as some of the important differences among them.

The Human Condition: Possibilities and Impediments

Anarchism centers on two basic beliefs. First, every individual human being is entitled to full freedom and dignity, simply by virtue of being human. Second, because we human beings are natural creatures, freedom means the unfettered flow of natural forces within and among us. Most anarchist thought emerges from the interplay between two ideals: the desire for maximum individual freedom and the desire to live according to nature.

For anarchists, a society is only the sum of the individuals who live in that society. Society has no separate existence or effects apart from the actions of individuals. So the idea that we should limit our freedom to abide by society's rules or to protect society's interests is spurious. It rests on the false premise that there is a "society" existing apart from and above the individuals who make up society. Since there is nothing but individuals, maximum individual freedom is the only logical ideal.

This does not mean that individuals should act purely randomly or chaotically. Rather, it is a call to follow the dictates of nature. Human life, like every other form of life, is a flow of creative energy that follows natural laws. True freedom means being free to develop organically by the laws of nature. By studying nature, we can learn the values that should guide human society.

What do anarchists see when they look at nature? According to an anarchist's view, nature is organic. All its parts are interconnected and constantly interacting, so each part influences all the others. Nature is spontaneous. It changes constantly, and the changes emerge naturally from the ever-changing interactions among its parts; the changes are never forced or commanded from above. Because it is organic and spontaneous, nature is diverse. Its changes are constantly producing new forms and ever greater variety; any attempt to stifle that diversity stifles the flow of life itself. Nature is cooperative. Contrary to the popular Darwinian view, anarchists believe that cooperation and not competition drives evolution; every individual creature naturally acts to promote the good of the whole species and the whole ecosystem. This cooperation, like everything else in nature, is spontaneous, not commanded by a central authority. Yet the result is not chaos. When individuals are totally free, they spontaneously create the forms of order that are best for them. So there is no conflict between the individual and the group; what is best for one is best for all.

According to anarchists, these qualities of nature can be applied to human society. When a society is organic, spontaneous, diverse, and cooperative, it is not only most rational but also happiest. To prove this, however, we must break down the huge groupings and institutions most of us live under today. We must live and work in small groups, where each individual can participate in making all the decisions that shape his or her life. In such small groups, the norms come from direct, face-to-face relationships. There is no central authority, so all actions can be voluntary. Everyone can see that the group is an organism in which every individual's acts affect all the others. So it is constantly evolving as its constituent members evolve. Therefore diversity flourishes. Everyone can see that what benefits one benefits all. There is no attempt to enforce one person's good over another's. There-fore cooperation flourishes.

Cooperation extends beyond the small group. Groups can relate to each other in the same way that individuals interact: naturally, freely, and spontaneously. When two groups can help each other, they will naturally form mutually helpful connections. On some occasions those connections may become relatively permanent, so that the union of two or more groups forms a larger group. That larger group may then link up with other larger groups, if it seems natural and mutually beneficial to do so. But these conjoined groups do not create centralized organizations or administrative structures that become ends in themselves. Their connections are not permanently institutionalized or legally binding. They last as long as they are needed to get something done that needs to be done.

In an anarchist community, as in any other, there is work that must be done. But work takes on a whole new meaning. It is not a way to get rich and accumulate material goods, to get power over others, or to exploit nature. Neither is work a way to change the world. Anarchists do not want to change the world, they simply want to be free to live in it. The only goal of their work is to meet basic human needs. But it turns out that relatively few hours of work are needed for that. Beyond basic needs, work is not goal-oriented at all. Rather, it is a spontaneous expression of each person's unique creative impulses. People work because it feels good, because they enjoy it, because they are doing or creating something intrinsically valuable to them.

If it is all so natural and seemingly easy, why don't we already live this way? Anarchists have nearly always agreed that the primary problem is centralized political authority, especially as it is embodied in the modern nation-state. The state is the root of all evil. The state, by its very nature, must rely on coercive force for its authority. Every political state claims that it alone has the right to define what kinds of force are legitimate. Logically, then, the state's own use of force is always held to be legitimate. And the state inevitably backs up its claims by the threat of force as the ultimate sanction. Thus, the state exercises tyranny over every individual. When individuals challenge the state in the name of their own freedom, the state will always use coercive force to prevent genuine social change. The state cannot make individual freedom its end, because it is always using coercion as its means. Freedom can only be attained through freedom; freedom must be the means as well as the end.

In modern industrial societies, the state is even more coercive because it is so intimately linked with capitalism. State power is obviously used to oppress the rights of workers. More subtly, capitalism infringes on the rights of all people to live fully human lives. It forces the natural diversity of life into its narrow channels of production and consumption. It forces us to measure the quality of life, and all qualities, by strictly economic measures of quantity and efficiency. The enormous size of modern institutions (required by capitalism's economies of scale) requires us to coordinate our lives under someone else's rules. Because we live under unnatural, abstract norms and institutions, all of our relationships become artificial, forced, and ultimately coercive.

Some anarchists extend their critique to include modern technology as a fundamental part of the problem. Technology is oppressive, they argue, for several reasons. It cuts us off from nature. It allows the people in authority to maintain their power. It reduces the mind to goal-oriented, problem-solving technological reasoning and treats that limited form of reasoning as the only source of truth. Thus reason imprisons us. Its strict rules impose uniformity of thought and stifle spontaneity. For these critics of reason, a spontaneous life is more valuable than the artificial categories created by the intellect.

Other anarchists have a much more positive view of reason and technology. Although anarchism has a reputation of being disorderly and irrational, it is largely a product of the eighteenth-century Enlightenment, which proclaimed that human reason can and should discover the orderly laws of nature. Many anarchists believe that reason, when used rightly, enables us to live a more natural life. The right use of reason is science, the most dependable source of truth. These anarchists see themselves applying scientifically proven laws of nature to human society.

Rationalist anarchists and scientists share the Enlightenment ideal of the free individual following his or her own reasoning wherever it may lead, unfettered by any authority. (The first anarchists were particularly concerned to free themselves from what they saw as the oppressive rule of religious authority.) For these anarchists, freedom is the ability to follow the dictates of reason. So they stress the central role of education in helping all people become rational. The positive view of reason often leads to a positive view of technology as the key to keeping a high material standard of living without a centralized economic system. It is also important to note that there has always been a third group of anarchists that sees the whole debate about reason as misguided. These anarchists believe that it is possible and necessary to create a new synthesis that will harmonize reason and nature, or mind and body.

Whatever their views about reason and technology, anarchists all agree on resisting the modern industrial state, which emerged in Europe and the United States in the nineteenth century. In that era, the movement had its greatest appeal among people who experienced in their own lives the shift from a predominantly rural, agricultural, decentralized society to the highly centralized, urban, industrial culture. This transition began in Britain and France in the early nineteenth century. By the later nineteenth and early twentieth centuries, its center of influence had shifted to eastern and southern Europe and the western part of the United States, where industrialization was just beginning and people could recall what preindustrial life was like. In each of these places, it appealed most to farmers, miners, lumberjacks, and skilled craftsmen, who were closest to pre-modern occupations. These people were most sensitive to the power of the centralized capitalist state, because they lived in places where it was newest and most obviously disruptive of the old, established way.

Anarchism is marked by a certain nostalgia for the past. Sometimes anarchists tend to romanticize the lives of peasants or "primitives," who supposedly lived a spontaneous life in tune with nature. It is easy for anarchists to project into this imagined past their ideal of small organic communities, free of external constraints. So they may imagine their movement as a return to some kind of primitive purity.

Yet anarchists who are committed to modern science and rationality recognize that modernity is inescapable. This also means that large-scale industry is inescapable. By the early twentieth century, anarchism in most places was adapting to industrial society. Increasingly, it focused more on economic than political forces. It developed an ideal of factories run solely by the workers, organized into small producer groups called syndics. Syndicalism became the most popular form of anarchism in the first half of the twentieth century. But it still appealed more to skilled workers than to the proletariat on the assembly lines.

Anarchism in Action

Analyzing the human problem and imagining creative new solutions is only half of the intellectual project of anarchism. The other half is figuring out how to bring down the all-powerful capitalist state and usher in the new era of organic, natural life. Wherever anarchists go, they tend to be in contact with one group of anticapitalist activists who think they have the answer: Marxists. Some anarchists want the workers to own and control all property. Some want to abolish all private property completely. But nearly all agree with the Marxists that, one way or another, the workers must be freed from capitalist oppression.

Anarchists do not embrace the Marxist solution, however, for a number of reasons. Marxists want humans to rule over nature, to manipulate nature for human ends. Therefore, they use their work as means to domineering ends. Anarchists want to live in organic harmony with nature and make work an end in itself. Marxists view society as an entity separate from the individuals in it, while anarchists argue that the whole can never be greater than the sum of its parts. Because Marxists deal with society as separate from individuals, they expect to change institutions, and ultimately change the world, by working from the top down. So they are eager to use centralized state institutions and the whole apparatus of state power to achieve their ends. To anarchists, of course, this "solution" only perpetuates the problem.

Anarchists claim that most Marxists have an unrealistically rigid view of history. Marxists believe that the capitalist state is withering away; it contains the seeds of its own destruction, which will blossom into revolution, according to iron laws of history. Anarchists, on the other hand, have much more respect for the immense power of the nation-state, the corporate economy, and the authorities who run them. They do not see the capitalist state containing the seeds of its own demise. However, unlike Marxists, anarchists do not think it necessary to create a totally new stage of human life. Rather, they argue that all the resources for a good life for everyone already exist now. Sadly, that universal good life is being blocked by the dominant economic and political institutions. All it takes to improve life radically is to remove the blocks.

In the anarchists' view, removing the blocks does not require a new powerful political structure that can launch a massive assault on the prevailing structure. Rather, anarchists generally believe that the small structures they create will, spontaneously, generate a decentralized alternative society. That society will provide people with everything they really need, without relying on the centralized structures of capitalism and the state. Those centralized structures will become irrelevant and gradually fade away.

These differences between Marxists and anarchists on matters of basic principle lead to tactical differences. According to anarchists, Marxists put far too much stress on a vanguard—"the party"—organizing to force the contradictions within the existing system to the breaking point. Anarchists fear that such an organized political assault on the state, even if it succeeds, will only lead to a counter-state that will be just as centralized and thus just as oppressive. (By the 1930s, Stalin had given the anarchists a perfect case in point.)

Anarchists' concern is with individuals, not whole systems. How, then, to change individuals' lives? In fact, anarchists say, there is nothing wrong with individuals' lives now, if they were allowed to live by their own innate natures. Again, it is only a question of removing the artificial structures that prevent people from living according to nature. Some anarchists would do this by letting nature work within the existing system. Nature wants small organic communities. So anarchists create such communities—at home, at work, at school, wherever people gather to share their lives. These small communities create alternative structures, independent of the state apparatus. As they grow, they gradually erode the power of the state from within.

Other anarchists imagine sweeping away the barriers to nature in one great radical act. Their motto is "direct action," that is, overt resistance that will challenge and weaken the power of the state and all centralized authority. Direct action is embraced not only as a means to social change but as the best way to exercise freedom, to demonstrate the individual's independence from the prevailing system. The most widely known type of anarchist direct action is the one promoted most by the Syndicalists: a general strike, shutting down the whole apparatus of production and consumption until the authorities capitulate. This would create a season of social chaos and anarchy. Indeed, anarchist critics of technological rationality justify irrational acts as the only way to act spontaneously and become free of the constraints of reason. But that is only a means to an end. Anarchism is a vision of a new kind of social order. Anarchy can be one means, perhaps the only means, to reach the new order.

Since anarchists insist on individual freedom as both their means and their end, it is hardly surprising that they disagree on the question of tactics. This disagreement leads directly to disagreement about the role of violence. All anarchists agree that violence is ultimately caused by the state and societal institutions, especially under capitalism. As long as our present system continues, there is no way to escape violence. And all agree that when anarchism prevails, violence will end, because its causes will have ended. But given the prevailing violence in the present, many anarchists justify violence as the only way to create change. They argue that their violent direct action is defensive and unselfish violence, taken only as a last resort to end the selfish violence of the powerful. It is a necessary means to clear the path to a future nonviolent society. Some want violence planned by small groups to start a mass revolt. Some want spontaneous violence done by individuals as direct action, especially efforts to kill state and corporate leaders.

There have always been some anarchists who have committed themselves to nonviolence, arguing that the means must match the end. If free action is the only way to a free society, then nonviolent direct action must be the only way to a nonviolent society. More important, perhaps, the whole movement stands in the tradition of resistance that runs from the Anabaptists and Quakers, through the Abolitionists and Thoreau, up to the present day. All anarchists agree that no person should be ruled over by another person. All understand that we can be ruled by another only when we allow ourselves to be ruled by another. All see resistance to illegitimate authority as the foundation of a good and free human life. Because anarchism centers on individual freedom understood in this way, and because it developed techniques of direct action that would later be widely used by nonviolent activists, it has an important place in the history of nonviolence.

For some idea of the diversity of anarchism and its influence in the United States, let us take a closer look at two well-known American anarchists from two very different eras: Emma Goldman and Murray Bookchin.

Emma Goldman

From the 1890s to 1919, when she was deported, Emma Goldman (1869–1940) was the most widely known anarchist in the United States. As she traveled around the country, speaking and writing, she gave detailed and often eloquent explanations of her views. The goal of anarchism, as she saw it, was for everyone to live the fullest possible life, with "the freest possible expression of all the latent powers of the individual." "Anarchism insists that the center of gravity in society is the individual—that he must think for himself, act freely, and live fully. The aim of Anarchism is that every individual in the world shall be able to do so. If he is to develop freely and fully, he must be relieved from the interference and oppression of others."[1]

When there is no interference from others, there is true equality; everyone has equal freedom and an equal right to full self-development. "Such free display of human energy being possible only under complete individual and social freedom, Anarchism directs its forces against the greatest foe of all social equality; namely, the State, organized authority or statutory law—the dominion of human conduct."[2]

People accept the authority of the state and its laws, Goldman claimed, because they are afraid of other people: "At its base is the doctrine that man is evil, vicious, and too incompetent to know what is good for him. On this all government and oppression is built." However, when people are free from external interference, they discover that they need not fear others, because free people naturally want to help each other: "The belief in freedom assumes that human beings can co-operate. They do it even now to a surprising extent, or organized society would be impossible. If the devices by which men can harm one another, such as private property, are removed, and if the worship of authority can be discarded, co-operation will be spontaneous and inevitable." When people are most free to develop their own individuality, they are also most free to cooperate. Then they can discover "the social bonds which knit men together, and which are the true foundation of a normal social life."[3]

In sum, according to Goldman, "the sense of justice and equality, the love of liberty and of human brotherhood [are] fundamentals of the real regeneration of society." Regeneration seems so hard because equality, liberty, and brotherhood are stifled by a "whole complex of authority and institutional domination which strangles life."[4] This complex includes the interlocking powers of government, capitalism, religion, and social convention.

Even in a democracy, government blocks the path to freedom: "It matters not whether it is government by divine right or majority rule. In every instance its aim is the absolute subordination of the individual." As long as the state depends on capitalism, the political system depends on the money of the rich. If truly good people tried to get elected to office, they would "either remain true to their political faith and lose their economic support, or they would cling to their economic master and be utterly unable to do the slightest good. The political arena leaves one no alternative, one must either be a dunce or a rogue." So there is no chance of gaining true freedom by constitutional means: "Man has as much liberty as he is willing to take. Anarchism therefore stands for direct action, the open defiance of, and resistance to all laws and restrictions, economic, social, and moral."[5]

Goldman argued that liberty must be taken in the economic as well as the political realm. Freedom "is only possible in a state of society where man is free to choose the mode of work, the conditions of work, and the freedom to work." In an anarchist society, "economic arrangements must consist of voluntary productive and distributive associations, gradually developing into free communism." So she joined the Marxists in attacking the oppressive features of industrial capitalism. But she went beyond the Marxists when she insisted that capitalism and the state are so intimately intertwined that both must be resisted together.[6]

Goldman went beyond many other anarchists when she insisted on another crucial realm where people must be free, perhaps the most crucial of all for her: the realm of love. "The most vital right is the right to love and be loved," she wrote. People cannot express all their latent powers and potentialities freely unless they can freely give and receive love: "Love in freedom is the only condition of a beautiful life. . . . Whether love last but one brief span of time or for an eternity, it is the only creative, inspiring, elevating basis for a new race, a new world."[7]

She was especially sensitive to the freedom to love because she was a woman. Like other feminists, she fought to end the oppressive restrictions that men imposed upon women. However, she rankled other feminists with her criticisms of their movement. In her view, women who demanded only the vote, equal legal rights, and access to all fields of work with equal pay were simply asking to participate fully in the oppressive state system. They were, in effect, legitimizing and reinforcing that system. Therefore, they were accepting the strict limits that society placed on women's ability to give and receive love freely:

Emancipation, as understood by the majority of its adherents and exponents, is of too narrow a scope to permit the boundless love and ecstasy contained in the deep emotion of the true woman, sweetheart, mother, in freedom. . . . Until woman has learned to defy them all, to stand firmly on her own ground and to insist upon her own unrestricted freedom, to listen to the voice of her nature, whether it call for life's greatest treasure, love for a man, or her most glorious privilege, the right to give birth to a child, she cannot call herself emancipated. How many emancipated women are brave enough to acknowledge that the voice of love is calling, wildly beating against their breasts, demanding to be heard, to be satisfied. . . . The greatest shortcoming of the emancipation of the present day lies in its artificial stiffness and its narrow respectabilities, which produce an emptiness in woman's soul that will not let her drink from the fountain of life. . . . To give of one's self boundlessly, in order to find one's self richer, deeper, better. That alone can fill the emptiness, and transform the tragedy of woman's emancipation into joy, limitless joy.[8]

Goldman scandalized audiences when she talked about love, because she made it quite clear that she meant, above all, romantic and sexual love, the kind of love that produces babies. She argued passionately that women should be free to love men without marrying them, to love more than one man at once, and to have children with men that they loved, whether or not they were married to those men. Indeed, she saw marriage as a major impediment to love. Most women feel forced to marry, she explained, because only a husband can provide them with economic security and social respectability. In return for those privileges, they must offer to their husbands their bodies and the children their bodies produce.

The ultimate price they pay is to sacrifice their freedom to love: "Love, the strongest and deepest element in all life, the harbinger of hope, of joy, of ecstasy; love, the defier of all laws, of all conventions; love, the freest, the most powerful molder of human destiny; how can such an all-compelling force be synonymous with that poor little State- and Church-begotten weed, marriage?" Love is genuine only if it is freely given, Goldman insisted. When charged with promoting "free love," she replied: "As if love is anything but free. . . . Man has conquered whole nations, but all his armies could not conquer love. Man has chained and fettered the spirit, but he has been utterly helpless before love. . . . Love has the magic power to make of a beggar a king. Yes love is free; it can dwell in no other atmosphere. In freedom, it gives itself unreservedly, abundantly, completely."[9]

Goldman's passionate defense of free love and free motherhood reveals the romantic streak that her critics, and some of her supporters, often failed to see. It also reveals the rebellious streak that marked her whole life. But her rebelliousness was not merely a psychological trait. It was also part and parcel of her theory of anarchism. She explained that, since liberty is every person's natural right, "it cannot be given; it cannot be conferred by any law or government. The need of it, the longing for it, is inherent in the individual. Disobedience to every form of coercion is the instinctive expression of it. Rebellion and revolution are the more or less conscious attempt to achieve it." Precisely because rebellion requires breaking laws, it is a sure path to freedom: "Everything illegal necessitates integrity, self-reliance, and courage. In short, it calls for free, independent spirits, for [as Thoreau said] 'men who are men, and who have a bone in their backs which you cannot pass your hand through.'"[10]

Every time individuals break a law, they are refusing to consent to the legitimacy of that law and the legitimacy of the government that promulgated the law. They are acting as if the state is irrelevant in their life. Thus they are weakening the state's power and taking one step closer to its collapse, because "no government can exist without the consent of the people, consent open, tacit or assumed."[11] In Goldman's view, withdrawing consent from the state is an act of freedom. It removes the barrier to the free expression of one's own fullest potential. It opens the door to one's own unique creativity, spontaneity, and love. Taking the state out means letting the life force in.

Emma Goldman knew that people were often frustrated because she did not describe specifically how things would operate under anarchism. But she could not offer such a description, she explained, because "anarchism cannot consistently impose an iron-clad program or method on the future." Anarchism "leaves posterity free to develop its own particular systems, in harmony with its needs. Our most vivid imagination cannot foresee the potentialities of a race set free from external restraints. How, then, can anyone assume to map out a line of conduct for those to come?"[12]

One topic that she left especially vague was the use of violence. She had no doubt that anarchism was ultimately the antidote to all violence, because the state itself was the ultimate source of all violence. She defined anarchism as "the philosophy of a new social order based on liberty unrestricted by man-made law; the theory that all forms of government rest on violence, and are therefore wrong and harmful, as well as unnecessary." The methods of anarchism were always based on "emancipation from all oppressive and limiting forces; in short, by libertarian principles. The methods of the State, on the contrary—of the Bolshevik State as of every government—were based on coercion, which in the course of things necessarily developed into systematic violence, oppression, and terrorism."[13]

Although coercion always leads to violence, in Goldman's analysis, not every act of violence is meant to coerce. Anarchists can do violence in order to express their freedom from the state or to trigger a radical social change that will undermine the power of the state. Yet, as she understood anarchism, it does not require or command violence. Anarchists who planned assassinations and bombings "were impelled, not by the teachings of Anarchism, but by the tremendous pressure of conditions making life unbearable to their sensitive natures." Their acts were "the violent recoil from violence, the last desperate struggle of outraged and exasperated human nature for breathing space and life."[14]

Moreover, it makes little sense to focus on anarchist violence while ignoring the much greater state violence: "Resistance to tyranny is man's highest ideal. So long as tyranny exists, in whatever form, man's deepest aspiration must resist it as inevitably as man must breathe. Compared with the wholesale violence of capital and government, political acts of violence are but a drop in the ocean."[15] That was her rationale, no doubt, when she helped her lover, Alexander Berkman, plan his attempted assassination of a U.S. Steel executive in 1892. (Berkman spent fourteen years in jail for that failed attempt.)

However, after Goldman was deported from the United States and spent two years in the fledgling Soviet Union, she came to doubt the efficacy of violent revolution. She saw the Soviet leaders merely replacing one centralized state authority with another, and using massive violence to do it. Reflecting on this experience, she wrote:

> It is one thing to employ violence in combat as a means of defence. It is quite another thing to make a principle of terrorism, to institutionalize it, to assign it the most vital place in the social struggle. Such terrorism begets counter-revolution and in turn itself becomes counter-revolutionary. . . . The one thing I am convinced of as I have never been in my life is that the gun decides nothing at all. Even if it accomplishes what it sets out to do—which it rarely does—it brings so many evils in its wake as to defeat its original aim. . . . If we can undergo changes in every other method of dealing with the social issues we will also have to learn to change in the methods of revolution. It think it can be done. If not, I shall relinquish my belief in revolution.[16]

She told Alexander Berkman that "violence in whatever form never has and probably never will bring constructive results."[17]

Goldman recognized that the Soviets had embraced violence because they assumed the principle that a good end justifies any means to attain it. "There is no greater fallacy than the belief that aims and purposes are one thing, while methods and tactics are another. . . . All human experience teaches that methods and means cannot be separated from the ultimate aim. The means employed become, through individual habit and social practice, part and parcel of the final purpose."[18]

It is not surprising that Goldman eventually endorsed nonviolence. Her anarchist views embraced the fundamental premises of the nonviolent Abolitionists. She believed that all people should be treated as equals because no one should have authority over another (though she stripped away the religious foundation of this belief and argued for it on strictly rational grounds). She believed that when people do have authority over others, they are coercing others, and thus they are bound to do violence. She believed that no one could achieve right ends by wrong means.

Her anarchism also foreshadowed important ideas that would later shape the nonviolence tradition. She believed that all power is based on consent. No one can impose his or her authority upon another. People are ruled by others only because they allow themselves to be ruled by others. It is always possible to withdraw consent, to refuse to be ruled. True freedom means withdrawing consent from all human authority. If enough people withdraw consent from a government or authority, its power will vanish, and it will fall of its own weight.

Many anarchists shared Goldman's analysis of power. They followed this line of reasoning to the same conclusions that Thoreau reached in "Civil Disobedience." (Many recognized their debt to Thoreau. Fewer realized that these ideas could be traced all the way back to *The Discourse on Voluntary Servitude*, written by the French philosopher Étienne de la Boétie in 1548.) Resistance to illegitimate authority is the foundation of a good and free human life. Social change comes most effectively not from working within the legal structure, but by acting freely—doing what one sees as right—outside the laws. In the twentieth century, this concept of direct action would be combined with other facets of nonviolence. The resulting ideas would be fully articulated and turned into fundamental principles of the tradition.

Near the end of her life, though, Emma Goldman showed that she valued revolution, by any means, above nonviolence. When Spanish anarchists, who had gained control of parts of Spain, were attacked and fought back violently, she actively supported and promoted their cause in the Spanish Civil War.

Murray Bookchin

In his youth, Murray Bookchin (1921–) was a factory worker, a union organizer, and a Marxist. He never abandoned the Marxist idea that people will not be truly free until private property is abolished and all goods are distributed solely according to need. However, by the early 1950s it was clear to him that Marxism had ceased to be the revolutionary force he and so many others had hoped it would be. The Soviet Union had not fulfilled the promise of a state truly run by and for the working class. In the United States and other Western industrialized nations, capitalism had raised the living standards of most workers and coopted revolutionary workers' movements. With no clear line separating capitalists from workers in the class struggle, the prospect of revolutionary class struggle was rapidly vanishing.

Bookchin turned to the anarchist tradition as a source of revolutionary thinking. He seized especially on the idea that the revolution should not be about gaining control of the state but about dissolving the state. But he lived in a world quite different from the world of the earlier anarchist writers. Most people now lived in big cities and suburbs. They were as likely to work in offices or stores as in farms or factories. Their lives were dominated by centers of power organized in huge anonymous bureaucracies: corporations, labor unions, the military, universities, media conglomerates, and so on. Government's role was now to coordinate all these bureaucracies. The state was the one huge conglomerate created by the interlocking of all these institutions.

Bookchin envisioned a world in which power would be decentralized and returned to the people by dismantling all these institutions. He came to see the structure of capitalism, with society divided between capitalists and workers, as just one example of a larger structure: the hierarchical structure, with society divided between dominators and dominated. Capitalism is only one of many forms that domination can take.

His most creative breakthrough came when he recognized the indissoluble link between human society and the natural environment. Humans are part of nature. Human consciousness evolved in the same way that every other organism's unique features evolved. Consciousness is part of nature. But it has the unique ability to develop a concept of nature, to think about its relation to nature. That gives humans a special responsibility to think about what is happening to nature and to take care of the natural environment.

As early as 1952 (far earlier than most other anarchists or non-anarchists) Bookchin began warning that humans were failing in this responsibility. The earth's environment, and the bodies of all people on earth, were being poisoned by industrial chemicals. "The principal motives for chemicals," he argued, were "shaped neither by the needs of the public nor the limits of nature, but by the exigencies of profit and competition." Generalizing from this point, he wrote: "The imbalances man has produced in the natural world are caused by the imbalances he has produced in the social world." Why? Because people who want to dominate each other also want to dominate nature. When people believe that humans should dominate nature, they soon come to believe that they can generate wealth only by dominating nature. [19]

This idea was especially dangerous when people recognized the fact of nature's scarcity. There simply was not enough to go around. So it was easy to believe that competition was inevitable. From this, it was another easy step to believe that competition was good, that it was the only way to encourage people to work their hardest and create the most wealth out of the natural resources at hand. Of course, competition meant winners and losers, dominators and dominated. "In order to harness the natural world, it has been argued for ages, it is necessary to harness human beings as well. . . . The myth of a 'stingy' nature has always been used to justify the 'stinginess' of exploiters in their harsh treatment of the exploited." [20] At the same time, the same ideas were leading people to treat the natural environment very harshly, too. This explains the direct link between hierarchies and destruction of the environment.

Bookchin went on to point out that, by destroying the natural environment, capitalism was creating an ultimate limit to its expansion and sowing the seeds of its own destruction. A revolution in human society would some day have to come, when humans could no longer survive physically in the polluted environment that the centralized power of capitalism had created. The only way to avoid environmental catastrophe, he insisted, was to let people reclaim control over their own lives in small, decentralized units. Humanity, he wrote, now faces the stark simple "alternatives of anarchism or annihilation." [21]

If decentralization must happen some day to save the human race and the earth's biosphere, why not begin it now? That was the essential argument that launched Bookchin's career as the most influential American anarchist in the second half of the twentieth century.

In developing his innovative approach, he allied himself with the side of anarchism that saw great value in rationality and technology. By the latter half of the twentieth century, he insisted, technology had advanced so much that everyone could have all the goods he or she would ever need. The principle of nature's scarcity, so basic to human civilization in the past, was simply no longer true. The end of scarcity meant that humanity could now be free from want, free from any lack of necessary material goods. This fact deprives the capitalist ruling class of its familiar excuses for domination. It also eliminates the need for arduous and tedious labor. Thus technology gives everyone enough free time to participate fully in community affairs and to enjoy life: "The human relationships and psyches of individuals in a post-scarcity society must fully reflect the freedom, security, and self-expression that this abundance makes possible. Post-scarcity society, in short, is the fulfillment of the social and cultural potentialities latent in a technology of abundance."[22]

Technology also allows every community to rely totally on renewable resources for its energy. However, "to use solar, wind, and tidal power effectively, the megalopolis must be decentralized." Bookchin called for decentralized, small-scale communities in which economic life would be totally cooperative and communal. Each community would be tailored to the distinctive features of its own natural environment. Humans would become sensitive to those features and adapt their technology to nature rather than trying to make technology control nature. They would learn to deal with nature "not like playing chess but like steering a boat."[23]

When Murray Bookchin began writing about his anarchist views in the 1950s, he was a lone voice. The anarchist tradition in the United States had waned after World War I; after World War II, it seemed to be virtually extinct. In the early Cold War years, it took great courage to express anarchist ideas. Since anarchism was widely associated with communism, it was suppressed by mainstream American society, which was quick to attack anything related to communism. Anarchist tendencies were also suppressed by the communists, who were under severe attack and trying to keep their own movement alive. Concern about the environment, from any perspective, was virtually unheard of. Bookchin could not know that, by the late 1960s, his thought would become appealing and influential to a new generation of young people creating a counterculture.

Eventually, the environmental concerns of the 1960s, which Bookchin had pioneered, became part of popular culture. But in the late twentieth century he criticized the environmental movement because it was not radical enough. It tended to view the environment as a collection of resources placed at the service of people. Its warning was only that these resources should be controlled and manipulated more wisely, so that they would last longer.

Calling his own outlook *ecology*, he explained that it "interprets interdependencies (social and psychological as well as natural) nonhierarchically. Ecology denies that nature can be interpreted from a hierarchical viewpoint. Moreover, it affirms that diversity and spontaneous development are ends in themselves, to be respected in their own right." He based his ecology on the principle that "each form of life has a unique place in the balance of nature and its removal from the ecosystem could imperil the stability of the whole."[24]

Bookchin also criticized ecofeminism and the deep ecology informed by spirituality because, in his view, they denigrated reason and science, which he believed were crucial to creating a good society. He was equally critical of what he called lifestyle anarchism. As he described it (perhaps not wholly accurately), this movement glorified the individual who had broken free of all social structures to express completely his or her deepest desires. To

Bookchin, this kind of freedom is an illusion, since the individual can never be free of the social structures that condition each person's life. The task is, rather, to change those structures so that they support and nurture a more genuine kind of freedom. "It must be a social anarchism that seeks freedom through structure and mutual responsibility, not through a vaporous, nomadic ego that eschews the preconditions for social life."[25]

Lifestyle anarchism, he argued, values passion and intuition above reason. But reason is necessary as "a guide to standards of progress and regress, necessity and freedom, good and evil." Bookchin's social anarchism "celebrates the thinking human mind without in any way denying passion, ecstasy, imagination, play, and art," the values celebrated by lifestyle anarchism. Social anarchism "is committed to rationality while opposing the rationalization of experience; to technology, while opposing the 'megamachine'; to social institutionalization, while opposing class rule and hierarchy; to a genuine politics based upon the confederal coordination of municipalities or communes by the people in direct face-to-face democracy, while opposing parliamentarianism and the state."[26]

Unlike some varieties of lifestyle anarchism, Bookchin did not call for a return to the state of nature. There would be no benefit in destroying urban life and vainly trying to return to nature. In his vision, town and country are not opposed. Rather, town and country must be skillfully blended, so that the best of human technology can be wisely integrated into a natural setting on a human scale.

Nor did he call for a return to a pre-urban tribal past. Tribal societies often overused nature, he pointed out. They had no concept of nature and therefore no conscious relationship with nature. So they could not make free choices about their relation to their environment. That is why they felt controlled by supernatural forces. Bookchin praised the era of the Enlightenment, with its stress on reason as the source of truth, partly because it gave humanity a concept of nature. For the first time, people felt empowered to choose freely how they would relate to their natural environment. However, he did see great value in remembering or studying the tribal past. Doing so could be a way to recognize "the past possibilities that remain unfulfilled, such as the far-reaching importance of community, confederation, self-management of the economy, and a new balance between humanity and nature."

The balance between humanity and nature was the central thread in all of Bookchin's writing. In many different ways he argued that the only way to save the environment is to find that proper balance; the only way to find the balance is to create genuine democracy; the only way to create democracy is through anarchism.

"The most creative feature of traditional anarchism," according to Bookchin, "is its commitment to four basic tenets: a confederation of decentralized municipalities; an unwavering opposition to statism; a belief in direct democracy; and a vision of a libertarian communist society." For him, direct democracy required what he called "libertarian municipalism." It would be "built around intimate groups of brothers and sisters—affinity groups—whose ability to act in common is based on initiative, on convictions freely arrived at, and on a deep personal involvement, not on a bureaucratic apparatus fleshed out by a docile membership and manipulated from above by a handful of all-knowing leaders."[27]

Affinity groups would coordinate with one another when needed, but always voluntarily. In each urban neighborhood or rural town, all of the affinity groups would assemble to debate and decide upon every aspect of their community's life, including the distribution of property.

People would find their real freedom in this ongoing rational discussion of their shared needs. Freedom depends on a real ability to make free choices in every aspect of life and act upon those choices. But Bookchin emphasized that free choice does not mean choosing what is best merely for oneself. Real freedom means the freedom to choose what is best for one's whole community: "The individual is, indeed, truly free and attains true individuality when he or she is guided by a rational, humane, and high-minded notion of the social and communal good."[28]

For libertarian municipalism to work, economic and social and political life would have to be scaled down to human dimensions. Most things would be done locally, in small communities where everyone knows everyone else and understands everyone's needs. The local assemblies would communicate with one another when matters of larger concern arise. They would form a series of confederations, chains of association that would grow larger and larger to deal with problems on a growing scale. But the confederations would always be voluntary, organic, and constantly changing. They would have no permanent structure, and nothing would be imposed from above. Such a series of confederations would act independently of the state, and in many cases simply ignore the state. As this process of confederated association grows, initiated from the grass roots, it would wield enough power to challenge the power of state. Eventually, the state and its institutions would simply become irrelevant to people's lives. This, according to Bookchin, is the only way to fulfill Marx's prediction that the state will wither away.

Murray Bookchin has been criticized in some anarchist circles because he has so often done just what we might expect an anarchist to do; that is, he has taken staunchly independent stands, stated his views freely and firmly, and vented his opposition to other views with full force, even when doing so led to antagonism and schisms in the anarchist community. At times, some of his critics say, he has misunderstood or misrepresented the varieties of anarchism that he criticized. Even those who disagree with him and have felt the sting of his critiques, however, often have paid their respects to him. They recognized that he kept the tradition of anarchist theory alive through an era when it otherwise seemed virtually defunct. He kept it alive by working with it creatively, adapting it to new circumstances, and thereby renewing it. He anticipated many of the key ideas that came to be associated with the 1960s. For the rest of the twentieth century, he kept up a vibrant, often contentious, dialogue with younger people who were inspired by his ideas and by his example of always bringing something new and fresh to the anarchist tradition.

6.

World War I—
The Crucial Turning Point

After the Civil War, Garrisonian nonresistance survived in the Universal Peace Union (UPU), founded in 1866 by Alfred Love. Women like Lucretia Mott and Belva Ann Lockwood were especially dedicated and influential members of the UPU. Of course, the abolition of slavery was no longer an issue. The UPU focused on the ultimate nonviolent reform: the abolition of war. Yet it struggled against powerful odds. There was little interest in any kind of reform movements in the post–Civil War era. Nonviolence never had much appeal in the South, and the Union victory in the Civil War led most Northerners to believe that war could be justified. Moreover, war hardly seemed worth worrying about. The United States was involved in very few international conflicts, and those were quite small. Most Americans assumed that the oceans would protect them not only from war but from the need to think about international involvements.

The 1890s saw an upsurge of interest in international affairs and therefore in issues of war and peace. The annual conferences of the UPU began to attract several thousand people each year. Although the UPU was bringing a new internationalist perspective to the nonviolence tradition, it was still dominated by traditional moral reformers, who saw war primarily as a product of individual sinful behavior. By the 1890s, though, the idea of ending war by persuading individuals to be more virtuous was rapidly becoming old-fashioned. So the UPU soon found itself on the margins of the peace movement.

The Progressive Era

The new approach to peace was the Progressive approach. To the Progressives, the nineteenth-century idea of moral reform appeared to be an oversimplifying effort to avoid facing the fact of change. The Progressives prided themselves on embracing technological, economic, social, and political change. But they wanted it to be rationally controlled change, guided by highly educated experts. These experts studied the makeup of public institutions like schools, factories, corporations, and legislatures. They were confident that they could find ways to reorganize all these institutions, to adapt them to constantly changing conditions, so that they would all serve the greater public good.

By and large, the Progressives were optimists who believed that once the causes of a problem are analyzed, a cure will soon follow. They had little doubt that cures would soon be found for every problem, leading to unlimited social progress. But they were upper- and middle-class people who had little sympathy with the discontented workers on the assembly lines in the new, huge industrial plants. Nor did they have great sympathy with the newly rich capitalists who were building those plants and becoming millionaires. They assumed that, if both workers and capitalists would abide by rational middle-class values, they could resolve all economic and social conflicts reasonably, peacefully, and easily. In retrospect, it appears that the Progressives generally ignored, or misunderstood, the new sources of domestic social violence in their day.

When Progressives turned to international conflict, they applied the same kind of thinking. War, too, is a public institution. But it struck most Progressives as an irrational institution that serves no public good. They created a large and influential peace movement, built on rational arguments against war and rational efforts to reorganize international affairs so that conflicts would be resolved reasonably and peaceably. Education was the key to peace, they argued. Since all people are rational, all can learn to see the folly of war and therefore move to end it. Their practical efforts for peace focused on new institutions: international conferences to resolve disputes, arbitration treaties between nations, disarmament agreements, legal institutions like a league of nations and a world court, and other programs to promote peaceful relations among nations. Progressives were especially enthusiastic about the power of free trade to end war, because they believed that trading partners would not run the risk of destroying each other.

Few Progressives advocated principled nonviolence. Their peace movements differed from movements for principled nonviolence in at least three ways. First, most Progressives allowed that there might be situations in which violence was unfortunate yet necessary. These situations would be evidence that one party to a conflict had failed to be reasonable. Second, the Progressive peace movements focused only on war itself. As long as nations were not fighting with each other, they would count their efforts successful. The nonviolence proponents held a higher standard of success, since they wanted to end all kinds of violence and coercion. Third, the Progressives rejected the UPU's focus on individual sin and virtue. They believed that society's problems arose from flaws in institutions and systems, not from individuals' immoral choices. Therefore the Progressives looked to institutional reform, imposed from the top down, to cure the ills of society.

Although Progressivism departed from the Christian moralism of the UPU, it helped to spawn a new mode of Christianity: the Social Gospel movement. The Social Gospel preached that it is a Christian's duty to feed the hungry and minister to the material as well as spiritual needs of the poor. That means changing the economic and social structures responsible for poverty. The Social Gospel saw sin manifest less in individual misbehavior than in unjust and degrading social conditions that lead individuals to antisocial behavior. It was heavily influenced by the Progressives' faith in progress through human reason, teaching that education is the way to motivate people to change their institutions and themselves. Everyone can learn, they assumed, because all people are innately rational and can be educated to change their behavior. There is no original sin blocking the path to improvement.

The Social Gospel advocates were so optimistic that they believed the kingdom of God on earth to be quite near. Yet they paid relatively little attention to issues of war and peace. Before World War I, there was little in the way of a distinctly Christian Progressive peace movement. Social Gospel Christians joined in the general Progressive trend toward pacifism. But they did not necessarily embrace principled nonviolence. (Because the mainstream Progressive peace movements were all called *pacifist,* it is useful to avoid that word when speaking of those committed to principled nonviolence.)

One noteworthy link between U.S. Christianity and the U.S. peace movement in the Progressive era came through the writings of a Russian, Leo Tolstoy (1828–1910). Renowned as the author of *War and Peace* and *Anna Karenina,* Tolstoy committed himself to a peasant-style life of manual labor and a Christlike life of absolute nonviolence. Christ's teachings "have now become identified with human conscience," he wrote. To be a Christian is to follow the inner voice of conscience, which is also the voice of reason. And the message of this voice is always an "intuition of love" for all of God's creation. Therefore, "the mutual interaction of rational beings upon each other should consist not in violence but in rational persuasion."[1]

All social problems are caused by violence and coercion; the only way to make social progress is to renounce coercion. On this, reason and Christianity agree: "Christianity is meekness, nonresistance, love." This was not an original insight, in Tolstoy's opinion; it was just saying in simple words what was obviously true, right, and well known. Ordinary people in all nations "have reached the period of reasonableness, have no animosity toward one another, and might decide their differences in a peaceful fashion." The kingdom of God is already beginning—if people choose it: "Its approach depends on us. We must do it. The Kingdom of God is within us."[2]

The real problem, Tolstoy insisted, is with the leaders of society. Professors, journalists, aristocrats, and industrialists have largely forgotten the simple Christian truths. So have priests. Christianity as practiced in the modern world, he argued, is nothing like its founder intended. But Tolstoy reserved his greatest scorn for government officials. Since the government's function is to rule, he argued, it will inevitably use force and never voluntarily give up either power or violence. The state is, in short, legalized robbery and murder. Therefore, true Christians, bound to love their enemies and renounce all violence, can have nothing to do with the state: "The words 'Christian State' resemble the words 'hot ice.' The thing is either not a State using violence, or it is not Christian." Most important, "a Christian, whose doctrine enjoins upon him humility, nonresistance to evil, love to all (even to the most malicious), cannot be a soldier; that is, he cannot join a class of men whose business is to kill their fellow-men." Thus a true Christian, and a truly rational person, must live life wholly apart from the state and its killing apparatus. The state might try to compel participation, especially through military conscription. Tolstoy's advice was to resist, regardless of the consequences.[3]

Tolstoy first developed these thoughts on his own. But he was overjoyed when he discovered the writings of Garrison and Ballou and learned that there were people in the United States still trying to perpetuate those ideals. He, in turn, passed them on through his writings and through conversations with the many visitors who sought him out in his farm retreat at Yasnaya Polyana. Among these were some of the greatest names in U.S. Progressivism. This indirect route helped to keep Garrisonian ideals alive in Garrison's native land.

World War I

The greatest spur to the idea of nonviolence, however, proved to be an outbreak of massive violence. In April 1917, the United States entered World War I and a new generation was forced to deal with issues of war and violence. Most Progressives supported the war effort. They accepted President Woodrow Wilson's claim that the United States was fighting a "war to end all war," to "make the world safe for democracy." They interpreted the war as one more Progressive reform movement, a rational way to use violence to improve the world.

There was significant opposition to the war, nonetheless. Some of it came from older peace activists who were skeptical of the president's claim. In the first years of the war, before the United States entered, many thought that American virtue and moral reform would put an end to this European sin. Once the United States entered the war, they were forced to think through their own views more carefully and to distinguish themselves from the pro-war Progressives. Therefore, they tended to take a more radically antiwar stand, which led many to reject all forms of violence. Some among them were devotees of the Social Gospel; thus this Christian movement was linked directly to nonviolence for the first time.

There was also a group of young adults who were thinking about issues of war and violence for the first time. Their names would soon become the "Who's Who" of the U.S. nonviolence movement: A. J. Muste, Kirby Page, Norman Thomas, Roger Baldwin, John Haynes Holmes, John Nevin Sayre, Devere Allen, Frederick Libby. The list also includes eminent women like Jane Addams, Carrie Chapman Catt, Dorothy Day, Emily Greene Balch, Jessie Wallace Hugan, Tracy Mygatt, Frances Witherspoon, and Dorothy Detzer. Women had certainly supported the peace movement before, but the World War I era was different because women were gaining a new level of political influence through the successes of the suffrage movement. (They would gain the right to vote just a few years later.) World War I saw the first U.S. peace groups led by, and sometimes consisting wholly of, women. The first antiwar march in New York City, within weeks of the outbreak of the war, was led by female suffragists. Jane Addams (the most famous of them) convened a meeting to organize the American Union Against Militarism. In early 1915 she became leader of the Women's Peace Party and led the U.S. delegation to the Women's Peace Conference at The Hague. Upon her return, this once revered icon of Progressive reform endured intense criticism. But she stuck firmly to her antiwar views.

Unlike Jane Addams, most of the antiwar activists, male and female, were too young to have participated in the heyday of Progressive reforms. They articulated their values mainly in terms of love and the supreme value of each individual personality. Through love, they believed, all humans can fulfill their highest potential. Love means each person helping all others to develop fully. One of their leading voices, Norman Thomas, said: "The central law of all wholesome life is reciprocity, mutuality. . . . [But] the group is valuable only as it permits personalities, not automatons, to emerge."[4] Although they advocated democracy, they worried that the majority might rule over the individual conscience.

One of their main reasons for opposing war was the likelihood that war would trample on individual freedoms. They saw this happening most clearly in the military draft. The expression of conscience they stressed most was the right to be a conscientious objector (CO). When COs were persecuted, they and their supporters became more convinced that war violates freedom of conscience and the worth of the individual personality. Many read the writings of social critic Randolph Bourne, who said that "war is the health of state." The state always wants to use authoritarian measures to enhance its power, Bourne argued, and war gives it the best opportunity. War allows even democratic governments to demand conformity, which enhances the state's authority. As evidence, he pointed to the U.S. government's massive public-relations (some would call it propaganda) effort to foster public support for the war. To Bourne and his readers, this demonstrated the inevitable link between military violence and violence to individual freedom of conscience.

The young war critics were coming to maturity just as the war was putting an end to the Progressive era. Yet Progressivism's influence was strong and lasting. When asked how love can help every individual to develop freely, Progressives generally answered that love will lead us to change the world in which every person lives. The crucial thing is to change social conditions by improving societal institutions. Morality must be a social process. Because humans are social creatures, true progress means making the world a single mutual society. The ideal of love should be a practical means of reform.

The Progressive influence also included a marked tendency to pragmatism, the view that ideals should be judged by their practical results. The antiwar movement had no doubt that war does more harm than good. It prevents the growth of global humanistic values. It creates a more authoritarian state. And far from ending all war, it leads only to more war, because violence always begets more violence. According to pragmatists, the way to put ideals into practice is to study how political, economic, and social processes work. Knowing how the processes work is a necessary first step to changing them effectively. The war seemed to offer a great laboratory experiment. If experts could figure out how and why the prevailing systems had led to war, they could then figure out how to change those systems to prevent another war. For the younger generation, it would no longer do to blame war on sin and immorality. They were more inclined to see war as the logical outgrowth of a maladjusted social order.

Analyzing the problem rationally, they quickly recognized that the social order of the enemy was very similar to and increasingly interlocked with the social order of the United States and its allies. Since all the nations in the war were parts of the same system, all were equally responsible for the war. So it made no sense to view war as a fight of good nations against bad nations. Since the same moral conflicts are found within every nation, they concluded, war always creates a single global struggle of the good against the evil. As they learned to think in terms of a single international system, the war critics reinforced their desire for a single global society, fostering humanistic values that transcend all national boundaries. Their ideal of peace was more than just individual moral purity. It was an ideal of institutionalized processes for nonviolent resolution of conflicts.

How could this ideal be realized? As pragmatists, they looked as deeply as they could into the system that had produced the war. What they saw was, above all, capitalism. This was no accident. The strongest organized opposition to the U.S. war effort came from the socialists. They argued that violence is always a product of social injustice. They saw their own society founded on the injustice of economic exploitation. Workers labored for long hours, often in dangerous conditions, for little pay and fewer benefits, so that their employers could get rich. The same exploitation was acted out on a global scale through imperialism. The war, they argued, was primarily a battle of imperial titans vying for economic and political power. Both sides were fueled by producers of weapons and military supplies, who were making fortunes. So the same forces that produced domestic social conflict were now producing an international war. Wherever one turns, they argued, capitalism must rely on, and increase, coercion and violence. The only way to peace would be economic justice, an equitable distribution of goods and resources in which every worker would receive the fruits of his or her labor. This argument received quite a hearing in the United States. In the November 1917 municipal elections, while thousands of young Americans fought in Europe, the Socialist Party earned its biggest vote ever. In fifteen Northeast cities it averaged 22 percent; in Midwest cities like Chicago and Toledo, it ran over 33 percent.

Among the young pacifists who championed love and the freely developing individual, many feared socialism because it seemed to promote state power and conformity. Yet many were drawn to socialism. It offered them the most convincing rational explanation of why the global system had produced such a horrific war. And it offered them a vision of a humane society that was pragmatic and hard-headed, yet also utopian.

Socialism, pragmatism, Progressivism, and the ideal of individual self-fulfillment were all powerful influences on the young antiwar movement. But most of its adherents were still Christians. Almost 90 percent of the COs in World War I based their claim on religious beliefs; virtually all were Christian and most were from the historic peace churches. As they reflected on why they would not fight, some drew on the teachings of the Social Gospel. They argued that because the political and economic system was unjust, it was also unchristian. They were an important factor in bringing the Social Gospel and peace movements together for the first time. Even some in the historic peace churches, particularly the Quakers and the Brethren, began to show interest in Social Gospel ideas. One very practical and enduring result was the Quakers' founding of the American Friends Service Committee (AFSC). To this day, the AFSC is active around the world helping people overcome the problems of hunger, disease, and poverty, as well as war and violence.

The new Christian war critics who were not based in the historic peace churches also founded an organization that is still active today: the Fellowship of Reconciliation (FOR). The founding principle of FOR was a Christian interpretation of the desire to build a society based on love. FOR members took Jesus as the model of perfect love. They looked forward to the coming kingdom of God, in which the whole society would follow that model and be guided by love. This was not merely utopian dreaming for them. They took it as a pragmatic criterion by which to judge the present. Clearly, the present would be found lacking. And that would motivate efforts to improve it. FOR was "a fellowship of those who, by the method of love, seek the triumph of justice and the establishment of a social order based upon the will of God revealed in Jesus Christ."[5]

The young Christians in FOR blended a religious appeal to the individual conscience with the Social Gospel's concern for reforming institutions. Their important innovation was to treat those two approaches as two sides of a single coin. The structures of society would be improved when individuals obeyed the voice of conscience and acted with moral virtue. But individuals would be far more likely to obey conscience if they lived within rational, humane, and just social structures. For many in FOR, that meant structures rebuilt along the lines of socialism (though there was no clear agreement on precisely how to implement socialism). FOR became the primary organization uniting Christian pacifism and socialism.

FOR members devoted much of their energy to traditional Christian practices of preaching and exhortation, directed at the individual soul. But their desire to change society sent them into the political arena, too. They had to strengthen their organization. They also had to ally with other organizations, both religious and secular. The persecution of antiwar activists made them feel isolated and thus drove them to organize for mutual support. In addition to AFSC and FOR, two other groups arose that endure and remain very active today: the Women's International League for Peace and Freedom (WILPF) and the American Civil Liberties Union (ACLU). These are the most long-lived, and thus the most widely known today, of many such organizations that emerged out of World War I. All were imbued with an optimistic hope that, once the war was over, their movement would lead U.S. society toward ever greater heights of social justice.

The 1920s

Most people in the United States soon decided that their nation had made a mistake entering World War I. Pacifism reached new heights of influence. This culminated in 1928, when the United States negotiated and signed the Kellogg-Briand Treaty, officially outlawing war as a way to resolve international differences. Although the peace movement was rooted in Progressive thinking, Progressivism as an organized movement actually lost much of its influence. Many people blamed the Progressives, with their optimism about changing the world, for leading the United States into war. Voters chose a succession of conservative Republican presidents who pledged to restore "normalcy."

Many of the young people who had committed themselves to nonviolence during World War I, however, retained that commitment. Because their views now stood out more clearly from the mainstream of public opinion, they were motivated to define their views more distinctly and affirm them more strongly. The nonviolence proponents wanted to see more than just an end to war. They wanted to end all kinds of violence and coercion. They were intent on building a society in which social order and progress would arise not from coercion but from cooperation. They were convinced that reciprocity was the key to order and progress; each individual could fulfill himself or herself only by participating in cooperative efforts that helped others to fulfill themselves too. Their favorite word to denote the ideal of reciprocal cooperation was *fellowship* (enshrined in the name of their leading organization, FOR). Coercion of any kind would lead society away from fellowship.

During the 1920s, nonviolence advocates saw little movement toward a society of fellowship. They wondered why the growing influence of pacifism was not leading in that direction. Their answer grew out of the line of thinking begun during World War I. Since violence and war are produced by the structures of society, violence and war will not end until those structures are radically transformed. During the 1920s, they deepened their analysis of the links between capitalism and violence. By the decade's end, most members of nonviolence movements were convinced that capitalism is the major obstacle in the path to a nonviolent society, and they were prepared to explain why.

The principal argument was that capitalism divides people into conflicting classes and dehumanizes the largest class, the working class. Workers have no power and therefore no individual dignity. They suffer from the economic downturns that capitalism always brings, while capitalists insulate themselves from personal suffering. So capitalism both causes and disregards human suffering. This is a form of coercion, hence violence. Inevitably and justifiably, it generates resentment among the workers, which leads to a cycle of violence and counter-violence. The only way to rid society of violence is to transform the economic and political system so that power is equally distributed among all.

This critique was now extended beyond economic structures to the emerging mass culture of Hollywood and radio. Socialists saw these as insidious new ways for bourgeois capitalism to discipline and pacify the masses. They also recognized that nationalism could be used in the same way. This argument was especially powerful in Germany, as fascism spread its popular appeal, but it was also heard in the United States. In general, socialists made the case that capitalism is always more concerned with social order than social justice.

The socialist analysis also reinforced the new understanding of war that had emerged during World War I. The powerful industrial nations still needed to compete with one another for control of international markets and raw materials. So another war was inevitable, they predicted. That would bring more waste of human life and material resources. In a war-torn world, there can be neither the morality nor the morale to create a socialist society. For all these reasons, war and capitalism are linked together; neither can be ended unless both are ended. The logical conclusion of this line of thinking is that nonviolence requires social change. It cannot be reduced to a merely passive abstention from violence.

The next logical question was this: Must nonviolence wait for that social change to happen, or can it be the means to social change? In other words, is it possible to end capitalism and its attendant ills without violence? This was a crucial question, because the world's only example of a socialist society was the Soviet Union, which had been born in a violent revolution and justified that violence as a necessary means. On the other hand, nonviolence advocates in the United States were beginning to hear about the great successes of a nonviolent anticolonial movement in India led by a man named Gandhi. This gave them a contemporary example of nonviolent means that might achieve a nonviolent end. In the United States, the idea began to catch on that nonviolence should be valued not only as an ideal goal but also as a concrete means to attaining ideal goals. This meant that nonviolence movements would be judged by their ability to change society.

In particular, since no war was being fought at the time, they would be judged by their ability to resolve domestic conflicts between capitalists and workers. For most members of nonviolence groups, resolving conflict did not mean capitulating or compromising on workers' rights. It meant securing those rights nonviolently. U.S. workers in the 1920s were not as militant as they had been before World War I. After the Red Scare of 1919, the socialism that had given much of the passion to labor organizing was widely seen as dangerous and un-American. Indeed, any kind of labor organizing could easily be discredited by associating it (rightly or wrongly) with socialism. Yet there were still unions, and there were still organized efforts, including strikes, to get a better deal for workers. As nonviolence was more and more closely linked to efforts for social change, the natural place to express that commitment was in support of nonviolent strikes and other organized labor actions. That became a focus for many who judged nonviolence by its ability to improve the lot of workers as they stood up against the bosses.

The focus on social change and organized labor raised a new question. The goal of a strike is to get more economic justice by changing the behavior of the bosses. But the bosses are not likely to change unless the strike forces them to, by depriving them of profits. Doesn't that make a strike a form of coercion? If so, can a strike really be called a form of nonviolence? This question engendered many debates, and every imaginable answer was offered, with no consensus ever achieved.

Christianity and Nonviolence in the 1920s

Most nonviolence adherents during the 1920s were still Christians, centered in FOR. For them, this new turn to energetic social change brought new perspectives on their religion. They explained their concern for social change as obedience to God. They believed that the moral order God created can fulfill the fullest potential of every creature. This shows that God's love is directed to every individual and that God wants every individual's greatest well-being. Since God is the Creator of all and cares about all, there is a spiritual unity binding all creation. A Christian must recognize this unity and feel responsible for the well-being of all other people. This leads directly to the ideal of fellowship. Individual fulfillment requires reciprocity and cooperation. When God's moral order is followed, it promotes individual fulfillment by fostering a humane, just, and life-enhancing society for all. Doing God's will means creating that kind of society—a genuine fellowship.

The duty of all Christians is to follow God's moral order and to enact it in fellowship. True Christians do that because they love God, moral order, and all creation. They want to promote the well-being of all creatures by promoting the divine order. The loving acts of Jesus are an authoritative model for every Christian's life. Each must be willing to sacrifice for others. Each can fulfill his or her own potential only by serving others.

Since all people are children of God (the argument continued), all are capable of choosing to follow God's moral order. Why do so many fail to make that choice? Because they live in sinful—that is, unjust and inhumane—environments. The divine moral order commands us to improve the social environment, so that all individuals can fulfill their potential for living good and productive lives. Therefore, obedience to God requires us to understand and respond to social problems. This directs our attention to history. The effects of one's environment are the accumulated effects of the past, acting themselves out in the present. Every social problem is a product of history.

FOR members assumed that God acts in history to make human life better. But human freedom means that it is up to human beings to do God's work on earth. So they concluded that history is not a story of smooth progress toward an inevitable happy ending. There is no guarantee that we will soon, or ever, live in the kingdom of God on earth. Rather, history is an endless struggle for love and justice against the continuing resistance of injustice and sin. Every social problem is a site of a power struggle. The unjust are always striving to concentrate their power in institutions that will oppress individuals. Inevitably, they use violence to achieve their goals. Just as inevitably, that violence exacerbates the conflict, creates more injustice, and leads to more violence. That, too, is part of God's moral order.

FOR's vision led to a new understanding of Christian nonviolence. It was no longer merely a "counsel of perfection," directed to individuals who wanted to live a heavenly life on earth. It was now seen as a method, indeed the best method, for improving life on earth for everyone. Christian nonviolence movements had been inching in this direction ever since the Quaker colonists had made the treatment of Indians and slaves a test of one's true Christian faith. But the decade beginning in 1917 accelerated that process tremendously. By the late 1920s, Christian nonviolence in the United States had taken on a new pragmatic and this-worldly tone. It denied perfectionism and other modes of absolute thinking. It viewed life as an endless series of contests among competing values, with some truth on each side. Therefore, every concrete situation is ambiguous. The Christian must always make subjective judgments about what to believe and how to act, with no absolute truth or rules to rely on except the rule of love. So the individual conscience, the starting point of this approach to nonviolence, becomes the end point too; everything depends on the free decisions of a free and loving conscience.

Yet relativism had its limits. In fact, FOR was split by debates between more and less compromising factions. Two questions were most divisive. First, can a Christian oppose war while living in and tolerating a sinful society, or must a Christian opponent of war oppose all forms of sin and injustice? Members who tended more toward absolute thinking insisted that all forms of sin must be attacked. They offered the pragmatic argument that all forms of injustice generate violence, so it would be foolish to clip off a few branches and leave the root intact. They were probably also personalities more inclined to insist on total and absolute solutions. Others argued that it was foolish to make the best the enemy of the good. An all-out attack on the entire social structure might be desirable, but it would probably fail on all fronts, allowing violence to continue in all its forms. And it would alienate other pacifist groups who were not as radical in their view of capitalism and social problems. Did it not make more sense to join with other pacifists to end war and then address others forms and causes of violence, one by one?

The other divisive question was whether nonviolence must have a strictly Christian basis. Some in FOR were staunch and pious enough to insist that only Christianity could create a truly nonviolent society. Others were pragmatic enough to say that social change was more important than Christianity, and social change would come more quickly if Christians and non-Christians allied together. The pragmatists were also more likely to see truth and value in nonreligious, humanistic ideas. After 1924, they could point to the newly founded War Resisters' League (WRL), the first group founded to promote principled nonviolence without any explicitly religious basis. By 1930, this debate had polarized FOR, and no resolution was in sight. So the organization issued an official compromise statement. It said that nonviolence needs a spiritual basis, but not necessarily a Christian basis. Non-Christian forms of spirituality were recognized as both valid and effective. Therefore, FOR said, Christians should support non-Christians working for peaceful change.

This was another step toward moving the focus from personal religiosity to group action and political organizing, from individual salvation to practical strategies for concrete social and economic change. Of course, most members of FOR would have denied this dichotomy. They would have affirmed that individual religiosity and salvation cannot be separated from efforts to build a more just and humane society. But this affirmation was itself evidence of how far Christian nonviolence had come from its roots in the moralizing of the early nineteenth-century spiritual revivals.

Another major change from the nineteenth-century roots was the uncontested importance of women in the nonviolence movement. Women assumed that their maternal instinct naturally gave them greater concern about peace. Some also wanted to promote a distinctly feminine movement in order to demonstrate women's new political power, once they had gained the right to vote (in 1920). With suffragism no longer the focal issue, peace offered a new and valuable focus. But the women's peace movement soon found itself suffering from internal divisions. WILPF grew and developed into the main vehicle for women concerned about peace. But WILPF was as socially radical as its male-dominated counterparts, like FOR and WRL. A group of more conservative Christian women split off from WILPF. They were led by Fanny Garrison Villard, a descendant of William Lloyd Garrison who wanted to remain true to his values. These women found more congenial allies in the mainstream peace movements seeking international agreements to outlaw war.

Debates of the 1930s

It is understandable that some advocates of nonviolence, both male and female, became frustrated. As the 1920s went on, they saw little reward for their efforts. The nation as a whole seemed to be staunchly conservative. The public was ready to support the more centrist and conservative peace efforts, but it paid little attention to movements influenced by a seemingly moribund socialist ideology. Organized labor fared little better. The 1920s saw great economic expansion, but the gains went disproportionately to wealthy and middle-class citizens. Whether or not they were committed to nonviolence, unions were not able to close the gap between the prosperous and the working class.

These frustrations were difficult to bear for some nonviolence adherents. They began to wonder whether an overly strict commitment to nonviolence was preventing progress toward economic justice. The onset of the Great Depression in 1929 only made these questions more urgent. With the economic pie shrinking so fast, there seemed little hope that workers would improve their situation by strictly nonviolent means. Some began to think that organized labor would have to be more coercive in order to make significant gains. In fact, some, like Norman Thomas and A. J. Muste, felt forced to choose between nonviolence and socialism, and they chose the latter.

By the early 1930s, these doubts were reinforced when the doubters looked abroad. They saw a coercive Soviet government apparently making progress. They saw a coercive fascism on the rise in Europe and a militaristic Japanese imperialism on the march in East Asia. In the United States, many thoughtful people were wondering whether the twin dangers of economic depression and political totalitarianism might squeeze the life out of American-style democratic capitalism. In FOR, a few influential members began to ask whether strictly nonviolent responses were adequate to such an emergency, among them J. B. Matthews, FOR's secretary, and Reinhold Niebuhr, who would soon be widely acclaimed as the nation's most influential theologian. The growing doubts sparked a major debate in the organization. Although the vast majority of members held to their commitment to nonviolence, they were forced to think through that commitment more thoroughly. Those whose nonviolence was based only on feeling had a difficult time. Those who had come to the commitment in large part through rational thought found it easier to maintain their beliefs.

But they still had to find a way to act on their commitment, to show that nonviolent means could effect social change. They were helped by the resurgent strength of organized labor during the Great Depression. They supported unions and workers' cooperatives, urging them to adhere strictly to nonviolence. Most important, they supported the new wave of strikes that spread in the late 1930s, encouraging workers to use new nonviolent techniques of direct action, like sit-ins and lie-ins. (There were only a few very limited efforts to use nonviolence to promote racial justice during the 1930s.)

The move toward direct action was aided by the growing awareness of Mahatma Gandhi and the movement he was leading in India. Among the most important influences on nonviolence in the 1930s was Richard Gregg, who had gone to India to study Gandhi's movement. When he returned, he began to teach nonviolence as a very practical technique for social change. (He said little about the religious basis of Gandhi's nonviolence.) Gregg explained peace and social change as processes. He argued that since a process has many steps, it would be right in some cases to use coercion as one step toward a larger reconciliation of opposing interests. He agreed with Gandhi that the means always determine the ends. But, as a pragmatist, he added that sometimes it is also necessary to let the ends have some say in determining the means.

Gregg's idea of peace as a process became very popular in nonviolence circles. For some, it was a sort of compromise on the question of coercive means. This was one more sign of the profound change that had come upon the movement in the two decades since World War I. The tendency was ever toward stress on economic justice, social change, and transforming the conditions in which workers and the underclass were forced to live. Nonviolence was increasingly judged by the pragmatic test of its ability to help bring about those changes. This is not to say that the pious and spiritual side of the movement disappeared. Far from it. The vast majority of adherents to nonviolence still based their commitment on Christian faith. But the shift in relative emphasis was plain for all to see.

By the late 1930s the nonviolence movement in the United States was therefore an amalgamation of different and sometimes conflicting motives. It based itself on religious values, which were held to be absolute and unchanging. Yet it tried to judge each situation of conflict in its own particular context, pragmatically. In other words, all cases were the same, yet every case was different. This seeming contradiction was linked to several others. On the one hand, Christians had to credit revelation and religious tradition as unchanging sources of truth. On the other hand, as pragmatic activists they judged every situation through the eyes of reason and promoted humanistic values. So it was never quite clear whether individual religious virtue or collective social change was the highest goal. This led to a more practical quandary: Should a group like FOR form coalitions with nonreligious groups to gain specific goals, or should it work alone and guard its ideological purity?

There were other contradictions that were not directly related to religion. They affected the minority in the movement whose nonviolence was not religiously based, too. The nonviolent response to World War I had emerged from an insistence on the value of free conscience and maximum individual freedom as the highest good. Yet the growing desire for social change put the focus on institutions and group behavior. The free individual might go off in any direction. But social justice required some sort of orderly coordination of everyone's behavior. So there was an implicit conflict between the ideal of freedom and the ideal of a more just social order.

To many in FOR, these were not especially troubling issues. Many denied that there were any such conflicts in reality. They were convinced that absolute religious values and practical efforts for social change went hand in hand, that neither one could be meaningful without the other. They were quite sure that people of goodwill could always resolve their conflicts by rational compromises that would point the way to a consensus satisfying for all. So they believed it possible to harmonize all these apparent contradictions in their actual practice of nonviolence.

The nonviolent activists of the 1920s and 1930s laid down the fundamental structures that still shape the idea and the practice of nonviolence in the United States. In their discussions and debates they explored the entire spectrum of options: from a focus strictly on individuals to a focus strictly on institutions; from a purely Christian nonviolence to an ecumenical or even totally secular nonviolence; from pure nonresistance to using outright coercion for social change. They, and their successors in the movement in later years, would wrestle with the same contradictions and ever-expanding range of options. There is little in the contemporary debates in nonviolence circles that was not foreshadowed, and often fully fleshed out, in that formative era many decades ago. Their efforts, and their faith in the ultimate triumph of peaceful ways, paved the way for the nonviolence movement of the present day.

7.

Mahatma Gandhi

Mohandas K. Gandhi (1869–1948) never set foot in the United States. Yet the man called Mahatma ("the great soul") had an enormous influence on the idea of nonviolence in the United States. During the 1920s, as he led the movement for India's independence, he became well known to all those who followed world affairs. In 1930, *Time* magazine made him famous by declaring him "Man of the Year." However, only a few Americans studied his ideas carefully and shared his commitment to principled nonviolence. They could be found largely in two groups. One was FOR. The other was the African American intellectual community. A number of African American thinkers traveled to India to meet Gandhi and learn about the movement he led. There was as much, and perhaps more, written about Gandhi in African American periodicals as in white periodicals. The African American intellectuals played a key role in bringing Gandhi's thought and work to the United States.

Most whites and blacks who shared Gandhi's commitment based their nonviolence on religious faith. Ironically, though, few of them paid much attention to Gandhi's religious foundations. They studied him as a brilliant political strategist who was showing how to make nonviolent resistance work. Most studies of Gandhi to the present day have followed the same course. The largest segment of books on Gandhi still pay little attention to the details of his religious thought. Therefore, they give a rather misleading view of this greatest of nonviolent activists. Gandhi himself said many times that his political work was merely a branch of his larger commitment to social change, and his commitment to social change was merely a branch of his fundamental life's work, his quest for spiritual truth. If he ever had to make the choice, he would give up his political work and even his social efforts rather than forsake his religious quest. Yet he could not imagine having to make such a choice. In his view, political and social life was inextricably tied up with religion, and vice versa.

Gandhi's collected writings fill more than one hundred volumes. Thus, it is not possible here to do more than hint at the complexity of his ideas on nonviolence. Many issues that he considered very important must be omitted. The following paragraphs aim only to suggest the basic foundations of his idea of and commitment to nonviolence. Gandhi will probably be a major influence as long as the nonviolence tradition continues, in the United States and around the world. So it seems best to explore his idea of nonviolence on his own terms, in the broadest possible context, in order to understand his fullest potential influence. That means beginning with his religious foundations.

To be true to Gandhi's own thought, it is not enough to say that his foundations were religious. More precisely, the basic foundation was in Hinduism. He was raised as a Hindu and never left that tradition. Yet he was open to other influences. As a youth he absorbed much from the Jain tradition, an indigenous religion of India that was especially popular in his native state of Gujarat. When he studied law in London in the early 1890s, he took a great interest in Christianity, especially in the New Testament. As a young lawyer in South Africa, he became the leader of the movement for legal rights for all Indian people living there, Muslims as well as Hindus. He received help from some Jewish friends too. This was the setting in which he first experimented with what he called *satyagraha:* nonviolent resistance and civil disobedience. But he soon recognized that, for him, political action had to be grounded in religious truth. Since his movement embraced Hindus, Muslims, Christians, and Jews, he developed a deeper appreciation of the resources of all these traditions.

When he returned to India in 1915 to lead the movement for independence, he had to deal directly with the tensions (often fanned by the British) between Hindus and Muslims. So he took a special interest in seeking common ground between the two religions. At the same time, he broadened his scope to encompass Buddhist and Parsi influences, finding in every religious tradition an avenue to truth. Still, living in India tied him even more closely to his Hindu roots, and Hinduism remained the foundation and framework of all his thought and life. Tragically, Hinduism was also the source of his death. Gandhi never felt bound by every detail of Hindu tradition. He claimed that the way to make it a living faith was to adapt it to changing circumstances. This outraged many Hindu traditionalists, who believed he was undermining essential elements of their religion. In 1948, just a year after India finally gained its independence, one of these outraged Hindus shot him.

The fact that one Hindu could kill another is a sharp reminder that Hinduism is not, and has never been, a single monolithic religion. It encompasses a tremendously wide variety of experiences, beliefs, and practices. To study Gandhi's religion is to study his own unique blend of traditional and modernized Hinduism. Ironically, Gandhi's blend was influenced substantially (probably far more than he knew) by the very British rulers who were his political foes. During the nineteenth century, middle-class Indian families like Gandhi's adapted to British rule by taking on many elements of Western culture in varying ways and to varying degrees. This often included a more or less Westernized understanding of Hinduism. Their religion was a rather abstract version of Hinduism, which could make sense to Western scholars and their readers. It was usually based on a philosophical interpretation of two classical sacred scriptures: a large collection known as Upanishads and a brief text, the Bhagavad-Gita, which Gandhi came to treasure as the most valuable of all scriptures. To understand Gandhi's idea of nonviolence, the first step is to understand Hinduism as he understood it.

Gandhi never wrote down his basic ideas in any unified, systematic way. He was not an abstract philosopher. He was too busy helping people organize to improve their lives, both spiritually and materially. He never thought that systematic theories were of much help in those efforts. So his writings were almost entirely letters, short articles, editorials, and the like. From this fragmentary evidence, though, it is possible to construct a fairly clear systematic picture of his idea of nonviolence.

Truth Is God

In the Upanishads, the spiritual essence of all that exists—the fundamental reality—is called brahman. "The wonderful implication of the great truth 'brahman is real; this world is not real' grows on me from day to day," Gandhi wrote.[1] Hindu thinkers have struggled for many centuries to define precisely the difference between the real and the unreal. Some say that brahman is literally the only reality; all else is illusion (in Sanskrit, *maya*), no more real than a dream or a hallucination. For most interpreters, though, *maya* is more than mere illusion. It has some existence. But it is impermanent; it has a beginning and therefore an end. Only brahman, the imperishable, is permanent. *Maya* is sometimes described as "spun out" from brahman, as a spider spins a web out from itself. Brahman is sometimes said to be the innermost essence, or the thread on which all reality is strung, like pearls. Brahman is also described as the sun, with *maya* being the rays of the sun. As this metaphor suggests, brahman pervades everything, yet is above and beyond everything. All interpreters agree, though, that only brahman is ultimately real; in Sanskrit, it is *sat,* that which really is.

To put it that way, however, gives a false impression of a static being, like the unchanging God of Western philosophy. Brahman does have a static aspect. And relatively Westernized Hindus like Gandhi felt perfectly comfortable using the English word *God* as a synonym for brahman. But since brahman is the essence of all reality, brahman is also the cosmic process. At times, Gandhi seemed to understand it as the pattern of relationships among all things, the way that all realities are bound together and interact as parts of the single ultimate reality. Those interactions are dynamic and constantly changing. Therefore, brahman is the eternal pattern of endless change. In this sense, brahman is not only the way things really are, but the way things really ought to proceed in the cosmos. It is the dynamic moral order at heart of reality.

"All the other forces are static, while God is the Life Force, immanent and at the same time transcendent." The word *transcendent* is important here. It warns against simply equating brahman with a collection of "everything in the whole world." Gandhi did write: "God is the sum total of all life." But God, or brahman, is not only the sum total of all reality that can be experienced, from the tiniest pebble up to the grandest god; brahman is also much more. Even a collection of "everything in the whole world" would ultimately perish; in that sense, it is unreal. Only the imperishable brahman is *sat,* the really real, the essential being of the endless process we call reality. Things come and go, but the pattern by which they interact is eternal.[2]

For Gandhi, the most crucial insight is that *sat* is truly real, the only real truth. In Sanskrit, the word for truth is *satya:*

> The word *satya* is derived from *sat,* which means that which is. *Satya* means a state of being. Nothing is or exists in reality except Truth. That is why *sat* or *satya* is the right name for God. In fact it is more correct to say that Truth is God than to say that God is Truth. But as we cannot do without a ruler or general, the name God is and will remain more current. On deeper thinking, however, it will be realized that *sat* or *satya* is the only correct and fully significant name for God. . . . Devotion to this Truth is the sole justification for our existence. All our activities should be centred in truth. Truth should be the very breath of our life. . . . God as Truth has been for me, at any rate, a treasure beyond price.[3]

Here is the crux of Gandhi's Hinduism and, as far as he could tell, of all religion. He repeated over and over again that religion is the lifelong quest for absolute Truth.

"Pure and absolute truth should be our ideal. . . . Reaching it is attaining *moksha.*" *Moksha* is the term used in the Upanishads for the highest state of spiritual perfection. A person who attains *moksha* experiences directly the key insight of the Upanishads: *tat tvam asi* (you are that). Your essential self (in Sanskrit, *atman*) is identical with that brahman. There is no difference at all. The *atman* transcends what we normally call the self (body, thoughts, feelings, personality, ego), just as brahman transcends all existence that is *maya*. As Gandhi put it: "One ought always to remember, while dwelling on Him, that one is but a drop, the tiniest of creatures of the ocean that is God." The goal of all spiritual life is to know oneself, totally and at every instant, as brahman, a spark of the divine, a drop in the infinite sea of Truth.[4]

What exactly does it mean to know oneself as brahman? Hinduism offers many different answers to this question, because it offers so many different interpretations of brahman. Since Gandhi never adhered to one clear and consistent view of brahman, he had no single view of the relationship of self to brahman. He sometimes seemed to say that the only way to know truth is for the individual self to disappear entirely: "Realization of Truth is impossible without a complete merging of oneself in and identification with this limitless ocean of life."[5] This suggests that the sense of separate self is totally illusory; *moksha* means experiencing the truth that brahman is the only reality.

More specifically, Gandhi could speak of this merger in terms of a cosmic consciousness: "Where there is Truth, there also is knowledge which is true. . . . To the man who has realized this truth in its fullness, nothing else remains to be known, because, as we have seen above, all knowledge is necessarily included in it."[6] In *moksha,* one's own knowledge becomes the ultimate Truth itself. One realizes that what we call the self is actually the sum total of all reality. One's own consciousness is the cosmic consciousness that is brahman. Our own knowledge, the limited truths that we discover in life, are all parts of the ultimate, infinite Truth. Whenever we know something to be true, and whenever we adhere to that truth in our thoughts and deeds, we participate in Truth, in the process that is brahman. "The most ignorant among mankind have some truth in them. We are all sparks of Truth. The sum total of these sparks is indescribable, as-yet-Unknown Truth, which is God."[7] From the instant of conception, we are all essentially drops of pure consciousness in the ocean of pure consciousness that is Truth.

Sometimes, though, Gandhi spoke of the individual self as if it had real existence: "We are all sparks of the divine and, therefore, partake of its divine nature."[8] If brahman is the force or pattern of relationships among all things, then each self must partake of the divine nature, simply by virtue of being alive. The individual is in some sense a separate self. Yet the essence of each individual's life is being woven into the cosmic web of endless interactions, which is brahman. The essence of life is not what separates one from all others, but what binds one to all others. The essential truth is not separation but interconnectedness; that is, my life is fully and eternally united with all life.

Sometimes Gandhi captured the ambiguity of his thought quite precisely: "The soul [*atman*] is unborn and indestructible. The personality perishes, must perish. Individuality is and is not even as each drop in the ocean is an individual and is not. It is not because apart from the ocean it has no existence. It is because the ocean has no existence if the drop has not, i.e., has no individuality. They are beautifully interdependent."[9] Had he been interested in systematic precision, Gandhi might have gone on to explain brahman in terms of this interdependence. But he was content to say different things at different times and let the question of self and brahman remain only vaguely answered. The essential point was not theoretical definition but a life devoted to realizing in direct experience the truth of *tat tvam asi* (you are that [brahman]). Once that realization is attained, Gandhi might have said, precise definitions are irrelevant.

Why does it take such strenuous spiritual effort to realize the truth directly? The simple answer of Hinduism is that we are ignorant of the truth. Why are we ignorant? To answer that question, Gandhi turned to his beloved text, the Bhagavad-Gita. The Gita's simple explanation for ignorance is, in one word, desire. Every desire stems from the mistaken notion that the person who desires is separate from whatever he or she desires. Every desire reinforces this mistaken notion of being a separate individual. Desire stems from and reinforces our sense of ego; when Gandhi spoke of desire, he always meant selfish, egotistical desire. Conversely, when there is no desire, there is no illusion of separate existence: "He who has achieved extinction of the ego becomes the very image of Truth; he may well be called the brahman."[10]

The way to Truth and to *moksha* is to restrain and control all desires, until ultimately there is no desire at all. "In working out plans for self-restraint, attention must not for a single moment be withdrawn from the fact that we are all sparks of the divine and, therefore, partake of its divine nature, and since there can be no such thing as self-indulgence with the divine it must of necessity be foreign to human nature." The divine has no desire because it is the totality of all the processes that make up reality. It lacks nothing; therefore, it can want nothing. Essential human nature—the *atman*—is that totality, so it too can want nothing. "If we get a hard grasp of that elementary fact," Gandhi continues, "we should have no difficulty in attaining self-control." That claim is rather misleading. In fact, Gandhi admitted that he struggled mightily his whole life to attain self-control: "It is always a case of intense mental struggle. It is not that I am incapable of anger, for instance, but I succeed on almost all occasions to keep my feelings under control. Whatever may be the result, there is always in me a conscious struggle." Traditional Hinduism has developed many different kinds of spiritual disciplines, all aiming at greater control of emotion and desire.[11]

Gandhi's great contribution in the realm of religion was his distinctively modern method of spiritual discipline: serving other people through organizing for social, economic, and political change. While Gandhi was not the first to do this, he was certainly the greatest and most influential exponent of this spiritual path. For Gandhi, the logic was clear. Ego is self-love. The way to transcend ego is to love others. Love of others is not primarily an emotion but rather an attitude translated into action. Love is most real when we put aside our own needs to serve others. "God is TRUTH. It is impossible to reach HIM, that is TRUTH except through LOVE. LOVE can only be expressed fully when man reduces himself to a cipher [i.e., a zero, nothing]. This is the only effort worth making, and it is possible only through ever-increasing self-restraint." "True development consists in reducing ourselves to a cipher. Selfless service is the secret of life. To rise above passions is the highest ideal."[12]

From the Gandhian perspective, it makes no sense to speak of balancing one's own needs against the needs of others. That would only foster the illusion that there is a separate self with its own separate needs. There should be no limit on service of others, because serving the needs of another person is actually serving ultimate reality itself:

> Realization of Truth is impossible without a complete merging of oneself in and identification with this limitless ocean of life. Hence, for me, there is no escape from social service; there is no happiness on earth beyond or apart from it. . . . The purpose of life is undoubtedly to know oneself. We cannot do it unless we learn to identify ourselves with all that lives. The sum total of that life is God. Hence the necessity of realizing God living within every one of us. The instrument of this knowledge is boundless selfless service.[13]

Service to others is the only way to merge with the limitless brahman, because the essence of brahman is service. *Sat* is a process in which the innumerable creatures sustain themselves by meeting their basic needs. Truth includes the truth that all beings should be able to sustain themselves in their particularly appointed ways. But *sat* is a single unified process in which all elements of reality are bound together. *Sat* encompasses the infinite web of interconnections and interactions that make up reality. Those interactions are essential for every creature's survival, since every creature depends on others to meet its own needs.

More specifically, Gandhi stressed, every creature survives only because others make sacrifices. Every manifestation of brahman requires and receives something from some other manifestation. Each helps to sustain all the others by sacrificing for others. All are linked in this endless chain of mutual giving. Love is the name of that chain, the force that binds all beings together. Each one of us exists only because others have already made innumerable sacrifices so that we could exist. Now we have the opportunity to sacrifice for others.

This opportunity is also our sacred duty. To do one's duty, by making the required sacrifice, is the only act of love; the only way to love is to do one's duty. Loving dutiful sacrifice is the eternally true pattern, the moral order at the heart of reality. Any act that helps keep that pattern going is participation in Truth and brings the doer closer to Truth. Therefore, serving others is not serving discrete individual beings. It is serving *sat,* ultimate reality itself. Any act that aims to serve *sat* is a manifestation of *sat.* It is *satya,* a true act, an act of Truth.

Seen from the spiritual perspective, reality "is an undivided and indivisible whole; and, therefore, what is or may be good for one must be good for all. . . . Never have I taken up any activity—be it sectional or national—which would be detrimental to the good of humanity as a whole."[14] The Gandhian path to *moksha* is to serve Truth by setting aside personal likes and dislikes and serving the totality by serving all creatures equally:

> Just as the sea accepts the water of all rivers within itself, purifies it and gives it back again, so you too, if you make yourselves as the sea, will be able to accept all people. As the sea makes no distinction between good rivers and bad, but purifies all, so one person, whose heart is purified and enlarged with nonviolence and truth, can contain everything in that heart and it will not overflow or lose its serenity. Remember that you aim at being such a person.[15]

Serving Truth also means overcoming fear. Fear and desire are two sides of the same coin of concern with self. When we desire something, we fear not getting it. Once we have it, we fear losing it. When we are afraid of something, we are usually just desiring to avoid the unpleasant consequences it can bring. To serve Truth, one must overcome fear as well as desire. "If you want to follow the vow of truth in any shape or form, fearlessness is the necessary consequence. . . . We fear consequences, and therefore we are afraid to tell the truth. A man who fears God will certainly not fear any earthly consequence." "Fear and love are contradictory terms. Love is reckless in giving away, oblivious as to what it gets in return." Love is also oblivious of what is risked or might be lost. Indeed, once we experience ourselves as ciphers, as drops in the ocean, we realize that there is nothing that can be lost, for we are already and always the sum total of eternal reality: you are that. "In order to be fearless we should love all and adhere to the path of truth."[16]

Truth and Nonviolence

The quest for Truth is the foundation of Gandhi's understanding of religion. Therefore it is also the foundation of his understanding of nonviolence: "A truthful man cannot long remain violent. . . . As long as there is the slightest trace of violence in him, he will fail to find the truth he is searching for." This was not an ethical assumption or presupposition. For Gandhi, it was a logical conclusion, based on his definition of violence. He used the Sanskrit term for violence, *himsa,* which means (in his view) acting toward others with selfish desire or intent, trying to force them to comply with one's own desire. Perhaps the best translation of *himsa,* as Gandhi used the term, is "coercion." "Coercion means some harmful force used against a person who is expected to do something desired by the user of the force." Thus coercion is always an expression of desire: "There is violence always in the attachment to one's ego. When doing anything, one must ask oneself this question: 'Is my action inspired by egoistic attachment [desire]?' If there is no such attachment, then there is no violence."[17]

When speaking of nonviolence, Gandhi typically used the Sanskrit term *ahimsa,* which literally means "without *himsa.*" Any action that is not motivated by selfish desire but instead aims to serve and benefit others is an act of love: *ahimsa. Ahimsa* is an attitude of full, conscious awareness that one is participating in *sat,* the process of reality, and that one can never separate oneself from the process of reality. Since each of us is already the fullness of reality, there is nothing to desire.

Ahimsa, or egoless action, "implies as complete self-purification as is humanly possible." But Gandhi had an extraordinarily high standard of what is possible: "Nonviolence is impossible without complete self-effacement." Gandhi never claimed that he had reached this state of perfection. Over and over again, he said things like, "I do not know that I have in me purification enough to realize true peace or nonviolence." But he never doubted that moral perfection was a valid and meaningful ideal[18]:

To say that perfection is not attainable on this earth is to deny God.
. . . There is no occasion for limiting the capacity for improvement.
Life to me would lose all its interest if I felt that I *could* not attain
perfect love on earth. After all, what matters is that our capacity for
loving ever expands. It is a slow test. How shall you love men who
thwart you even in well-doing? And yet that is the time of supreme
test.[19]

The test is the one posed by Jesus in the New Testament: Can we love our
enemies? More precisely, according to Gandhi, the question is: Can we love
those who consider themselves our enemies? "For one who follows the doctrine of *ahimsa*, there is no room for an enemy; he denies the existence of an
enemy."[20] Those who follow *ahimsa* are acting on the truth, the oneness of
all reality. They know that their own best interests can never be separated
from the best interests of all reality, including every other person. To love,
to want the best for the entire process, is also to want the best for every
individual part of the process. Those who coerce others in order to gain
advantage are acting untruthfully. By treating their own well-being as something separate from the well-being of others, they are denying the essential
truth that self and other are facets of the same single reality. Denying that
truth is the basis of all evil and suffering.

But when others consider themselves enemies and try to do us harm, then
we are put to the test. Can we continue to serve them and want their best
interests, too? As in the New Testament, it is a matter of inner attitude as
well as outward action: "You may not harbour an uncharitable thought . . .
wishing that some harm should be done to the enemy, or that he should be
put out of the way. . . . If we harbour even this thought, we depart from this
doctrine of *ahimsa*."[21] This is not only a matter of moral precept, but also
of simple logic. If we do not experience ourselves as separate beings with
separate interests, then we cannot want to promote our interests over others. We cannot want to defeat others or get the best of them. We can only
want what is best for all, what the infinite process of reality itself requires.
Therefore, we must do *ahimsa*—act without desire.

Gandhi was quick to recognize the obvious problem here. Different people
have different ideas of what is best for all. If everyone's truth is a part of the
ultimate Truth, how is it that one person's truth can flatly contradict
another's? Who is to decide what the truth really is? In so many conflict
situations, each side is sincerely convinced that it is in the right. All too
often, that certainty leads one group to impose its views upon the other. Yet
what is the alternative? Should we simply stand by and watch others do
something that we are sure is morally evil or unjust?

To resolve this dilemma, Gandhi said, it is necessary to distinguish between essential and nonessential truths. On nonessentials, it is best to compromise for the sake of peace and harmony: "The test for brotherhood is that each party always makes allowances for the weaknesses of the other, and I know that on the Judgment Day that party will win the day which will be able to show that it has always surrendered on non-essentials."[22]

But if an essential truth or moral principle is at stake, a person should not compromise. To give up resisting at that point is cowardly; Gandhi called it "the nonviolence of the weak." He insisted, many times, that "it is any day better to use brute force than to betray cowardice."[23] "The nonviolence of the strong" is nonviolence that keeps resisting, even to the death, rather than compromise on a matter of fundamental principle. ("Nonviolence of the strong" also implies that one has the capacity and the courage to do violence but refrains from violence on principle.)

This does mean insisting on one's own view of truth. But there is no alternative for a person of conscience. As long as people are nonviolent,

> there is nothing wrong in every man following Truth according to his lights. Indeed it is his duty to do so. Then if there is a mistake on the part of anyone so following Truth, it will be automatically set right. For the quest of Truth involves *tapascharya*, self-suffering, sometimes even unto death. There can be no place in it for even a trace of self-interest. . . . The question is asked why we should call any rule unjust. In saying so, we ourselves assume the function of a judge. It is true. But in this world, we always have to act as judges for ourselves. That is why [the nonviolent person] does not strike his adversary with arms. If he has Truth on his side, he will win, and if his thought is faulty, he will suffer the consequences of his fault.[24]

By taking all the risk of suffering upon oneself and protecting the other against any threat of suffering, one maintains the attitude of love. And, if there is a mistake, only the person who made it will suffer, since no suffering is imposed on those with a different truth. So "the absolutist's sphere of destruction will be always the narrowest possible."[25]

An uncompromising yet nonviolent struggle for one's truth is also the only way to come closer to absolute Truth. "Absolute truth alone is God. It is beyond reach. At the most we can say it is *neti, neti* [not this, not that; neither this truth nor that truth is the full truth]. The truth we see is relative, many-sided, plural and is the whole truth [only] for a given time."[26] Even those truths that seem most certain must be viewed as tentative. It is always possible that a wider perspective will open up, revealing what we held as true to be false. So it is always a mistake to feel absolutely certain about anything. Every time we affirm some truth and act on it, we should consider it as an experiment. Indeed, Gandhi titled his autobiography *The Story of My Experiments with Truth*.

If the "experiment" is going to be valid, there must be no selfish motivation in the quest for truth. "There is no scope for vanity in it and the only way of reaching it is through *ahimsa*."[27] This was one of Gandhi's main arguments for *ahimsa*. If we coerce others to promote our own view of truth, then we are acting as separate individuals and detaching ourselves from the totality of reality. We are more concerned about winning the contest than discovering Truth. Then we close ourselves off to the possibility of discovering new truth; doing so moves us further away from absolute Truth. When we pursue Truth for its own sake, not motivated by any desire, we participate in the desireless totality, which is Truth itself. Thus we come closer to the absolute Truth. And being desireless means being nonviolent. The sole motivation of *ahimsa* is to discover Truth, not to gain a victory. That is the only way to have a valid experiment with truth.

Ahimsa means remembering that everyone's truth is partial, that there is always another way to interpret the situation and to respond to it. The nonviolent person "gives his opponent the same right of independence and feeling of truth that he reserves to himself, seeing if he wants to fight for truth he will do so by inviting injury upon his own person."[28] Therefore, the nonviolent person never coerces another, no matter how wrong the other appears to be.

In a sense, the opponent is secondary in any conflict situation. The real test is between Truth and the person committed to nonviolence. It is an experiment to discover the depth of commitment to a particular truth. The real question is: How much suffering can we endure for the sake of what we now hold to be the truth? If we value our pleasure, our well-being, or even our life more than this truth, then this truth turns out to be something other than ultimate Truth and should be abandoned. But if we impose our truth upon another, we can never truly test our own relationship to this truth. If every conviction of absolute certainty is seen as an experiment with ourselves rather than a battle against an enemy, then absolutism and tolerance can coexist. This approach to truth combines uncompromising certainty with tolerance for differences. It offers the virtues of both absolutism and relativism simultaneously. Again, though, the price is to take all the suffering in the situation upon oneself.

Self-suffering is a fundamental part of all spiritual purification, Gandhi assumed. The less sense of ego or separate self we have, the more suffering we can endure, and the more we are free from the fear of suffering. Conversely, the more we accept suffering in a spirit of love, the more we learn to overcome fear and the illusion of ego. The more we transcend the illusion of ego, the closer we come to Truth itself. Only those who are willing to endure suffering even unto death can totally transcend ego and know Truth.

Attachment to the body is the last barrier to Truth and therefore to *ahimsa*. "The body exists because of our ego. The utter extinction of the body is *moksha*." *Moksha* means a life of perfect love, because it is the end of all desire to possess anything, even our physical being. However, "in actual life, we can hardly exercise perfect love, for the body as a possession will always remain with us. Man will ever remain imperfect, and it will always be his part to try to be perfect." As long as we live a bodily existence, we must destroy some other life (even if only vegetable life) in order to live. We must do *himsa*. "Still we have to live a life of *ahimsa* in the midst of a world full of *himsa*, and we can do so only if we cling to Truth. That is why I can derive *ahimsa* from truth. Out of Truth emerge love and tenderness. A votary of Truth, one who wold scrupulously cling to Truth, must be utterly humble. His humility should increase with his observance of Truth." *Ahimsa*, by taking all suffering upon oneself, teaches one to let go of attachment to the body. It brings one closer to the ideal of *moksha*. Therefore, it teaches love and Truth.[29]

Satyagraha

From Gandhi's perspective, the only vital question in any situation is: How can I be more perfectly selfless and loving and thus come closer to absolute Truth? The answer, he insisted, always turns upon the way one conducts oneself, not upon the outcome of the situation. He pointed out that we cannot control the outcome of any situation, in any event. The only thing we can control is our own decision-making process. We can choose to think and act more or less selflessly. Once that choice is made, the true significance of the occasion is already determined. Everything else is secondary. As the Bhagavad-Gita puts it: "You have the right to act, not to the fruits [results] of the act." That is why nonviolence should always be judged by the intention, not the outcome: "A votary of *ahimsa* . . . will strive for the greatest good of all and die in the attempt to realize the ideal. . . . That he may therefore make grievous mistakes is irrelevant to the fact of the motive."[30]

It is not quite accurate to say that Gandhi focused on means and ignored ends. He put it more precisely when he said: "Nonviolence is the law of life for human beings. For me it is both a means and an end."[31] In other words, there is no essential difference between means and ends, for at least two reasons. First, the outcome of a situation is basically determined by the means used to achieve it. To take one especially important example: whenever violence is used as a means, the result will always embody violence and therefore lead to more violence. Whenever nonviolence is used as a means, the result will always embody nonviolence and reduce future violence.

There is a second reason that the means is the end. If a loving motive is the only thing that really matters, then the process of acting lovingly, for the good of all reality, is the goal in every situation. As long as one intends the good of all and acts on that intention, then nothing more can be desired. The goal has already been achieved. Gandhi admitted that it is possible to deceive oneself. That is why, all his life, he set an example of the most careful (sometimes agonizing) self-scrutiny.

He also admitted that the results of an action should not be totally ignored: "To be detached from fruits of action is not to be ignorant of them."[32] If every act is an experiment in truth, it makes sense to pay attention to the outcome of the experiment. That can help give a more accurate understanding of what the good of all demands: "One should never be content with one's purity of motive alone. The necessity of knowledge [that is, knowing the results of an action] has been accepted for the reason that one may not commit an error in spite of a pure motive."[33] Still, as long as an action is done with the best of loving intentions, it should be considered strictly nonviolent, and thus the right thing to do. The rightness depends on the motive, not the result. Therefore, a person should never avoid or abandon an action simply because the contemplated results may not follow.

Many people may ask: If I am not motivated by desire for some gain or benefit, what would motivate me to act at all? How can I know what to do unless I aim at some desired outcome? Even the most ordinary act seems to have some goal. How can I live a full, rich life without being goal oriented? Gandhi tried not to think about life in these terms. In any situation, he tried to ask only: What is my duty here and now? The Bhagavad-Gita teaches that all people must do the duty imposed on them by their particular caste identity. Although Gandhi did not reject the caste idea completely, he applied it very flexibly. Most notably, he waged a vigorous campaign to end oppression of the very lowest caste, the so-called untouchables. (This was one of his most grievous offenses, in the eyes of some Hindu traditionalists.)

However, Gandhi's idea of duty was much broader than caste duty. He assumed that at every moment every person was aware of some basic need in the world that that particular person could help to meet. Whatever need is closest to hand, our duty is to try to fulfill it, which means always to act

with love. Gandhi taught that political action, even among the most oppressed, should aim not at securing rights but at responsibly discharging
duties: "All rights to be deserved and preserved come from duty well done.
Thus the very right to live accrues to us only when we do the duty of citizenship of the world."[34]

There are certainly times, however, when the clearest duty of every person is to stand up for human rights. As a subject of the British colonial
empire for virtually his whole life, Gandhi was acutely aware of the evils of
political and economic oppression. He was convinced that all forms of oppression are wrong because they are untruthful. Truth, or *sat*, as a universal
moral order, includes the freedom for individuals, groups, and nations to
make the fundamental decisions that shape their lives. Gandhi called this
swaraj (literally, "self-rule"). Anything that abridges *swaraj* denies the proper
moral order and hence denies Truth. To serve Truth, then, is to serve and
promote *swaraj*. Beyond the physical suffering it inflicted, British colonialism was evil because it worked every day to deprive the Indian people of
swaraj. So he focused primarily on the quest for *swaraj* in India—so much
so that many people understood *swaraj* as a synonym for Indian independence.

For Gandhi, though, political independence was merely one facet of
swaraj: "I am not interested in freeing India merely from the English yoke.
I am bent upon freeing India from any yoke whatsoever. . . . Hence for me
the movement of swaraj is a movement of self-purification. . . . Work of
social reform or self-purification of this nature is a hundred times dearer to
me than what is called purely political work." Gandhi worked to purify
India of the social prejudices that set some Indians oppressing others. He
worked to purify India of ignorance, illiteracy, greed, and all the other factors that perpetuate massive poverty.[35]

Ultimately, though, his idea of *swaraj* was a religious one. He defined it
as "disciplined rule from within."[36] Freedom, self-rule, and self-control would
be achieved only by purification from all forms of desire. Gandhi drew a
direct link between freedom and overcoming desire. Anyone who is motivated by desire is controlled by that desire. Since all people are interconnected in society, it is usually hard to fulfill a desire without involving some
other person. That other person then has it within his or her power to be-
stow or withhold the desired reward or the feared punishment. So, people
motivated by desire usually bend to the will of the more powerful. They will
follow the course of action dictated by the more powerful in order to reach
their desired goal. In most cases, therefore, desire means being controlled
by another person.

Real freedom, for Gandhi, meant inward freedom, the freedom to do
what is true and right in any situation, regardless of the consequences. People

who are truly free will pay attention to the responses of others, but they will never let their own actions be dictated by the responses of others. People who have inward freedom cannot be coerced. They may face an oppressive government with a huge army and other trappings of political power. They may have deadly violence directed at them. But the oppressors have no power over them, for there is no way to coerce inwardly free people—not even with deadly violence. "The outward freedom therefore that we shall attain will only be in exact proportion to the inward freedom to which we may have grown at any given moment. And if this is the correct view of freedom, our chief energy must be concentrated upon reform from within. ... Everyone's freedom is within his own grasp."[37] In other words, *swaraj* and *ahimsa* are two sides of the same coin. Violent people are motivated by their desire for a particular goal. Therefore, they are enslaved to others. Only through nonviolence and detachment from desire can one be free to do the right thing, regardless of the consequences. For Gandhi, that was the only genuine freedom.

Gandhi applied this principle to India. He said that the Indians were enslaved to the British only because they let themselves be. On the day that they chose to embrace nonviolence, rise above their fear, and refuse to follow British rules and rulers, they would begin to act like free people. Then they would, in fact, be free. Having taken back their own rights, they would begin to fight for the rights of others too: "Through the deliverance of India, I seek to deliver the so-called weaker races of the earth from the crushing heels of Western exploitation in which England is the greatest partner."[38]

Gandhi saw nothing wrong with fighting when basic rights were being violated. He refused to speak of *ahimsa* as "passive resistance," because he wanted to stress that it must be an active process of continual, forceful resistance to injustice. Indeed, for him the word *ahimsa* meant not simply "without *himsa*" but actively being "against *himsa*." He insisted that it is better to resist moral wrongs violently than not to resist at all. But resistance can serve Truth only if it is done nonviolently, for the sake of promoting the truth rather than for the sake of winning victories. For this kind of resistance, he coined the term *satyagraha*, which he sometimes translated "truth force" or even "soul force." Literally, it means "hanging on to truth," or "persevering in truth." Perhaps the best translation is "persisting in truth" or "persistence of truth."

In practice, *satyagraha* means organized efforts to resist nonviolently any kind of political, social, or economic wrongs. In order to be genuine *satyagraha*, the resistance must be for selfless reasons. "Whatever is done with a selfish motive cannot be called *satyagraha*. That would be like insisting on untruth."

So *satyagrahis* (those who practice *satyagraha*) are motivated by their duty to serve others, not by any desire to secure their own rights or privileges. Having no desires, they depend on no one to satisfy their desires. Therefore, they rule themselves; they alone have *swaraj*. "Real *swaraj* is possible only where *satyagraha* is the guiding force of the people." Because *satyagraha* is by definition selfless, it is also by definition nonviolent. Where there is no desire, there can be no enmity. "*Satyagraha* is gentle, it never wounds. It must not be the result of anger or malice. . . . It is a breach of *satyagraha* to wish ill to an opponent or to say a harsh word to him or of him with the intention of doing harm."[39]

Satyagrahis do what is right, regardless of consequences. They do not try to force others to bend to their will. They simply go about their business of seeking truth and doing truth, allowing others to choose freely how they will behave. In effect, a *satyagrahi* says to others, no matter how violent or oppressive they may be: "It is not my place to tell you how to act. That is up to you. But regardless of how you act, I will do what I believe is right." If that involves refusing to follow laws or receiving physical violence, *satyagrahis* accept whatever consequences come their way. But the consequences do not affect their own actions. So they can never be coerced.

Precisely because *satyagrahis* are not seeking to change others' behaviors to achieve their goals, they actually have more power to change others' behaviors and achieve their goals. "The truth is that power resides in the people. . . . Imagine a whole people unwilling to conform to the laws of the legislature, and prepared to suffer the consequences of non-compliance. They will bring the whole legislative and executive machinery to a standstill." The judicial machinery may still function; *satyagrahis* show their respect for law and order by lovingly accepting whatever punishments are meted out. They never try to avoid punishment, because they never try to avoid suffering: "*Satyagraha* cannot proceed a step without fearlessness. Those alone can follow the path of nonviolent resistance who are free from fear, whether as to their possessions, false honor, their relatives, the government, bodily injuries or death."[40]

Since *satyagrahis* are not swayed by fear or desire, their inward freedom will bring them outward freedom as well. There is nothing anyone can do to force them to deviate from the way of Truth, as they see it. Sooner or later, the oppressors will see that they are powerless to impose their will. The judicial punishments and the oppression will then cease. The oppressors' violence and punishments will only speed up the end of oppression. Gandhi was sure that the sight of nonviolent people suffering unjustly, yet still loving their tormenters, would "melt the stoniest heart."[41] He was sure that showing friendship and compassion to even the harshest oppressor was the fastest way to end the oppression.

Yet he never advised *satyagrahis* to love their enemies or provoke unjust suffering as a tactic to gain sympathy and thereby win the battle. *Satyagrahis* must never calculate their actions in order to achieve a certain result. Letting the end justify the means always leads eventually to compromise, even if the means are peaceful. In *satyagraha*, the sympathy and the victory will come of themselves, Gandhi affirmed, as long as the right means are strictly followed.

Some critics have charged that Gandhi did not always focus on means rather than ends. His words sometimes make it sound as if he based his decisions on political goals. For example, although he once wrote, "I am not interested in freeing India merely from the English yoke," he also wrote: "I long for freedom from the English yoke. I would pay any price for it."[42] Some have also charged that Gandhi focused on results, not principles, when he needed to enlist the Indian masses in the independence movement. His ideal of nonviolence was simply too demanding for most people (and still is), these critics contend. So he sometimes argued for nonviolence based on the results it could bring, although he always denied he was doing so. Related to this charge is another: Gandhi's political strategies did cause the British to suffer and thus were coercive. The British gave India its independence not because they were persuaded that Gandhi was right, but because Gandhi made the cost of colonialism too high. In sum, the critics say, his political practice contradicted his spiritually based theory.

Clearly, Gandhi was a first-rate political strategist, always finding ways to undermine British power. He knew that in politics there is always a strong temptation to do whatever it takes to achieve the goal. There is an equally strong and related temptation to maximize power. The best way to maximize power is to choose whatever means are most likely to achieve one's goals, that is, whatever means are most likely to coerce the other side to capitulate. And if capitulation is not possible, the politician's temptation is always to compromise. Politics is often defined as the art of the possible.

Knowing all this, Gandhi walked a fine line. He tried to chart effective political strategy without letting politics determine his choices, without intending to coerce, without admitting a difference between means and ends. He knew what a great challenge this is, and how easy it is to go astray. At times he may have slipped off the fine line. In Gandhi's defense, though, it should be said that he viewed all people as free agents. If many Indians decided to use nonviolence merely as a tactic, or if the British decided to leave India because they wanted to avoid suffering, those were decisions they made. It is at least logically consistent to say that he was not responsible for those results, because he never shaped his own decisions to force others in those directions; he merely did what he thought was right at every moment. Perhaps not even Gandhi himself could ever know for sure exactly what his motives were. But it is logically possible for someone to be concerned always with means, never with ends.

Gandhi's approach to nonviolence has been criticized for other seeming contradictions, too. For example, he seemed to have contradictory views about bodily needs. On the one hand, he took a vow of poverty and owned little more than he could carry in his two hands. Yet he pointed to the vast poverty of India as one of the worst results of British rule. He was tormented by the thought of millions having too little to eat and no decent place to live. Why care about poverty if the body is the primary barrier to perfect Truth?

Gandhi tried to resolve this contradiction by distinguishing between voluntary and forced poverty. The millions of poor who have not chosen their poverty have been coerced into it by those who control and profit from the economic system. Mass poverty is therefore a manifestation of structural violence—coercion and suffering woven into the fabric of society. Voluntary poverty, according to Gandhi, is the best way to serve the needs of the masses forced into poverty. But he may have been trying to synthesize the Hindu ideal of detachment from the body and the world with the Christian ideal of sympathy for those who suffer in the world. He may never have escaped from that contradiction.

Gandhi's vow of poverty opened him to another criticism. He adopted poverty to help him toward the ideal of having no physical desire. But perhaps he carried it too far. His writings include long discussions of his efforts to eliminate physical desire. To overcome all desire for food, he spent a great deal of time seeking a diet that would keep him healthy with the minimum of food. He was also quite concerned with finding ways to eliminate sexual desire. Is all this necessary to transcend selfish desire? Or is it actually an indirect way to remain preoccupied with oneself? Indeed, critics say, such strenuous efforts to transcend desire actually make us more preoccupied with desire and thus more tied to the self and its individual desires.

In response to this and other criticisms, Gandhi would surely have admitted that he may have been guilty of logical contradiction. He was not a strict rationalist. Reason is a useful check to tell us when we are veering away from truth, he said. But reason alone cannot bring us to truth. That is ultimately the task of religious faith. So he was willing to tolerate some inconsistency in his experiments with truth. And surely he would have admitted that his experiments sometimes failed. He was the first to insist that he was just as imperfect as everyone else. The only difference, he would say, is that he never stopped striving for the ideal of perfection. An individual's failure should cast doubt on the individual, not on the ideal. The important thing is to keep on experimenting with truth. Gandhi's great achievement, in his own eyes, was not that he attained perfect Truth, but that he dedicated his whole life to the experiment. Yet he could keep on experimenting, and discover *satyagraha* as a new mode of spiritual life, only because he had faith that perfect Truth, however elusive, can ultimately be attained.

8

Reinhold Niebuhr

During the 1930s, some nonviolence advocates in the United States were encouraged by the news of Gandhi's successes in India. Others, however, paid more attention to the declining fortunes of the working class and the rise of totalitarian communism and fascism. They found it hard to sustain their faith in the efficacy of nonviolence as a means for social change. There was a growing body of opinion saying that conflicts are never resolved without some degree of coercion. This view was promoted especially by those who saw all conflict rooted in the gap between rich and poor. They were convinced that the rich would never give up any of their riches and privileges unless they were forced to. That would take a revolution. And successful revolutions always require violence. By 1932, those who took this view were eagerly reading its most profound theoretical statement, Reinhold Niebuhr's classic book *Moral Man and Immoral Society*.

Niebuhr (1892–1971) was a young Protestant minister who committed himself to nonviolence and socialism in the wake of World War I. His brilliant mind and many talents soon made him a leader in FOR. But during the 1920s he devoted most of his energy to the church in Detroit that he served as pastor. As the decade went on, more and more of his congregation consisted of assembly-line workers in the rapidly expanded automobile factories. So he saw firsthand how the new system of industrial mass production worked. Henry Ford and other company owners grew fabulously wealthy. Middle managers and technical professional lived comfortable suburban lives. Meanwhile, the vast majority of workers, the people who actually made the cars, were overworked and underpaid. They spent their days sweating in dangerous factories. They spent their nights and Sundays crowded into substandard housing. Their efforts to unionize, so that they could have the power to demand a fair share of the wealth, met constant resistance from the bosses.

As Niebuhr grew more sympathetic to the workers he served, he grew more and more doubtful that they could attain power through strictly nonviolent means. He began to suspect that he would have to choose between economic justice and nonviolence. He had adopted the nonviolence position largely because he was repelled by the senseless slaughter of World War I; the principled arguments were not his main motive. Through the 1920s he continued to see nonviolence as the better alternative, but by no means ideal. One hallmark of Niebuhr's thinking throughout his life was skepticism about ideals and absolutes. He was always quick to see the dangers in any viewpoint or action, no matter how good it might seem. He did not deny that absolute ideals could be found; he denied only that they could be acted out consistently in the real world. Every effort to act out ideals brought with it unintended ironic consequences. So, for example, he pointed out that the widespread pacifism of the 1920s helped to maintain the status quo, which served U.S. political and economic interests. FOR, by supporting the broader pacifist agenda, unwittingly served the same interests.

As early as 1923, Niebuhr said that principled nonviolence was too ideal for this sinful world. By the early 1930s, when he had become a professor at New York's Union Theological Seminary, he chose the world over the principle. Justice for the workers was the most important goal, he affirmed. To obtain justice, some violence would inevitably be necessary, because the rich would never be peacefully persuaded to share their riches. But if violence was the way to justice, so be it. Niebuhr resigned from FOR and set about explaining his new direction in theological terms.

The result was *Moral Man and Immoral Society* (1932). That book remains the most influential, and probably the most trenchant, critique of nonviolence ever written in the United States. Many people who are strongly committed to nonviolence will agree that no one should make the commitment without seriously considering Niebuhr's arguments against it. Anyone who works through his arguments carefully and still opts for nonviolence will have a stronger intellectual (and probably emotional) commitment for having done so.

Niebuhr did not write his book primarily to criticize nonviolence. He saw Christian nonviolence in the United States as merely one part of a larger trend of liberal Christianity, typified by the Social Gospel movement. That larger trend was his principal target. Liberal Christianity, at its extreme, trusted that people could learn to become so reasonable that they would work together for the good of all and create the kingdom of God on earth. Niebuhr vigorously rejected this. As always, he argued on both practical and theological grounds. Practically speaking, he saw no grounds for utopian hope. With liberal democratic capitalism so imperiled by economic depression and rising totalitarianism, the optimism of liberal Christianity struck him as totally unrealistic. He wanted Christians to take a more "realistic" approach to getting justice for the working class. The commandment to love must be acted out in real history, he asserted, in organized efforts to seek justice for the oppressed. That means using the political system—pitting power against power—rather than always treating the powerful with perfect love.

Theologically, he pointed out that, while the New Testament commands Christians to perfect love, it also assumes that no one will follow this commandment perfectly. So there is no Christian basis for such utopian hope. To support his argument, he went back to the most influential of all Christian theologians, Augustine of Hippo (who wrote in the early fifth century). Augustine's ideas had fallen out of fashion among liberal intellectual Christians. In the history of U.S. Christianity, Niebuhr's greatest achievement was to bring Augustinian theology back to center stage. He created a modernized version of Augustinian thought, informed by current intellectual trends like existentialism and psychoanalysis.

Human Nature and the Limits of Reason

Niebuhr's theory, as presented in *Moral Man and Immoral Society*, is based on Augustine's understanding of human nature. It begins with the fact that human beings are both similar to and different from other animal species. Like other species, we have an innate will to survive; we will do whatever it takes to fend off challenges to our survival. (Here he drew on the rather simplistic view of Darwin's theory, still popular in his day, as "tooth-and-claw" survival of the fittest.) Unlike other species, though, we are consciously aware of ourselves. We can think about our place in the universe. As soon as we do, we immediately recognize the vast gulf between the infinite scope of the cosmos and our finite individual selves: "Self-consciousness means the recognition of finiteness within infinity. The mind recognizes the ego as an insignificant point amidst the immensities of the world." This humbling realization is disturbing, perhaps even unendurable, Niebuhr assumes. Therefore, "in all vital self-consciousness there is a note of protest against this finiteness."[1]

There are two ways to cope with our radical finitude. One is the mystical path, "the desire to be absorbed in the infinite." Niebuhr mentions this option in one brief sentence and then forgets about it. The other way of coping, which is the foundation of his entire theory, is "man's effort to universalise himself and give his life a significance beyond himself."[2] In short, this is the human condition. We all know we are insignificant, and so we look for ways to enlarge and aggrandize our sense of self, so that we can feel more significant.

This is the root of selfish desire (Augustine called it original sin), which is the mainspring of most human activity. We may try to feel more significant by gaining more power, wealth, prestige, or sensual pleasure. We may do it in more socially constructive ways, by creating a great work or building a social institution that improves the lives of others. Perhaps the most common way is simply to get married and raise a family; we imagine our lives extending forever in an endless chain of descendants. All the ways in which we struggle to survive can easily become ways of making ourselves feel greater. "There is therefore no possibility of drawing a sharp line between the will-to-live and the will-to-power."[3]

The selfish desire that motivates all these efforts begins in the mere fact of self-consciousness. It grows through the other uniquely human endowment: imagination. Once we start desiring, we can imagine our desires being fulfilled. But we can also imagine going beyond that to have even more, and more. In imagination, there is no end; that is where we get a sense of infinitude, which is always what we really desire. "Man's lusts are fed by his imagination, and he will not be satisfied until the universal objectives which the imagination envisages are attained. His protest against finiteness makes the universal character of his imperialism inevitable."[4] Sometimes we imagine getting more for ourselves by getting more than our neighbors. Sometimes we imagine getting more for ourselves by joining with our neighbors to get more than another tribe, or another nation. Indeed, we feel bigger when we join with others in pursuit of a shared desire. So the larger the group, the more our selfish desire and imagination come to dominate us. On every scale, from the household up to the whole world, desires come into conflict. Because each of us is driven to self-aggrandizement, we resist compromise as much as we can. We would rather fight—if we see some chance of winning.

Fighting is irrational, because we need each other. Humans must live in groups in order to survive. We can hardly afford to tear apart the social fabric that sustains us. It would make more sense to take only as much as we need of the material, social, and psychological resources available to the group. Then others could have what they need too, and we could all live together harmoniously. We are all somewhat rational, so we are not totally oblivious to this fact. When we think reasonably about any conflict situation, we usually see that compromise is the best solution. When we think reasonably about material goods, we usually realize that it makes no sense for some to starve while others stuff themselves; it makes no sense for millions to be desperately poor while a relative handful grows fabulously wealthy. The more rational we are, the more we recognize that justice demands an equitable distribution of goods. "There is a general tendency of increasing social intelligence to withdraw its support from the claims of social privilege and give it to the disinherited. In this sense reason itself tends to establish a more even balance of power."[5] (When he wrote *Moral Man and Immoral Society*, Niebuhr still viewed the Marxist ideal of equality as the most rational of all social goals. He would abandon this view a few years later.)

The problem is that a person's selfish desire and imagination are nearly always stronger than reason. "In his sanest moments he sees his life fulfilled as an organic part of a harmonious whole. But he has few sane moments. . . . There is no miracle by which men can achieve a rationality high enough to give them as vivid an understanding of general interests as of their own."[6] And when people get together with others, they are even less likely to be reasonable. Crowds amplify emotion and crowd out reason.

If reason is not strong enough to teach us how to get along with one another, what is to prevent our conflicts from tearing society apart? Niebuhr's answer is that this is why every group is structured in a social hierarchy. "Unity within an organized social group, or within a federation of such groups, is created by the ability of the dominant group to impose its will."[7] Leaders often take the desires that individuals might turn on one another and divert them to a common enemy. But that is never enough to quell brewing conflicts within the group. Ultimately, the leaders must impose their rules on the members of the group by force. If people are to get along, they must accept the authority of leaders.

In return, the leaders typically get the lion's share of political power or material wealth (and often both). "The same force which guarantees peace also makes for injustice."[8] But this is the price we must pay in order to live together. The alternative is anarchy, which means there are no constraints on the struggle for power. That is always a recipe for greater injustice. An orderly society has a chance to move toward greater justice. But an anarchic society, no matter how just at the moment, is bound to degenerate into rule by the most powerful.

No matter how orderly a society, the masses who are ruled are never very happy about the arrangement. If they can, they will oust the leaders, even if they have to do it violently. Naturally, the leaders will fight back. Or they will try to divert the masses' anger onto some other group (foreigners, minorities, and so on). But if the masses succeed in getting rid of their rulers, some of the masses will have to become the new rulers and use force to suppress the others. There is no end to the cycle. (In 1932, Niebuhr already saw the Soviet revolution as an obvious example of this cycle in action.) "The selfishness of human communities must be regarded as an inevitability. Where it is inordinate it can be checked only by competing assertions of interest; and these can be effective only if coercive methods are added to moral and rational persuasion." "Thus society is in a perpetual state of war."[9]

This argument leads to a conclusion that was, in Niebuhr's view, the book's most important point. The liberal Christian ideal of a society where everyone is reasonable, and therefore all live together harmoniously working for the good of all, is utterly unrealistic. So is the hope of getting justice for the workers by redistributing the wealth nonviolently. The facts of human nature doom these efforts to failure. Conflict, force, and injustice are permanent facts of life. The best to hope for is to reduce these enough that society can survive. The only "realistic" goal is "a society in which there is enough justice, and in which coercion will be sufficiently non-violent, to prevent his [collective man's] common enterprise from issuing into complete disaster."[10] Again, it is important to remember that, in the United States of 1932, the complete collapse of all social structures seemed to many a very real possibility.

The Limits of Religion

Niebuhr's analysis surprises many readers who assume that concern for the poor and oppressed comes less from reason than from emotional feelings of love, empathy, and human connectedness. Niebuhr said just the opposite. He was suspicious of emotion, because it is so wrapped up with desire and imagination, which are the sources of injustice and violence. He found reason, not emotion, to be the way to justice. As a Christian minister, though, he could not deny that love must play some role in human life. After all, the gospel that he preached proclaims love as the highest Christian value. So he analyzed the role of love and of religion in general to show both their possibilities and their limits.

Taking Christianity as his model for all religion, Niebuhr asserted that the highest value in religion is always a perfectly good will, that is, perfect selflessness. Religion moves people to set aside their own desires and give to others through its emphasis upon love of others. Because love sees the infinite divine value of every individual, it sees every individual as equally valuable. So it protests against inhumane treatment of any person.

However, religion can actually undermine efforts to improve society, for at least two reasons. First, religion often makes people feel attached to an infinitely powerful God or perfect being who is still a person, much like ourselves except greater in every way. Religious people believe that this absolutely powerful person gives them special care and support. So religion can encourage people to assert themselves in extremely powerful ways. This can be especially dangerous when whole nations believe they have God "on their side."

Second, religious people may be so focused on their ideal of perfect goodness that they see everything in the world as evil. Therefore, they may not protest against particular evils in the world. The classic source for this idea in Christian theology is Augustine's idea that human life is divided into two realms, the heavenly "city of God" and the earthly "city of man." These are totally opposed to each other: "Self-love in contempt of God created the earthly [city of man]; love of God in contempt of one's self created the heavenly [city of God]. The first seeks the glory of man, and the latter desires God only, as the greatest glory." Since everything that we call human society is part of the "city of man," it is all inherently evil. It is "regarded as too involved in the sins of the earth to be capable of salvation in any moral sense. Usually the individual is saved by the grace of God while society is consigned to the devil; that is, the social problem is declared to be insoluble on any ethical basis. Thus Augustine concludes that the city of this world is 'compact [made up of] injustice,' that its ruler is the devil, that it was built by Cain [the first murderer, in the Bible] and that its peace is secured by strife. That is a very realistic interpretation of the realities of social life."[11] The last sentence in this quotation shows Niebuhr's sympathy with Augustine.

But Niebuhr immediately adds that there is a problem with this view: it can lead people to despair of doing anything good in this world. Since all individuals have some degree of selfishness in all their actions, every action falls short of God's standard of perfection. From this point of view, for example, building shelters for the homeless is no better than building overpriced mansions for the rich. This can easily create defeatism; people feel thwarted in their efforts to improve the world before they even try, so they don't bother to try. This can lead people who love individuals very much to accept unjust social institutions as inevitable.

The other quality of religion, its ideal of love and goodwill, also has serious limits in our efforts to create a more moral society. We can easily love members of our families and other intimate small groups, people we have direct ties to. Paradoxically, we can also love total strangers, because they exist purely in our imagination, so we never have to deal with their reality. But when we are dealing with the real people in our society who are not intimate with us, we have to use our cold reasoning rather than our feelings and imagination. Then love, or the warm feeling most people think of as love, has distinct limits.

In fact, love can also lead us to give up in our efforts to improve society. Love is concerned with pure motives, not results. So it can end up supporting actions that lead to bad results, because the motives are good. And the pure motives it demands may be unrealistic: "The demand of religious moralists that nations subject themselves to 'the law of Christ' is an unrealistic demand, and the hope that they will do so is a sentimental one. Even a nation composed of individuals who possessed the highest degree of religious goodwill would be less than loving in its relation to other nations."[12] The same goes for other groups, especially economic classes. Again, religious idealists can easily fall into defeatism; they may say that since perfect love can't be realized in society, no social efforts are worthwhile.

This kind of defeatism is not good, because it accepts injustice. But "there is a certain realism in this defeatism, and it has its own virtues."[13] People with a high ideal of love, trying to make the world live by their ideal, may easily convince themselves that their efforts are having more effect than they really are. They then become too sentimental or tenderhearted, believing that everyone is really pure and good. This is the trend that Niebuhr saw in liberal Christianity and set out to combat, since it was the most common trend in his day. To point up what he saw as its dangers, he stressed the virtues he saw in Augustinian realism, despite its defeatism.

Sentimental liberals are dangerous, Niebuhr says, because they are unrealistic. Since they think they are improving society more than they really are, they may be content with rather feeble efforts at reform and never get at the real injustices in society. In fact, they may never even *see* the real injustices, since their view is so unrealistic. If they do see the problems, they won't do anything effective to solve them, because they misunderstand their causes. They mistakenly think that society is made up of loving people. So they don't see that social problems arise from unavoidable conflicts and require radical solutions. This same mistaken idea leads to perhaps the greatest danger, in Niebuhr's view: sentimentalists think they can change society without using coercion. Naturally, he argues, their efforts at change are ineffective, because all change requires some degree of coercion.

Still another danger is that the wealthy and powerful will attach themselves to the liberal reformers and support their efforts. In this way they will use religion to legitimate their own power and oppression. The poor and powerless will correctly see this as hypocrisy and reject the religious reformers' efforts completely. In Niebuhr's opinion, the dangers of sentimentalism are so great that it is necessary to make Augustine's view central in Christian thought. He wanted a movement for social change that would be hopeful, avoiding Augustine's defeatism, yet be based on Augustine's "realistic" idea of human society.

Niebuhr finds great value in religion, despite this subtle critique. It can move individuals, families, and small groups to the highest levels of moral behavior. Because religious love demands absolute goodness and perfection, it leads people to imagine an absolutely good and loving society. This can motivate people to work for a better society, even when it seems hope-less. "Religion is always a citadel of hope" for achieving that moral ideal. But it is a citadel "built on the edge of despair," and with good reason. "In their most unqualified forms, these hopes [for a perfect society] are vain." "As individuals, men believe that they ought to love and serve each other and establish justice between each other. As racial, economic, and national groups they take for themselves, whatever their power can command."[14]

Thus the highest levels of morality may be attainable by individuals but never by large groups. There may be a moral man or woman, but such a person will always live in an immoral society. For the individual, the highest value is the religious ideal of selfless love: all for you, nothing for me. But for a society, the highest value is the rational ideal of justice: the same for you and for me. Perfect justice is unattainable. The best society can hope for is that it will be sufficiently rational to mitigate the worst injustices and maintain some minimal level of justice as well as harmony.

Coercion and Violence

Even to attain that minimal level of justice and social harmony, society must accept the use of force, according to Niebuhr. Those who say force, compulsion, and violence are always immoral are misguided. They are ap-plying the standard of individual and religious life—the law of love—to the group's social, political, and economic life. In the group's life, the law of love can never be fulfilled, so it is more reasonable to be governed by the law of justice. In group life "the good motive is judged by its social goal. Does it have the general welfare as its objective?" If it does, it aims at greater justice. Therefore, it is rational and good to follow that policy, even though it will require some kind of force. "There is no moral value which may be regarded as absolute." "Immediate consequences must be weighed against ultimate consequences." So it may be rational to sacrifice any value for the sake of another value that seems, at the moment, more important. Even killing a human being may sometimes be justified, if it can be proven that a greater good will result. No matter what people say, when it comes down to actual decisions, society always acts on the maxim that "the end justifies the means."[15]

Once again, the individual's religious values are clearly different from the group's social values. Individuals may be right in following the absolute principle of selfless love at every moment, even though their efforts prob-ably will not improve their society very much. But the group must be more practical, more concerned about seeking the relative advantage of greater justice.

Individuals may aspire to the absolute with more justification and less peril than societies. If the price which they must pay is high, the probable futility of their effort involves only their own losses. . . . But societies risk the welfare of millions when they gamble for the attainment of the absolute. And, since coercion is an invariable instrument of their policy, absolutism transmutes this instrument into unbearable tyrannies and cruelties.[16]

Therefore, when it comes to policies for the whole society, it is safer to stop chasing absolute values like love or nonviolence. It is wiser to admit that we must always compromise, always let the ends justify the means, always use some force, and therefore always live in conflict. "Equality is a higher social goal than peace." Although perfect equality will never be achieved, a rational society will keep moving toward it and keep employing force against anyone who resists equality. People resist equality because they want to preserve their own special privilege and superior status; they will not give this up unless they are forced to. It is rational, and therefore perfectly ethical, to force them, because nothing else works. "Every effort to transfer a pure morality of disinterestedness to group relations has resulted in failure."[17]

"Once we admit the factor of coercion as ethically justified, though we concede that it is always morally dangerous, we cannot draw any absolute line of demarcation between violent and non-violent coercion." Every action that works to break down inequality is coercive. "As long as it enters the field of social and physical relations and places physical restraints upon the desires and activities of others, it is a form of physical coercion." There is such a thing as pure nonresistance, the spiritual virtue taught by Jesus. That is the path chosen by the historic peace churches, and it is one logically consistent way to be Christian. But it does not fulfill the Christian duty to help others who are suffering. Precisely because it does not resist the existing situation, including all its evils, it makes no improvement in the situation. In order to combat injustice, it is necessary to use force.[18]

It is not necessary to use violence in every case. For Niebuhr, violence is a specific kind of coercive force, the kind that results in intentional destruction of life or property. "Non-violent conflict and coercion may also result in the destruction of life or property and they usually do. The difference is that destruction is not the intended but the inevitable consequence of non-violent coercion."[19] Some people confuse nonviolent resistance with spiritual nonresistance, because they use the word *nonviolence* to denote the religious ideal of selfless love. But as soon as nonviolence becomes a tactic in the service of social change, Niebuhr said, it is a means to an end and therefore a form of coercion. And then someone ends up getting hurt, either physically, economically, or psychologically.

As long as the hurt moves the whole society toward greater justice, it is rational and therefore morally acceptable. In Niebuhr's view, even Gandhi was willing to cause harm to others because it served a greater good. For example, his boycott of British textiles caused many British workers to lose their jobs. Niebuhr saw nothing wrong with this. He objected only to Gandhi's claim that the boycott was not coercion and intended no harm, a claim he found dishonest and hypocritical. If Gandhi had read Niebuhr's book, he might well have objected that the author took a few passages from Gandhi's voluminous writing, tore them out of context, and misinterpreted their meaning. It does seem that Niebuhr first decided that every leader must be coercive and then went looking in Gandhi's writings for evidence to support his preconceived belief. This does not necessarily mean that Niebuhr was wrong, however.

Nor does it negate Niebuhr's warning that principled nonviolence can always entail a risk of self-righteousness. Those who believe in the possibility of perfectly loving political action may be tempted to identify their own cause with perfect love and their opponents with absolute evil. They may forget that all parties to any struggle are equally involved in the same web of good and evil; none is sinless.

Niebuhr was not against nonviolence. Having devoted over a decade to the cause, he understood its value very well. In *Moral Man and Immoral Society* he insightfully explained its advantages as a tactic to reach a goal. Nonviolence "protects the agent against the resentments which violent conflict always creates in both parties to a conflict." It also "proves this freedom of resentment and ill-will to the contending party in the dispute by enduring more suffering than it causes." This allows nonviolent resisters to see things more objectively. They can "discriminate between the evils of a social system and situation and the individuals who are involved in it." This reduces animosities even more, because the individuals doing the evils may not feel personally attacked.[20]

Nonviolence also makes it clear that people who want to promote justice are not attacking the peace and order of their society. In fact, it improves chances for peace and order during the conflict: "It preserves moral, rational and co-operative attitudes within an area of conflict and thus augments the moral forces without destroying them." "Non-violence is a particularly strategic instrument for an oppressed group which is hopelessly in the minority and has no possibility of developing sufficient power to set against its oppressors. The emancipation of the Negro race in America probably waits upon the adequate development of this kind of social and political strategy," Niebuhr wrote prophetically.[21]

Niebuhr mentioned in passing that, if there are ever enough "religiously inspired pacifists," they "might affect the policy of government." And if their example spread to opposing groups, it might "mitigate the impact of the conflict without weakening the comparative strength of their own community." But he did not see much hope for this development to be significant in group relationships, especially in his own time. The trends in industrial society "aggravate the injustices from which men have perennially suffered. . . . They obsess us therefore with the brutal aspects of man's collective behavior. . . . We can no longer buy the highest satisfactions of the individual life at the expense of social injustice. We cannot build our individual ladders to heaven and leave the total human enterprise unredeemed of its excesses and corruptions."[22]

Having analyzed both individual religious morality and group social morality, Niebuhr concluded that there is no realistic way to blend or harmonize the two. "It would therefore seem better to accept a frank dualism in morals. . . . It would make a distinction between the moral judgments applied to the self and to others; and it would distinguish between what we expect of individuals and of groups."[23] We should still expect selfless love of individuals. But of groups we should expect coercive force, even violent force when it seems justified, to move society toward greater justice.

In the last paragraph of his book, Niebuhr returned to his primary target: the liberal Christians who believe that they are leading their society toward perfect justice. His whole argument aimed to persuade them that their unrealistic beliefs and aspirations make it harder to get the small victories that the working class needs to improve their lives even a little bit. At the very end, he acknowledged that the unrealistic illusion of perfect justice is useful, because it inspires religious people to work for justice. But it is also "dangerous because it encourages terrible fanaticisms. It must therefore be brought under the control of reason. One can only hope that reason will not destroy it before its work is done."[24]

Niebuhr's Later Career

Moral Man and Immoral Society made Niebuhr one of the most influential U.S. theologians of his day. Over the next two decades he produced a series of books and essays that made his influence preeminent. In these writings he developed more insights to support the fundamental position he had announced in 1932. He extended his Augustinian explanation for the innate selfishness of all human beings, and he cast it in a more psychological mode.

The innate dignity and worth of every human being are based not on the capacity for reason but on the fact of human freedom, he now argued. Humans are radically free to choose either good or evil. Reason tells us what is good, but it does not necessarily lead us to choose the good. Life is always uncertain. Evil is an ever-present possibility and thus always part of everyone's life. And we are responsible for every choice we make. Awareness of all this naturally makes us anxious. The anxiety is compounded because we are finite beings aware of infinitude. We must deal with the concrete particularity of each moment, having no fixed structures to restrict us. So we have no way of knowing our own limits, for evil as well as good.

One way to avoid this anxiety is to accept our finitude and the fact that God loves us despite our finitude. But precisely because we are finite, we never trust God's love perfectly. So we look to other sources for security. We take the finite values that give meaning to our lives and treat them as if they were infinite. In this way, we pretend to be self-sufficient, as if we have no need of God. In other words, we try to become God. To sustain this fiction, we try to wield infinite power. Of course, everyone else is doing the same. So we want more power to protect ourselves against others. The resulting conflicts are bound to make us feel less secure. And the more power we amass, the more we have to lose, so the less secure we feel. Then we seek more power. The vicious cycle just goes on, making the liberal Christian hope of a genuinely good society impossible.

All of these ideas fit perfectly well with Niebuhr's analysis in *Moral Man and Immoral Society*. But by the late 1930s he had renounced one of the crucial premises of that book. He no longer believed that the industrial working class has any special value or a special claim on the concern of Christians. He no longer believed that socialism's aspiration to equal distribution of resources is the most rational ideal. He no longer believed that people can be motivated by a desire for economic justice, rather than their own power. By 1940 he had quit the Socialist Party, for a variety of reasons. He was distressed by the reports of Stalin's atrocities and by Stalin's nonaggression pact with Hitler, which made the world communist movement oppose a war to stop Hitler. Convinced that only power could stop power, Niebuhr was equally convinced that Hitler could be stopped only by war. He chastised pacifists and socialists, as well as communists, for evading the political responsibility to fight the fascist evil.

There was also a theoretical reason for his political change. There was an unresolved tension between the lines of *Moral Man and Immoral Society*. On the one hand, the book clearly argued against the possibility of resolving conflicts and ending injustice by human means. On the other hand, it showed the author's fervent wish that human problems could be resolved, or at least mitigated, so that a general framework of justice would prevail. Occasionally that wish was even expressed as a genuine hope. A thinker as rigorously logical as Niebuhr could not long sustain such a contradiction. Under the press of historical events, he opted for pessimistic realism.

Socialism was too utopian, he decided. Instead, he embraced the political theory of democratic liberalism, which had become popular during the New Deal era. According to this theory, it is a misunderstanding to view politics as the rational pursuit of ideals. Rather, politics is an arena of competing pressure groups. Of course, all of these groups have sinful motives. And the best they can produce is an imperfect, somewhat unjust arrangement. But each counterbalances the others, so that no one group can permanently prevail. That is why liberal democracy is preferable to the totalitarian tyranny of fascism or communism.

This theory fit well with the ideas in *Moral Man and Immoral Society*, where Niebuhr argued that even the most loving person must make compromises. The Christian commandment of perfect love cannot be a guide for political action. Precisely because the ideal of perfect love cannot be fulfilled in society, it can remind all people that they are sinners and that the societal structures they create are always imperfect. It can judge every human ideal and condemn it as less than absolute. Thus it can produce humility and avoid the self-righteousness that breeds fanaticism. In politics, a true Christian will accept the kind of pragmatic compromises and small improvements that liberal democracy offers, rather than trying for an impossible perfection.

Niebuhr's opposition to socialism and embrace of liberal democracy was a fateful step, because it was directly related to the origins of the Cold War. During and after World War II, U.S. foreign policy was shaped by men like Dean Acheson, George Kennan, and John Foster Dulles, who took Christianity seriously and were greatly influenced by Niebuhr. (Kennan called Niebuhr "the father of us all.") They took his writings as a religious seal of approval on their uncompromising stance against the Soviet Union. By the late 1940s they were creating a permanent national security state dedicated to an all-out war against communism. They justified this transformation of American life with Niebuhrian arguments. An intelligent Christian would realize that the world's two superpowers would inevitably seek preeminence, and that meant they were bound to fight each other. A devout Christian would fight on behalf of the democratic capitalist superpower, which allowed individual freedoms, including freedom of religion, against an atheistic totalitarianism that denied individual freedom for the sake of absolutist ideals.

Their theological mentor soon began to complain that they had missed his point. They viewed themselves as representatives of absolute good, acting as if the United States were somehow set apart from the world's sin. So they felt perfectly entitled to create the most powerful military machine in world history, with a nuclear arsenal that would soon grow beyond all rational bounds. Niebuhr protested that his ideas were being used to justify the kind of self-righteousness that he most opposed. He pointed out "the irony of American history" (the title of one of his best-known books): the United States, claiming a mission to purify the world of sin, often acted sinfully; in its effort to protect the "free world," the United States often perpetrated injustices as bad as those it was opposing. In the last years of his life, he criticized the Vietnam War as the most egregious example of U.S. good intentions gone awry.

But it was too late. Niebuhr's words had helped to set in motion political changes that he could not control. Ironically, his own theories explained why this had happened and why it was inevitable. He always appreciated the ironies of human life. For him, they were the clearest evidence that we are all finite, fallible creatures whose best efforts for good are always mixed with evil, beyond our control. Yet he could never accept the irony that his Christian realism and his rejection of nonviolence, however well intentioned, had helped to bring the United States to moral disasters like the Vietnam War, and the world to the brink of nuclear destruction.

However, this outcome may be less ironic than it appears. There is a clear logical line leading from Niebuhr's initial premises to the horrors of the Cold War and the nuclear age. Niebuhr's thinking starts out from a world divided between one transcendent, infinite Creator and many lowly, finite creatures. It is a hierarchical world, with an inevitable tension between the ruler and the ruled.

The same kinds of divisions and tensions mark the relationships among the creatures. They experience themselves as essentially separate from one another. They are like the separate pots produced by the potter, all lined up on the shelf. They have no preexisting connections as part of their essential being. So they must struggle to make connections. But precisely because they feel so small and isolated, each creature tries to aggrandize itself at the expense of others. So the struggle to make connections becomes an arena of conflict and domination. The hierarchical structure of the cosmos is replicated in every human society, from the nuclear family up to the family of nations making nuclear weapons. The ruler dominates, hoping to preserve at least a minimal degree of order. The ruled resist domination. The cycle of conflict and violence has no end.

What is to prevent such a world from degenerating into all-out chaos? The only answer Niebuhr could offer is some combination of a bit of reason and a bit of humility, as preached by religious leaders like himself. But his own theory predicts that reason and humility will always be overwhelmed by human passions. The only real limit to the destructiveness of social conflict is the limit set by the state of destructive technology. Unfortunately for Niebuhr, during his lifetime technology surpassed all limits in its ability to destroy. The specter of nations threatening each other with total obliteration, using weapons on hair-trigger alert, was actually Niebuhr's own picture of human society as a jungle, taken to its extreme.

From the viewpoint of the nonviolence tradition, this tragedy flows inexorably from Niebuhr's premises. If the basic fact of reality is not connectedness but separation, if the basic structure of reality is not freedom but subjection to hierarchical authority, then there is no way to escape from conflict, violence, and destruction. Niebuhr often described the human condition as "tragic." The nonviolence tradition suggests that the tragedy is not in some unalterable human condition, but in a description of human life that makes tragedy the only possible outcome. The fate of Niebuhr's writings, leading to results he neither expected nor approved, shows that every view of human life can become a self-fulfilling prophecy. Any words that describe human life and human society help to create the kind of life and the kind of society that they describe. The nonviolence tradition is based on descriptions of human life quite different from Niebuhr's. They allow the possibility of escaping from tragedy into a more cooperative, harmonious, and peaceful life. And precisely because they allow for that possibility, they may make it more possible.

9.

A. J. Muste

One of of the great leaders of the nonviolence movement in U.S. history was A. J. Muste (1885–1967). But his path to nonviolence was not smooth. For many years, it seemed he might take a route as far away from nonviolence as Niebuhr's. Like Niebuhr, Muste was among the most gifted and articulate of the young Protestant ministers who committed themselves to nonviolence during World War I. After the war, like Niebuhr, he became deeply involved in the workers' movements for unionization and labor rights. His concern for the working class moved him increasingly toward socialism, and ultimately to communism. By the late 1920s, he was convinced that coercion and force were the only way to gain justice for working people. He aligned himself with the followers of the communist leader Leon Trotsky and spent a number of years actively promoting violent revolution. He even went a step further than Niebuhr: seeing no way to be both communist and Christian, he left the church for over a decade.

Then one day in 1936, while visiting a European church as a tourist, Muste felt an overwhelming conviction that the church was, and would always be, his true home. He broke with communism and recommitted himself to Christianity. He had always believed that true Christianity requires a Christlike commitment to the way of love and nonviolence. As a Marxist, he felt unable to make that commitment. Returning to the church, he also rejoined the Fellowship of Reconciliation (FOR), where he soon became a leader once again. From his reconversion until his death in 1967, he remained firmly committed to nonviolence. During those years he was generally acknowledged as the outstanding figure in the white U.S. nonviolence movement. He provided leadership for a broad range of progressive movements and causes, including eventually the opposition to the Vietnam War. He was widely respected, not only for his dedication and his articulate voice, but for his wisdom and his ability to bring disputing factions together.

127

When Muste wrote about the basis for his nonviolence, he was inspirational but not profoundly intellectual. He did not analyze the logic of his ideas in great detail; he was more of a preacher than a theologian or theorist. "We believe that there are rational and pragmatic arguments to support our pacifism," he wrote.[1] But they are not the most basic source or ultimate reason for that commitment:

> When we deal with ultimate things, with God, we all necessarily speak in symbols [rather than abstract concepts]. . . . In one sense this may mean limitation, yet in another sense greater effectiveness. . . . There is nothing wise or "broad" about not trying to talk to folk in "their own language." Neither is the difficulty met by talking exclusively in abstract technical language which bears no freight of emotion. No movement of any sort, and certainly no religious one, can "move" if it becomes thus over-intellectualized.[2]

Muste had been a Quaker in the years after World War I, and he explained the source of his religious commitments in Quaker terms: "It rests finally upon arguments based on the direct insight of the soul into the nature of Truth and Goodness, an insight interpreted as a revelation through Divine Light and Life." That insight must be accepted "not by the mind alone but by the entire being in an act of faith and surrender."[3]

Much of Muste's writing dealt not with religion but with the political, economic, and social sources of conflict and the concrete advantages of nonviolent alternatives. When he turned to these topics, he was strikingly rational, pragmatic, empirical, and well informed. In the subtlety of his hardheaded analyses, he could match any political scientist of his day. He was an effective leader partly because he so skillfully blended detailed rational analysis with inspirational preaching. But his approach to any specific issue always began from, and ultimately returned to, his Christian faith.

God Is Love

Although Muste tried to avoid abstraction, there was an abstract logical theory undergirding his nonviolent Christianity. He took it as a given that "obviously man did not create himself. He is the product or creation of something, Some One." He identified that "Some One" as God, the essential or ultimate or most basic reality of the universe (and he easily shifted from personal to impersonal understandings of that basic reality). Humans are unique among all species, he argued, because each one of us can have a direct relationship to "the living source and end of his being, which is deep within and yet infinitely beyond himself." That relationship allows us to make conscious decisions. This is the basis of all freedom and morality: "Only, therefore, if men stand in a living relationship to God, to a Moral Reality beyond themselves, can they live a life of freedom."[4]

Because we are free, we can always choose to do good. There can be no original sin, which condemns us to choose evil, for then we would be neither responsible nor free. But freedom also means that we can deny the source of our existence. We can choose to believe that we are self-sufficient, to act as if we had created ourselves. This is the most fundamental choice that any person makes: whether or not to acknowledge a relationship with the higher spiritual reality. The essence of all religion is to reject self-sufficiency, to accept relationship with the divine and let it become the guiding force in one's life. "The religious man can, less than anyone, live as an isolated atom." In religion, people are "delivered from imprisonment in the self and become conscious of unity with the whole, united with God, with moral reality beyond themselves . . . a faith that transforms and saves them, gives them eternal resources to live by and values to live for." Reflecting back on the time that he left the church and on his return to it, Muste wrote that, for a while, he had believed he was self-sufficient: "Now I know that I was not and am not; that I live by the grace of God and stand straightest when I am on my knees."[5]

A person who is open to this spiritual relationship can understand its nature in a "direct insight of the soul." Muste did not claim that every true insight would have to find the same truth. But he staked his own work and his own life on one overpowering insight: "Life is built upon a central truth . . . God is love, love is of God. Love is the central thing in the universe." "The most real thing in the universe, the most powerful, the most permanent is love." Although he recognized that others might disagree, for him this was the indisputable essence of the Christian message.[6]

Love, as Muste used the word, is not merely a psychological feeling or a human attitude. It is a cosmic force, which people not only sense but participate in whenever they act lovingly toward others. If God is love, then to have a relationship with God is to link oneself with that cosmic force. This is what he understood as the meaning of Christian salvation. But because love is the fundamental reality of everything in the world, it must be expressed not only in relation to God, but also in relation to the world. "Since it is precisely to love, to the apprehension of our unity with mankind, to the kingdom of God, that we are won, we must carry this dynamic and method into every relationship."[7] To love is to create a connection with others. But even more, it is to recognize the connection that already exists, binding all people together. To love is to experience that connection in a sense of fellowship, of human community, of the unity of all humanity.

It was self-evident to Muste that violence is the very opposite of love. Therefore, a true Christian, or anyone who is truly religious in the sense that Muste understood religion, will be strictly nonviolent (or, to use his terminology, a pacifist). "Pacifism is religious—is religion!" Here, again, he made no great effort to define his terms precisely or to argue his case with tight logic. But it is clear throughout his writings that violence is always aggressive, always an expression of a desire to dominate others. "The source of evil is the 'I,' 'me,' 'mine.'" To love a person is to want the best for that person, to want as much good for the other as for oneself. Love excludes any egotistical desire to benefit or dominate. So every expression of love must be nonviolent; anyone committed to living and acting lovingly must also be committed to nonviolence, on principle.[8]

To love is to experience all human beings as children of the same God, created by the same force of love. "The human family is therefore in the profoundest sense one; 'the neighbor' is my 'other self' and I can therefore no more think of wanting to put him in the wrong, to outwit him, to injure or destroy him than I can think of wanting to do these things to myself." Ultimately, then, nonviolence means much more than merely refraining from violence and rejecting war. It means escaping from the sense of isolation that is at the root of all violence and acting upon a profound awareness of unity: "To break out of the hard shell of the Self, which is all the time seeking to defend itself against its brothers and therefore commits aggression against them, to know in one's inmost being the unity of all men in God; to express love at every moment and in every relationship, to be channels of this quiet, unobtrusive, persistent force . . . that is the meaning of pacifism."[9]

Love, as Muste understood it, is the real effective power at work whenever human beings act constructively in the world. Because God is Love, there is "an inexorable moral order," which dictates that in any endeavor good results come only from acts of love: "The law that evil can be overcome only by its opposite; i.e., by a dynamic, sacrificial goodness, is so basic in the structure of the universe." Since nonviolence is essentially participation in this cosmic process, nonviolence is more than a moral ideal or mere abstention from evil. It is an active force at work in the world; it is a way—indeed the only way—of acting in harmony with the fundamental structure of reality. Love and goodness must be sacrificial because they always involve setting aside one's own selfish concerns to care for the good of others. "Only a love that does not think primarily of itself, that has the sensitivity to feel the need of others in concrete situations which cannot be blue-printed beforehand, is adequate to human need."[10]

That selflessness is precisely why nonviolence is effective. Cooperation is the only way to approach other people (or even animals, he noted) if we want to get something done with them. And cooperative efforts require "gentleness, selflessness, non-aggression." "Men who are essentially self-seekers will not build a cooperative commonwealth." "Every human organization and institution will be able to endure and to function in the degree that this divine, creative element of love, of fellowship, is embodied in it and promoted by it. On the other hand, any institution—family, economic system, state, church—will fall to pieces in so far as it embodies fear, envy, domination, exploitation, strife, and not fellowship." At its highest level, selflessness is the willingness to risk even death in order to do good. And when people are not checked by their fear of death, anything is possible. Therefore, "whenever love that will suffer unto death is manifested . . . unconquerable power is released into the stream of history."[11]

To say that nonviolence is always effective is not to say it is merely a means to an end, a technique for achieving results. On the contrary, Muste argued that "pacifism must also be an inner experience, an inner attitude, a way of life, not merely a tool or device which the individual uses in certain circumstances."[12] Anything that is just a device may be set aside in some situations where another device seems more effective.

> Begin by assuming that, in some degree, in some situations, you must forswear the way of love, of truth, must accept the method of domination, deceit, violence—and on that road there is no stopping place. Take the way of war and there is war—not only between nations, classes, individuals—but war, division and consequent frustration within your own soul. . . . The way of peace is really a seamless garment that must cover the whole of life and must be applied in all its relationships.[13]

Nonviolence becomes a seamless garment only when it is followed consistently in every situation, no matter what the results.

To say that nonviolence is always effective is not to say that its results will be seen right away. Love's effects are not always apparent. "The deepest reality, the most vital force always works quietly, unobtrusively, steadfastly, works through patience and gentleness and humility. God, life in its deepest sense, does not work through thunder, bluster, aggression, strife." For this claim, as for so much else, Muste drew his proof from his Christian faith. When God faces opposition and sin, he does what any father would do dealing with his children: "He keeps on loving the sinner. He does not seek subjects or victims. He is Love and can find no joy save in answering love. But love alone can invoke love." The process of love answering love goes on forever. So no matter how slowly it works, it cannot stop. Ultimately, it can never be overcome by any opposing force. Even among the most evil people, love will eventually appear. "It is somehow in this divine drama of love that will not let men go that we are given our profoundest insight into the heart of God, the nature of the universe." To be a Christian is to stand in constant relationship with this undefeatable force of love, to "be in league with destiny itself." To choose nonviolence is to act on the belief that love is ultimately more powerful, as well as more constructive, than hate.[14]

But the message of the Christian story is that "if you keep on loving in the face of rejection and evil and sin, then you suffer. . . . There was no other method save this of suffering love to redeem us." Whenever humans participate in the cosmic force of love, they must expect to suffer. This is what Christians have traditionally called the imitation of Christ. It means not only accepting one's own suffering but actively sharing in the suffering of others. A truly nonviolent person must do more than refuse to do the evils that others do. Such an individual must also "creatively and at whatever cost serve his fellows . . . provide channels for the positive and sacrificial service of human need." The task of love is to manifest the unity of humanity. This means working for reconciliation whenever that unity is not being manifest. "There is no reconciliation through the medium of any partial love, but only through a love that is prepared to pay the final price. . . . Human enmities are healed and human communities are built only through the process of costing, sacrificial love." So "we must indeed do our utmost to remain in fellowship" with others, even when they oppose us. To distance ourselves from others in times of conflict and suffering is to break the bonds of community, which would mean rejecting the unity of humanity. So "we must seek to identify ourselves with their need and suffering."[15]

Individual, Society, and the Truth

Muste spoke eloquently of the personal transformations demanded by, and produced by, nonviolence:

If you want a revolution, you must be revolutionized. A world of peace will not be achieved by men who in their own souls are torn with strife and eagerness to assert themselves. . . . Often it is true we cannot speak or act where conflict rages and evil is being done, because we do not love enough. We know that our eye is not single, that we are not disinterested, that we desire the satisfaction of setting somebody right rather than the right itself. . . . He who would save men and heal strife must unite in himself both reconciliation and a new order.[16]

He had abandoned Marxism largely because it seemed to ignore that personal dimension. Having gone through his own reconversion to nonviolence, he could never forget that the movement depends on personal commitments made by individuals, one by one: "In 1929, I believed that the way to bring in a new world was basically—virtually exclusively—a matter of 'social engineering,' changing 'the system,' economic, political, social. Today I recognize that we neglected too much the problem of what happens inside the human being."[17] Nonviolence requires, and depends on, a belief in free individuals making free and responsible moral choices. That is why, for Muste, nonviolence requires a democratic political system.

While exploring the personal dimensions of nonviolence, Muste never abandoned his concern for transforming societal institutions. He remained true to his roots in the generation of World War I, always focusing on the interactions between individual and society:

> Those of us whose roots go down into the Jewish-Christian prophetic tradition cannot evade the call to pray and work for the realization of the Kingdom of God on earth. We must resolutely carry out the political task to its end, the organization of all life on true foundations and for worthy ends. . . . We must carry this [nonviolent] dynamic and method into every relationship—into family life, into race relations, into work in the labor movement, political activity, international relations.[18]

Citing Gandhi as a model, Muste argued that the nonviolence movement "must give much attention to the ordering of the economic life." "A political organization must always embody what is at the time a progressive and mutually beneficial economic base or the former will be hopelessly unstable." Here, too, his former commitment to Marxism was evident; he often traced the roots of social problems back to capitalism and the inequalities it creates. But he criticized Marxism for postponing a new economic order until after the revolution was won "by any means necessary." Like so many other nonviolence thinkers, Muste argued that good ends cannot be achieved by bad means. Nonviolence is the better way, he claimed, because it teaches us to make our means match our ends. As he put it (in what have become his most famous words): "There is no way to peace. Peace is the way." Thus he urged people to live now in the way they hope to see all the world living some day, in economic relationships as in everything else: "Men who have entered into the spirit of community will inevitably be driven to seek to give expression at once to their inner spirit in economic relationships."[19]

Muste spoke of the kingdom of God as both a spiritual transformation and a social, political, and economic revolution. He saw no difference between the two, for each implied the other. Nonviolence is the key to that single, radical change, he argued. Capitalism depends on violence to repress progressive forces; every resort to violence strengthens capitalism and repression. On the other hand, "the system of economic exploitation and imperialism is bound to fall to pieces if it is deprived of its military machine, if it can no longer find an escape from its contradictions in war." "Were any nation today to accept avowedly pacifist leadership, disband its army, offer to join with all others in really establishing a new order, the effect would be revolutionary." Other nations would be surprised to learn how many of their soldiers would refuse to invade such a nonviolent nation; its example would be infectious.[20]

For Muste, the goal of nonviolence must be nothing less than the total transformation of all human society. "We must resolutely carry out the political task to its end, the organization of all life on true foundations and for worthy ends." In religious language, this goal is the kingdom of God on earth, "a kingdom based not on power but on ethical foundations, on a love (covenant) relationship between men and God and men and men . . . infusing a spiritual principle, the saving social principle of brotherhood, into this great politico-economic structure."[21]

He was well aware that this was a utopian vision. But because he believed that God's perfect love is the central reality of the universe, he saw no reason to doubt the possibility of creating the kingdom of God: "If in the final analysis it is such love as this with which we have to deal, then all things are indeed possible." "Either we believe our own words when we say that love, nonviolence, community form the basis on which all human associations must be founded—and in that case we must do our utmost to achieve such an order . . . or we do not really believe what we say." He was well aware that he was setting an infinitely high moral standard. As he saw it, Christianity demands the perfection of the kingdom of God precisely because it offers a utopian hope for the kingdom of God. Without this utopian hope, people too easily give up any hope of moral improvement. They accept the status quo with all its injustices. There is nothing unrealistic about aspiring to a radically better life. No one knows what is realistically possible until it is tried, and the element of human faith is just as much a part of reality as all the violence and evil in the world.[22]

The hope for perfection does not mean that a Christian, or anyone committed to nonviolence, should claim to be perfect. On the contrary, those who set out to live truly nonviolently must immediately realize and (if they are honest) confess their failure to meet the standard of perfect love. Nonviolence is an endless challenge: "The moral life is infinitely complex and we must be on our guard against feeling self-righteous, complacent, or superior." Humility is a crucial part of nonviolence. Those who acknowledge their own imperfection will not project all wrongdoing onto others and use that as an excuse to hate. It will be "impossible for you to hate him with the implacable hatred of the self-righteous. Like yourself . . . he is caught in the toils of evil. Thus, as it were, you take on your soul the burden of the enemy's sin too, you suffer for him." An awareness of common sinfulness creates a bond between both sides in a conflict; in nonviolence, the goal of the conflict is to redeem both sides together. The nonviolent strive for that redemption by taking upon themselves all the suffering generated by the sins of both sides.[23] Yet Muste argued that the acknowledgment of imperfection does not invalidate the absolute truth and demand of nonviolence. If I fall short of a standard, he said, that means there is something wrong with me, not with the standard.

There is a strong tone of absolute certainty in Muste's writings, for which he did not apologize. Rather, he argued that absolute truths are necessary. Without a belief in eternal objective truth, people are likely to follow the latest popular fads in truth, yield to the strongest person's truth, or simply stop believing there is any truth at all. "Only the belief in objective rational truths and moral values can preserve freedom; for it is only through the right of appeal to objective standards that men can judge the actions of their government and resist them when they believe them to be wrong. It is those and only those who bow the knee to God who do not bow the knee to any man." Those who stop caring about truth also stop caring about other people. If "they really believe there is no objective Good for which they can live; no law of reality to which high and low are truly subject . . . then they cannot respect and trust themselves or one another. The bond of community is broken and life flies apart." There is a more practical value to absolute certainty, too. Nonviolence means a readiness to suffer all. To endure that suffering, one must have a powerful conviction that one's own beliefs are true.[24]

To believe in absolute objective truth is not necessarily to believe that anyone can possess this truth in its totality. Muste recognized how easily belief in objective truth can lead to self-righteousness and then to oppression of others who hold different truths. One way to guard against this is "to discipline ourselves to discern and renounce our prejudices." Another way is to listen to people who disagree with us. "In each of the diverse positions which men hold there will be something that is valid, that represents an effort to respond to the situation, a fidelity to the truth as they see it. Recognizing this is a way of achieving at-oneness with our fellows." Violence prevents this "at-oneness." Violence is typically justified by the claim that I am wholly right and my opponent wholly wrong, or that my opponent is the aggressor and I am merely the defender. The nonviolent person recognizes that the opponent is probably making pretty much the same claim. The truth of the matter only appears by seeing things from both points of view. That will usually reveal some right and some wrong on both sides. This is especially true when two nations prepare to go to war.[25]

Anyone who closes his or her ears and mind, claiming to have the entire truth, is probably more interested in self than in truth. "We seek to divest ourselves of any notion that our knowledge is sufficient and final. . . . When we think of our insights as having finality, as something to be possessed and defended, we set up a wall against God who is the Source of Light and whom we can receive only if we become infinitely receptive."[26] That means being open to receiving truth from any source, including people who espouse a radically different truth.

The challenge of nonviolence is to admit that our own truth is always limited, yet avoid passivity; to keep our minds open to new truth, yet take a stand and act against injustice and oppression. Like Gandhi, Muste met this challenge by insisting on a commitment to nonviolence as an integral part of his commitment to truth—to suffer and die for the sake of the truth, but never to inflict suffering and death. Nonviolence means clinging steadfastly to an objective truth and disagreeing with others. But it also means loving those others and wanting only the best for them, never forgetting that even the bitterest opponent remains part of the single human community. If love itself is the objective truth, the only way to adhere to truth is to love. And that means to be, in every relationship and at every moment, nonviolent.

The Challenge of World War II

Although Muste had a rich theoretical foundation for his nonviolence, he was not primarily concerned with explaining or defending that foundation. His true goal was to promote the practice of nonviolence by blending the personal and societal dimensions. His greatest strength as a thinker, writer, and leader was his ability to explore that blend in all its subtle complexity. As a psychologist, sociologist, and political scientist of nonviolence, he was probably unequaled in the U.S. tradition. He always set his discussions in the context of the immediate issues of the day. Yet the points he made always transcended the context, and they still hold enduring interest.

One particularly important example of his skill is his response to the onset of World War II. When Germany invaded Poland in September 1939 and World War II broke out in Europe, the idea of nonviolent resistance became increasingly unpopular in the United States. To most people it seemed that the United States would either have to stay strictly uninvolved or else prepare to fight. As the war went on, the U.S. public gradually came to embrace the idea of U.S. entry into the war. Even within FOR, many members despaired of finding institutions that could promote revolution and stem the rise of fascism without violence. So they turned to a new focus on individual religious life.

Muste led the relatively small group who remained concerned with society and politics yet rejected the option of war. They were not isolationists (as their critics often claimed). They wanted the United States to take responsibility for helping to solve problems and improve situations abroad. Indeed, Muste wrote that no religious pacifist who believes that one God is the Father of all people could approve "our traditional policy of isolation from peaceful co-operation with other nations for the economic and political ordering of the world."[27] The nonviolent were as eager as anyone else to defend democracy against fascism. But they continued to reject war as a means to that end. They wanted to set foreign relations on a nonviolent foundation. And they were convinced that nonviolence is the best way to preserve the individual rights and freedoms that are the foundation of democracy.

Could they make a plausible case? This is a particularly important question for the whole nonviolence tradition. Critics of nonviolence invariably point to World War II, arguing that nonviolence would not have "worked" against the Nazis. And they often jump from that claim to the much more sweeping claim that the whole notion of principled nonviolence is mistaken or impossible. This jump is a dubious leap in logic. Even if it could be proven in a specific case that nonviolence would not "work," that would not invalidate the whole approach. It would be just as logical to say that if one house burns down, even though the fire department tried to save it, we should abolish the fire department.

But what about World War II? To be sure, if they are honest, the nonviolent will confess that the case of Nazi Germany poses a difficult challenge. But Muste pointed out that nonviolence never claims to offer a simple solution. The critics often take that to be an admission that nonviolence is useless. Of course this is unfair. The world has largely ignored the teachings of nonviolence for centuries. Then, as Muste said, "when a crisis develops, people turn upon the pacifist, figuratively hold a gun to his head, and demand: 'Now how would you pacifists stop this thing?'—in five minutes and painlessly."[28] It is usually the violent who want simple, instant solutions. The nonviolent recognize that there are never any simple solutions to society's problems.

Actually, there is no way to know what a massive, disciplined campaign of nonviolence against the Nazis might or might not have achieved. The fact is that it was scarcely tried. When the teachers in Nazi-occupied Norway refused to follow Nazi orders, many were imprisoned. But eventually the Nazis gave up their efforts to control the schools. When German soldiers refused to obey orders to kill civilians, they rarely received harsh punishment. Suppose that kind of refusal to obey had been practiced throughout Europe? Surely many would have died. But, of course, many died in the violent resistance too. So there is no reason to assume that nonviolent resistance would have been futile; what would have happened will forever remain unknown.

But that was not really the issue, for Muste. He knew that the blunt question, Could nonviolence defeat the Nazis?, makes the whole issue rest on a false premise. It assumes that the Nazis are an irrational, implacable force coming from outside civilization, like some monster from outer space. It takes the war out of its historical context, as if nothing had happened before the Nazis invaded Poland (or even, for Americans, before the United States entered the war). "It is never possible to take the case of Big Power A versus Little Power X and isolate it in space and time. It must be seen in its setting in world history and contemporary conditions."[29] The setting for Germany's invasion of its neighbors is the whole history of European capitalism and imperialism, the centuries of oppression of the weak by the strong.

The burden of Muste's analysis is that war is never caused by one "evil" nation attacking another "innocent" nation. War between nations is always an extension of class warfare. He wanted to apply to international conflict the model of nonviolence that FOR and others had developed for resolving class and labor conflicts. This means, first and foremost, recognizing that all parties to a dispute are parts of a single system of relationships:

> In the deepest sense, the "enemy" is not a person, someone whom you can shoot and thus "solve" your problem. . . . You are living in a civilization under a political-economic system of which your nation and the enemy nation are alike a part. . . . Its foundations were largely laid in greed and injustice and violence; and, at any rate, it is now everywhere unable to function unless basic economic changes are made. . . . [War] is both an outgrowth and an expression of that decay and an agent for terribly accelerating it.[30]

Muste condemned the evils of Hitler and the fascists as vigorously as anyone. But he recognized that the fascist nations and the United States were parts of a single system, whose evils the United States had done little to remove. "Our business in America is, however, primarily that of recognizing and repenting of the evil in ourselves and our associates among the nations. . . . We must recognize that we too are a war-like and imperialist nation."[31] By going to war, he argued, the United States would self-righteously avoid recognizing the real causes of problems in the world system: capitalism, imperialism, colonialism, militarism. And the United States would avoid its most basic moral task: creating economic justice within its own borders.

Every country fights wars only for its own advantage, Muste pointed out. Britain and its allies had not been forced to war. They had chosen war because they saw it as a way to maintain the status quo. They wanted to prevent socialist movements from having any success. Even more important, they wanted to hold on to their far-flung colonies. Britain and France refused disarmament proposals as flatly as Germany. If the United States had made "a great national effort . . . to participate honestly in providing equitable access to the earth's resources, for all peoples, instead of vainly seeking to protect ourselves behind tariff and immigration walls,"[32] fascism would probably not have come to power in the first place.

So it was a mistake to view the war as a fight between the peace-loving and the aggressive nations. Rather, it was a fight between "satiated powers determined to hang on to the 85 percent of the earth's vital resources which they control, even if that means plunging the world into another war, and another set of powers equally determined to change the imperialist status quo."[33] But the imperialist system was doomed, in Muste's opinion. For practical as well as moral reasons, it soon had to come to an end. Going to war to maintain it was self-defeating, because the costs of war would make it impossible for European powers to keep their colonies. Muste suspected that U.S. leaders understood this. They wanted to wait until all the other major powers had exhausted themselves and then enter the war, leaving the United States as the greatest postwar world power.

The United States would be hypocritical if it claimed to fight for freedom and prosperity for all, he argued, since so many people in the United States did not yet have freedom or prosperity. Moreover, if the United States really were fighting for abstract ideals like freedom and democracy, why not fight for them everywhere? In fact, U.S. policy ignored many oppressed peoples and called for war only when "our own imperialist concerns or native economic lords required that particular war."[34] And all too often, when it served these imperialist or economic interests, the United States went to war to support nations that were far from democratic. So the idealistic reasons most often given to justify U.S. entry into World War II could hardly be taken at face value. Yet society always applauds the individual soldier who enlists to fight on behalf of those ideals, as long as the soldier really believes in them. Why not applaud the pacifist, Muste asked, since he or she believes just as sincerely in the ideal of nonviolence.

At the same time, though, he insisted that both pro- and antiwar forces were not idealistic but realistic. The U.S. leaders moving the nation into war were guided by motives of power and profit, not by their professed concern for democratic ideals. And the nonviolent critics of the war, like himself, were offering the most realistic assessments of both motives and probable outcomes. Although their opposition to the war was ultimately rooted in religious and moral ideals, their arguments were as concrete, political, and logical as those of the most hardheaded realist.

For example, Muste analyzed an aspect of the situation that most people missed. Having studied the theory of nonviolence, he understood that ultimately a person chooses whether or not to obey authority. When the consequences of obedience are bad enough, people will resist. Even the most totalitarian government must maintain the support of its people. That is particularly difficult in war, when the government demands that people endure the most terrible horrors. In 1941, Muste, like many others, saw the war in Europe settling into a prolonged stalemate like the trench warfare of World War I. He said that the German and Japanese military successes had helped their people feel relieved of their international stigma and inferiority complex. At the same time, Germans and Japanese were already seeing the costs of war. Therefore, those governments were beginning to feel popular resistance to the war. This made the time right for a peaceful negotiated settlement, as long as it responded to the legitimate claims of the Axis powers. At least it was worth exploring this possibility, he claimed. But if the United States entered the war, it would make a settlement impossible. And he suspected that the United States would put all the blame for the war on the Germans and Japanese. That would allow people in the United States to deny their own nation's role in the causes of the war. But it would only anger the German and Japanese people, spurring them to give even more support to their governments' war efforts.

Arguing from yet another angle, Muste urged people to look beyond the war. If the United States entered and the allies won, the postwar world would look much like the world after World War I, but worse. Efforts at limited war would inevitably lead to full-scale war, because violence inevitably leads to more violence. Given the military technology available, full-scale war would be incredibly destructive for every nation. Yet there would be no way to stop the destruction, no matter how horrendous. No nation would make or accept any peace if it was losing the war. So there could be no negotiated peace. The war would end only with total victory by one side and unconditional surrender by the other.

Muste pointed out that if the United States destroyed Germany, it would have to impose a long military occupation and deny democracy to the Germans, or else risk another war. Moreover, the victorious Allies would inevitably resume their domination of the world's economic resources, perpetuating the inequities that had led to the war in the first place. Listening to the pronouncements of U.S. and British leaders during the war, Muste heard a vision of "American-British military domination of the earth" to protect their economic advantage. Indeed, he said, all possible outcomes of the war would lead to more enmity, not the world community that U.S. leaders publicly advocated. Capitalism would be preserved and its rule strengthened. A return to the familiar prewar capitalist system, buttressed by a massively militarized state, would lead to more economic depressions. (Many pro-capitalist observers agreed with him on this point.) Then there would be either "a period marked by chaos and incalculable woe," or the imposition of totalitarian-style controls—the very thing the war was supposed to prevent. Eventually, just as after World War I, the bitterness and hardship created by this war would sow the seeds of the next.[35]

Every war is more technologically sophisticated, and thus more lethal, than the last, Muste pointed out. World War II saw the first massive use of aerial bombing, which requires soldiers to detach themselves emotionally from the act of killing and from the victims. This dehumanizing experience would make it more likely that there would be more technological killing after the war, too. No one could expect people to seek unconditional surrender through violence in war and then immediately after the war become generous and democratic. The means one chooses to gain one's ends inevitably shape the ends that are achieved.

Once people become accustomed to use force during war to gain their ends, they would want to use force after the war, too. So they would continue the world system of dominators and dominated, the very system that created the war in the first place. They would feel less secure, with good reason, and build up their military forces. But "piling up armaments means piling up insecurity and terror." So the cycle would repeat itself, until eventually another war would erupt. "War for whatever purpose waged in these days creates more insecurity both while it lasts and as its inevitable aftermath. The pacifist believes therefore that at the present time the most positive thing he can do for the safety and the material and moral well-being of his countrymen and of all mankind is absolutely to refuse support to any war."[36]

The crucial task for the nonviolent, Muste insisted throughout the war, is to avoid adapting to the demands of the state, to keep on insisting that the state and all of society must adapt to the way of love and nonviolence. That way, "the hope of the world, the one means of salvation," remains.[37] Perhaps, he speculated, the war's devastation would be so complete that, when it ended, people would see the folly of their ways and turn to a wholly (and holy) new leadership group: the small band of pacifists who retained their principled commitment throughout the war. Though he did not think this likely, neither did he think it totally unrealistic.

Some of Muste's predictions about the postwar era were accurate. The European imperial systems did collapse. There was a new war. Although it was a "cold" war, it did bring a vast militarization of U.S. society. And it brought more insecurity to many millions of people. But it would be hard to argue that World War II created, in any sense, the kind of total disaster or world "suicide" that Muste predicted. He took the post–World War I era as his model, expecting it to be replicated on a larger scale. But it did not happen that way. There was no economic depression. Nor were there social revolutions in Europe. And the defeated nations made no effort to strike back at the victors militarily. Muste's views proved to be excessively apocalyptic. This was true, in part, because the U.S. government made sure it did not happen. Ironically, U.S. leaders were acting out of apocalyptic fears surprisingly similar to Muste's, though of course they blamed the supposed threats on quite different factors than he did.

It is not surprising that Muste saw the war in such apocalyptic terms. Despite his pleas for tolerance and his great ability to look at a situation from many angles, he tended to think, speak, and write in absolutes. He saw nonviolence as the salvation of humanity and of the Christian church. If the church did not adopt the strict nonviolent stance called for in the Sermon on the Mount, he predicted, it too would face disaster.

Much of Muste's writing was directed to internal Christian debates about theology, ethics, and the future of the church. Although those issues are not directly relevant here, one deserves brief mention. Muste was the most persistent and probably the most persuasive critic of Reinhold Niebuhr's views on nonviolence. Though he criticized Niebuhr in a number of different ways, his most telling argument was rather simple. He agreed with the great theologian that a Christian must say that everyone is a sinner. But, he argued, Christians believe that God loved the sinful world so much—enough to sacrifice the Son, precisely in order to triumph over sin. Christians believe that the death and resurrection of Christ broke the power of sin, making it possible for humans to live genuinely good lives. This is never effortless; faith and goodness are always a challenge. But if we cannot be perfect as our Father in heaven is perfect, then there is no point in Christianity or in being Christian. And if perfection is an ideal worth striving for, then nonviolence is the only way to approach it, and Niebuhr's arguments against nonviolence are all called into question.

Muste's absolutist style, and his concern for the church and theology, reflected the most fundamental fact about his commitment to nonviolence: Christianity was the unswerving center of his nonviolence, his writing, his activism, and his life (except for his few years as a Marxist). Yet he was a leader of the entire U.S. nonviolence movement, both Christian and non-Christian. He himself pondered the question of how nonviolent Christians should relate to others. He always urged tolerance of different paths to the same goal, but he implied that different religious groups might achieve that tolerance only by limiting their talk to practical matters and avoiding discussion of religious differences: "There is a unity underlying all differences. In 'the silence' we find it together." As soon as we start speaking, especially about religion, there is a danger of forgetting this unity, because we take our particular symbols as ultimate and total truth. We should "divest ourselves of any notion that our knowledge is sufficient and final. . . . When we think of our insights as having finality, as something to be possessed and defended, we set up a wall against God who is the Source of Light."[38]

Nevertheless, Muste continued, if we want to say anything meaningful we must use the symbols of a particular religious tradition. He adopted distinctively Christian language because his own life had been shaped and reshaped by specifically Christian religious experiences. Therefore, he always expressed himself in the concrete language of his own Christianity. He defended this choice quite explicitly:

> If we hold the religious pacifist position we must necessarily assert its centrality. We shall be profoundly convinced that the core of any effective movement against war must be composed of those who by the grace of God and a genuine religious experience have put the spirit of domination and strife out of their own hearts . . . who really believe in the overcoming power of prayer and humility and sacrifice. This does not mean that we cannot work whole-heartedly on many things with those who do not share our faith. But in any such organizations we must necessarily be a distinctive force and must proclaim the faith that is in us.[39]

It is right, he continued, for non-Christians always to ask whether this is a form of Christian arrogance. Christians can answer not with words but only by demonstrating humility, self-effacement, and constructive goodwill. And they can have these virtues in full measure only by rooting themselves ever more firmly in the church.

But did Muste push the question far enough? When he returned to nonviolence in the late 1930s, it was not a terribly important question, for the vast majority of the nonviolent were Christians. By the time he died, in the midst of the Vietnam War, the antiwar cause was bringing thousands to nonviolence, many of whom were not Christians. Indeed, some actively rejected the fundamental symbols of Christianity, such as a monarchical male deity who gives laws and punishes those who break these laws. These new adherents of nonviolence might or might not accept Muste's premise that love is the central reality of the universe. But those who were not Christian could not take that claim as an article of faith. They would have to find some other basis to believe it. Or they would have to find some other basis entirely for their commitment to nonviolence. For increasing numbers of people, that other basis was simply a concern for justice and the well-being of other people. They were more concerned with changing the world politically than changing themselves spiritually. Some were impatient with any teaching that the former depended on the latter. So they were likely to measure their nonviolence by outcomes, not by their own inner state.

Muste's years as a Marxist taught him to look carefully at the question of means and ends. He was always devoted to the cause of improving the world, making life more just and humane for all. But that was never his central motivation. Rather, his central motivation was always to live a good Christian life, to follow the way of Christ as he understood it. He tried to find the perfect balance between the socialists' concern for ends and the traditional Christian concern for means by living a Christlike life as an end in itself. Ultimately, though, the inner voice of conscience in obedience to God, not the outward results, was his fundamental guide for action. By the end of his life, the question was unavoidable: Is this any longer an adequate basis for building a strong, enduring nonviolence movement in the United States?

10.

Dorothy Day
and the
Catholic Worker Movement

It would be an exaggeration to say that Dorothy Day, all by herself, created the Roman Catholic nonviolence movement in the United States. But it would not be too much of an exaggeration. For nearly half a century, she was the most famous, most influential, and most energetic voice proclaiming that Catholics could and should be nonviolent, precisely because they are Catholic. As founder and leader of the Catholic Worker movement from its creation in 1933, Day (1897–1980) insisted that the movement affirm nonviolence as a basic principle. She inspired many Catholics to commit to nonviolence and to explore specifically Catholic ways of expressing and explaining their commitment.

Dorothy Day's own journey to nonviolence was long and sometimes difficult. Like A. J. Muste and so many others of her generation, her journey began during World War I. Unlike Muste and the others, though, she did not begin with religious faith and then move toward peace and justice in the political realm. Her path was quite the opposite. From her childhood, she showed a powerful love of ordinary working people and of nature. During and after World War I, she was a radical political journalist, espousing the cause of workers' rights and an anarchist-socialist revolution. She denounced World War I and preparations for future war as the inevitable fruit of capitalist imperialism. But she wrote about all this on a purely secular basis.

At the same time, Day was gradually drawn toward the Catholic church, where she was baptized in 1927. She became a Catholic, she said, because her love of and joy in the human and natural world led her to want even greater love and joy, the supernatural love and joy that she could find only in God and God's church. She wanted to live a saintly life, one in which every moment would be filled with the kind of love that, she believed, could be found only in a religious life. She also became Catholic because she wanted to escape a life that was, in her own words, "doubting and hesitating, undisciplined and amoral." In the church she found the certainty, order, and discipline she craved. But she never considered leaving the natural world behind. She knew that she wanted to combine pious Catholicism with active organizing efforts to create a new society, one that would alleviate poverty and offer justice for working people: "How I longed to make a synthesis reconciling body and soul, this world and the next."[1]

When the Great Depression impoverished millions of workers, she was more convinced than ever that capitalism was an evil system that had to be overthrown. But at that time Catholics were universally, and often bitterly, opposed to communism because of its militant atheism. She still could not see how to link her political and religious beliefs in order to be both a Catholic and a revolutionary. After covering a workers' protest march in 1932, she went into a church and prayed that God would show her some new way "to work for the poor and the oppressed."[2]

When she returned home, a visitor was waiting who was to answer her prayer—an itinerant, left-wing, French Catholic preacher and agitator named Peter Maurin (1877–1949). For Maurin, it was self-evident that a Catholic not only could but should be a social revolutionary. Yet the revolution Maurin promoted, to whoever would listen, was quite different from the revolution of Lenin and Stalin in several important respects. With Maurin providing the inspiring ideas, and Dorothy Day the written words, organizing skill, and driving passion, the Catholic Worker movement was born in 1933.

Along with it was born, for the first time in the United States, a Catholic organization promoting nonviolence as the authentically Catholic way of life. The basic principles of this movement would be familiar to members of FOR and other Protestant nonviolence activists. The Catholic Worker movement put rich flesh on the bones of those abstract principles by drawing on all of the resources of Roman Catholicism, with its ancient, rich, and very detailed doctrine, language, symbolism, ritual, and church hierarchy. For Dorothy Day, though, it was not a matter of caring about workers' rights or nonviolence and then seeking a religious framework. She always cared, first and foremost, about the religious truth and life she found in the church.

Nor was it a matter of theoretical analysis followed out to its logical conclusions. Her commitment came far more from her heart and direct religious experience than from any intellectual theories or religious doctrines. Indeed, like so many great nonviolence leaders, she never developed her beliefs in any systematic theological or theoretical way. Her writings, while never irrational, were always more inspirational than analytical. They communicated feelings that could not be reduced to specific ideas. They inspired because they were filled with her own personal experience, which at every moment seemed to reflect her abiding concern for all other people.

Not surprisingly, the Catholic Worker organization that Day founded was also based on mobilizing feelings of love and translating them into action, rather than adherence to a specific set of beliefs. Day herself set the tone, not only with her words but with the example of her tireless activities. Sometimes she seemed to dominate the movement because of her charisma and prestige. But she rarely tried to produce anything like dogmatic statements of belief that would be mandatory for all Catholic Workers.

The anarchistic flavor of Catholic Worker life was largely intentional. It reflected the founders' conviction that anarchism could help point the way to a new kind of society. Dorothy Day certainly shared the utopian impulse that fueled anarchism. But she expressed that utopia in strictly religious terms: "I must see the large and generous picture of the new social order wherein justice dwelleth. . . . The new social order as it could be and would be if all men loved God and loved their brothers because they are all sons of God! A land of peace and tranquility and joy in work and activity. It is heaven indeed that we are contemplating." In that heaven on earth, no person would rule over any other, because each would serve all: "These are the words of Christ, 'Call no man master, for ye are all brothers.' . . . Never to be severed from the people, to set out always from the point of view of serving the people, not serving the interests of a small group or oneself. . . . We must and will find Christ in each and every man, when we look on them as brothers."[3]

She took the anarchists' utopian impulse and translated it into the Catholic idea of "counsels of perfection," understood not merely as ideals to strive for but as commandments to be obeyed: "Perhaps St. Paul defined the Catholic Worker's idea of anarchism, the positive word, by saying of the followers of Jesus, 'For such there is no law'"— except the law of perfect selfless love. "Philosophical anarchism, decentralism, requires that we follow the Gospel precept to be obedient to every living thing . . . to serve others, not to seek power over them. Not to dominate, not to judge others."[4]

Many people wonder how the Catholic Workers could combine their anarchist social and political views with their devotion to a church that is so hierarchical and in some ways authoritarian. For Day, this was not a problem. She was convinced that Catholics could create a socially and politically anarchist society supported by the structure and authority of church. She insisted on freedom to express herself and to quarrel with church authorities. But she stopped short of claiming the right to contradict the authorities when they spoke officially on matters of spiritual doctrine. Moreover, she saw no contradiction between anarchism and orderly discipline: "All the anarchists I have met have been the most disciplined of men, lawful and orderly, while those who insist that discipline and order must prevail are those who out of plain contrariness would refuse to obey and are most unable to regulate themselves."[5] In Day's ideal society, people would cooperate willingly because they feel responsible for each other, and those who are Catholic would accept church order willingly because they love God and the church.

The Works of Mercy and the Body of Christ

Although Dorothy Day never set out to develop a theory, she always drew heavily on the very theoretical and rational theological traditions of Catholicism. Her writings, therefore, provide the resources for a theoretical explanation of her view. One place to start is with the doctrine of the works of mercy, which all Catholics are supposed to perform. There are two types of works of mercy: spiritual and corporal (material, physical). The spiritual works of mercy are "to instruct the ignorant, to counsel the doubtful, to admonish the sinner, to comfort the sorrowful, to bear wrongs patiently, to forgive all injuries, and to pray for the living and the dead." The corporal works of mercy are "to feed the hungry, to give drink to the thirsty, to clothe the naked, to ransom the captive, to harbor the harborless, to visit the sick, and to bury the dead." Dorothy Day wrote: "When Peter Maurin talked about the necessity of practicing the works of mercy, he meant all of them."[6] Maurin helped her to see that the spiritual and corporal works could not be separated. From then on, she never doubted this principle, which became the foundation of the Catholic Worker's unique approach.

Why must the spiritual and the material go together? For the Catholic Workers, the answer flows logically from the center of Catholic life: attending Mass (the worship service) and receiving the Eucharist, the bread and wine sacramentally transformed into the body and blood of Christ. In the Eucharist a Catholic receives God's grace, according to the theological doctrine that all Roman Catholics affirm. Among the many symbolic meanings found in the Eucharist, one is that material things like bread and wine should not be rejected or abandoned; they should be transformed into a higher, spiritual level of existence. "We are working for 'a new heaven and a new *earth*,'" Day wrote. "We are trying to say with action, 'Thy will be done on *earth* as is it in heaven.' . . . This work of ours toward a new heaven and a new earth shows a correlation between the material and the spiritual, and, of course, recognizes the primacy of the spiritual."[7]

The correlation of material and spiritual, as experienced in the Eucharist, is reinforced by another theological doctrine central to the Catholic Worker movement: the Mystical Body of Christ. According to that doctrine, the church—the community of all believers—is bound together in a mystical (that is, mysterious, more than rational) way. The believers are a single organism; the church is itself the body of Christ, Christ made visible. The act that creates and holds together the body of Christ is taking the Eucharist. So the body of Christ is not merely a spiritual analogy to a physical body; it is actually based on a material reality transmuted into spiritual reality.

The Catholic Workers moved this doctrine in a particular direction by taking most seriously an idea found in the writings of the theologian Augustine. Since God transcends all time, what we call the past and the future are just as immediately present to God as what we call the present moment. Therefore, from God's perspective, anyone who may in the future take the Eucharist as a Catholic is already part of the body of Christ. The body of Christ includes all potential as well as actual members of the Catholic church. For Dorothy Day, this meant that every human being is part of that single body. Since Christ and every person are parts of the same body, Christ is present in every person. So a Catholic should be "seeing Christ and serving Christ in friends and strangers, in everyone we come in contact with." "A hard lesson to take," she admitted, "to see Jesus in another, in the prodigal son, or members of a lynch mob."[8]

Yet in Day's view, Catholics are commanded to aim at nothing less than this level of spiritual perfection. She took literally the last words of the Sermon on the Mount: "You shall be perfect as your father in heaven is perfect." She said that all Catholics should aim at being saints (though she also said that she did not want to become an official saint of the church, because she didn't want to be dismissed that easily!). Saints make perfect love of God their only purpose in life. But there is no separation of spiritual and material. So loving God must mean loving all of creation as Christ loved it, always willing to give up our own life for others: "We must be ready to give up everything. We must have already given it up, before God can give it back, transfigured, supernaturalized."[9] Through such perfect love, the natural material world is transfigured, given supernatural meaning and value, just as it is in the Eucharist. Therefore, the corporal works of mercy, which are the fruit and expression of love for others, are inseparable from the spiritual works of mercy.

Peter Maurin taught the pursuit of perfection according to a theological trend that he brought with him from France: personalism. In this theology, every person has infinite value because every person is (as the Bible says) created in the image of God. Every person should be cared about and cared for. But every person has a personal responsibility to show that care to all others in direct ways. No one can wait for others, or for the church or the state or any institution, to do it. Dorothy Day was inspired not only by

Maurin's ideas but by his daily life. "He loved all," she said, "saw all others around him as God saw them. In other words, he saw Christ in them. . . . He saw in them what God meant them to be." "He made you feel that you and all men had great and generous hearts with which to love God. . . . It was having faith in the Christ in others without being able to see Him."[10] Once Maurin explained personalism and demonstrated it in his life, Day never doubted that it was the true Catholic path to sainthood, the way to transform natural society into a supernatural community of universal love.

Maurin's personalism emphasized that the abilities as well as responsibilities of individuals are fully manifest in face-to-face relations. So he readily agreed with the anarchist emphasis on decentralization: "Governments should never do what small bodies can accomplish." "Because his love of God made him love his neighbor," Day recalled, "he wanted to cry out against the evils of the day—the state, war, usury, the degradation of man." Maurin saw a society where "man fed himself into the machine." He wanted, instead, a society "where it is easier for people to be good," because it is easier for people to love one another and freely respond to one another. Like all anarchists, Day and Maurin felt that institutions encourage people to rely on rules made by others rather than to take personal responsibility. In particular, they urged noncooperation with the state in all its aspects. (For example, Dorothy Day never voted in elections.) Indeed, Day admitted quite frankly the Catholic Worker's "efforts to do away with the state by nonviolent resistance."[11]

To Build a New Civilization within the Shell of the Old

Dorothy Day never left any doubt that she intended the Catholic Worker movement to be a revolutionary force: "We are trying to change the social order." "We would like to change the world—make it a little simpler for people to feed, clothe, and shelter themselves as God intended them to do." "We must try to make that kind of a society in which it is easier for people to be good. Man needs work, the opportunity to work." She brought to the movement a great deal of the world view she had developed in her years as a secular revolutionary. The fundamental problem with the existing order was the oppression of workers by capitalism and capitalists: "The class structure is of *our* making and by *our* consent, not His, and we must do what we can to change it. So we are urging revolutionary change." She continued to support the struggle of organized workers to be treated as full human beings and as the partners, not the property, of the bosses. She continued to admire the mutual caring and solidarity she saw in organized labor, calling it an earthly manifestation of the spiritual unity of the Mystical

Body of Christ. The unions, like the church, taught that there were ultimately no boundaries separating one person from another. Since all are united in the Mystical Body, an injury to one is an injury to all. She even praised the communists for acting upon the same ideal of universal brotherhood, and she endorsed their slogan, "From each according to his ability, to each according to his need."[12]

Day rejected communism because of its atheism. Maurin persuaded her of another reason to oppose it: communists held it necessary to destroy the old order before the new could be created. It would be better, he argued, "to build a new civilization within the shell of the old."[13] This approach fit better with their personalist and anarchist tendencies. Marxists of their day generally envisioned a revolution from the top down, a highly organized vanguard destroying the existing institutions and replacing them with new institutions controlled by a new state apparatus. A personalist-anarchist approach would encourage individuals to do what needed to be done each day, on a person-to-person basis, outside the framework of the existing institutions. Those institutions would eventually fall of their own weight and uselessness, not from a direct frontal assault in a class war, but by patiently performing the works of mercy.

The problem was how to create this new civilization of personal love inside the shell of the old. Peter Maurin came to Dorothy Day with a three-point program in which he fervently believed: education and consciousness-raising by round-table discussions; caring for the poor and needy in Houses of Hospitality; teaching the poor and needy to feed themselves and become economically self-sufficient on cooperative farms (Maurin called them "agronomic universities"). He knew that it would take far more than faith and ideas to change the world. He found in Day someone with the skills to turn his ideas into an organized program for change. Day offered her journalistic skills, her organizing ability and experience, and most important, her unlimited enthusiasm.

The Catholic Worker movement that emerged was based on Maurin's program, although the education came more through the movement's most famous vehicle, its newspaper *The Catholic Worker* (edited and largely written for many years by Day herself). There were a number of Catholic Worker farms, though these were never very successful economically (and only a few still operate). There were many more Houses of Hospitality (over 150 in the United States as of 2003).

The Houses of Hospitality were and are the center of Catholic Worker life. From them come all the activities of a progressive Catholic left: organized protests and demonstrations, active resistance to injustice, educational efforts to explain systemic oppression and the path to a better world. However, Day knew that it would take a very long time to bring the better world into being. Meanwhile, there is immense suffering all around that must be alleviated: "While we are trying to build a new civilization within the shell of the old, we must perform the works of mercy and take care of our brothers in need."[14] So the day-to-day activities of the Houses of Hospitality center on caring for those in need in whatever ways possible. Above all, they feed the poor.

From the very beginning, Dorothy Day and the Catholic Worker movement focused on the needs of the poor. They were not offering charity. The state could give charity, but that only made the poor more dependent on state institutions. They wanted, rather, to create a new societal structure for dealing with systemic poverty, replacing charity with justice. More important, for them, they wanted to be true Christians: "We felt a respect for the poor and destitute as those nearest to God, as those chosen by Christ for His compassion." To care for the poor was not simply to imitate Christ; it was to see Christ in the poor, following the gospel's words: "For inasmuch as you have done it unto one of the least of these My brethren, you have done it unto me." "I firmly believe," Day wrote, "that our salvation depends on the poor with whom Christ identified Himself." "The mystery of the poor is this: That they are Jesus, and what you do for them you do for Him. It is the only way we have of knowing and believing in our love."[15]

Working daily with poor people, she discovered that many were kept in poverty by physical, mental, and emotional infirmities. Those who refuse to see Christ in the poor, the sick, the insane, and the alcoholic are the real atheists, she insisted. Christ is in them all, because all suffer with him: "We are, here in our community, made up of poor lost ones, the abandoned ones, the sick, the crazed, and the solitary human beings whom Christ so loved and in whom I see, with a terrible anguish, the body of his death."[16] In eloquent words like these, she used *The Catholic Worker* newspaper to spread to others her deep emotional connection with the poor, a connection based more on love and human feeling than on any abstract logical concepts of economic justice. Sometimes, she wrote about the special affinity between women and the poor. As bearers and nurturers of life, she suggested, women are especially aware of God's gift of life. So they are especially concerned to see that everyone has enough food, shelter, and the other basic necessities of life.

Day followed her thoughts on poverty to their logical conclusion. If Christ is encountered most fully in the poor, then the way to encounter Christ most fully is to be among the poor. It was not enough, for her, to live among the poor and care for them. Catholic Workers had to be poor themselves. "Whatever we have over and above what we need belongs to the poor, we have been told again and again by the Fathers of the Church." "What is superfluous for one's need is to be regarded as plunder if one retains it for one's self." "We cannot even see our brothers in need without first stripping ourselves. It is the only way we have of showing our love."[17]

For Catholic Workers, voluntary poverty is also a very secular recognition that everyone is part of the same economic system that keeps millions in poverty. All people are guilty of perpetuating that system unless they actively remove themselves from it. Through the suffering of voluntary poverty, people can atone for their complicity in the oppressive system. At the same time, they can weaken the grip of the economic system and of the state that supports that system. Voluntary poverty is perhaps the ultimate act of noncooperation with the state, the ultimate way to start building the new civilization within the shell of the old.

The praise of voluntary poverty also reflects the distinctively Catholic quality of the movement Dorothy Day founded—its emphasis on sin and suffering. In Protestant Christianity, there may be a strong sense of personal sinfulness (though this has generally not been so evident in twentieth-century Protestant nonviolence circles). But the Protestant response is always rooted in the biblical words that Martin Luther cited to launch the Protestant Reformation: "The righteous are justified [that is, set right with God] by faith alone." Catholics, on the other hand, live a life of striving for perfection, always knowing they have failed to be perfect, confessing their sins, and doing "works" (actions) that serve as penance for their sins. The utopianism of a Catholic like Day is tempered by a constant sense that sin is an inescapable part of life, because all people are sinners. Therefore each person must take personal responsibility for all of the world's ills. Penance is always some form of self-suffering, understood as an act of love and an imitation of Christ's ultimate act of love, his self-sacrifice on the cross. Redemption is a process of suffering being freely offered in response to suffering. Becoming poor voluntarily is choosing to suffer as the poor suffer, as Christ had suffered.

A Catholic Nonviolence

From the outset, Dorothy Day set the Catholic Worker movement on a course of strict principled nonviolence. (It is not clear how firmly Maurin himself was committed to this principle.) She was even less concerned about logic and theory in this area than in others. So she left no sustained arguments on behalf of nonviolence. Yet her writings offer a rich reservoir for constructing a Catholic argument for nonviolence.

For Day, the inescapable starting point (and in some sense the end point) of the matter is the Sermon on the Mount. To achieve perfection, Jesus clearly said, we must love our enemies, return good for evil, and turn the

other cheek. Unlike most Catholics, Day took these words directly, in their
plain meaning, without any interpretation through the lens of church tradition. She rejected the official Catholic view that Jesus' counsels of perfection could not always be applied literally, that sometimes war is justified
and therefore necessary. Even before the development of nuclear weapons,
Day argued that there is no such thing as a just war. In an era of total
warfare, there is no way to protect innocent civilians, as the just-war theory
requires. After the bombing of Hiroshima and Nagasaki showed the power
of the new weapons to kill indiscriminately, she had an even more powerful
case. Just-war theory requires the killing to be proportional to the evil being
fought against; nuclear weapons make disproportionate killing inevitable.

Day went beyond war to reject all forms of coercion, because as she read
the New Testament, she saw Jesus setting an example of never coercing
others. Instead, he relied on the power of self-sacrificing love. "Love is not
killing," she said simply. "It is laying down one's life." Those who truly
follow Christ have "given up all ideas of domination and power and the
manipulation of others." In other words, Jesus provides a model that shows
the necessary link between nonviolence and anarchism. A future anarchist
society of voluntary cooperation would have to rely on love, not force.
Since the means must suit the end, anyone working for such a society would
have to rely on love, not force, in the present: "We will be pacifists—I hope
and pray—nonviolent resisters of aggression, from whomever it comes, resisters to repression, coercion, from whatever side it comes, and our activity
will be the works of mercy. Our arms will be the love of God and our
brother."[18]

Day criticized the communists for their contradiction of means and ends:
"They are protesting against man's brutality to man, and at the same time
they perpetuate it. It is like having one more war to end all wars." They set
the capitalists apart from the rest of humanity, declaring them enemies to be
liquidated, rather than respecting their dignity as fellow human beings to be
redeemed through love. "We love God [only] as much as [we love] the one
we love the least," she quoted one of the priests who was inspired to develop a theology of nonviolence. Then she added: "What a hard and painful
thing it is to love the exploiter." Day often quoted the words of her favorite
novelist, Dostoevski: "Love in action is a hard and dreadful thing compared to love in dreams." She wanted Catholic Workers to learn "not only
to love, with compassion, but to overcome fear, that dangerous emotion
that precipitates violence." "We must love our enemy, not because we fear
war but because God loves him."[19]

The doctrine of the Mystical Body of Christ made clear to Dorothy Day
the folly of all war and violence. She applied Jesus' words, "Inasmuch as
you have done it unto one of the least of these, you have done it unto me,"

to killing in war. During the Vietnam War, she wrote: "We are all one body, Chinese, Russian, Vietnamese, and He has *commanded us to love one another*."[20] If all human beings are members of one body—if an injury to one is an injury to all—then war can result only in injury to all, never in good. War is, in effect, a single body attacking itself and tearing itself to pieces.

The same theological doctrine also argued against war from another perspective. If all people are members of a single body, not only do all suffer from any act of violence, but all share the responsibility and the guilt for any act of violence. From Dostoevski she took words that captured her own sentiments precisely: "Every one of us is undoubtedly responsible for all men and everything on earth, not merely through the general sinfulness of creation, but each one personally for all mankind and every individual man." Applying this belief to the political reality of the present, she commented: "We cannot ever be too complacent about our own uncompromising positions because we know that in our own way we, too, make compromises. . . . We are all part of this country, citizens of the United States, and share in its guilt." "We must all admit our guilt, our participation in the social order which has resulted in this monstrous crime of war."[21]

As a Catholic, Day assumed that while all humans are sinners, all also can perform acts of penance that will atone for sin. Indeed, this is the only way to truly emulate the love of Christ, whose self-sacrifice atoned for all sin. "Christ continues to die in His martyrs all over the world, in His Mystical Body, and it is this dying, not the killing in wars, which will save the world." "'An injury to one is an injury to all,' the Industrial Workers of the World proclaimed. So an act of love, a voluntary taking on oneself of some of the pain of the world, increases the courage and love and hope of all."[22]

However Dorothy Day's nonviolence, like her concern for the poor, did not stem principally from theological belief. Indeed, it might be more accurate to say that her nonviolence stemmed principally from her concern for the poor. Her first encounter with war, during World War I, convinced her that war, violence, and the sufferings of the poor were all symptoms of the same disease: state-sponsored capitalism. Protesting against war, she wrote, was also protesting against "the terrible injustice of our capitalist industrial system which lives by war and by preparing for war."[23] She never changed that view. She only strengthened and amplified it in the context of her adopted Catholic faith.

She pointed out that the corporal works of mercy—providing food, clothing, and shelter—are diametrically opposed to "the works of war which starve people by embargoes, lay waste the land, destroy homes, wipe out populations."[24] Throughout her life she watched the military budget steadily increase and the poor continue to line up at the Houses of Hospitality, waiting for food and shelter. In her mind, the contrast always remained vivid and bitter. Day, and all Catholic Workers, lamented all the resources that could have gone into wiping out poverty rather than people. When they explained their activism against war and militarism, they almost always put it in the context of their mission to care for the poor and alleviate the systemic roots of poverty.

Day's response to war was the same as to poverty: to acknowledge her own guilt and use that guilt as a spur to greater efforts toward peace and justice. Self-suffering love would be the key to solving both sets of problems: "Our whole modern economy is based on preparations for war, and that is one of the great modern arguments for [voluntary] poverty. If the comfort one has gained has resulted in the deaths of thousands in Korea and other parts of the world, then that comfort will have to be atoned for. . . . Whatever you buy is taxed, so that you are, in effect, helping to support the state's preparations for war exactly to the extent of your attachment to worldly things of whatever kind."[25] To detach from the state by voluntary poverty would also be detaching from the wars of the state.

But voluntary poverty would not be enough to end the scourge of war. Day and the Catholic Workers intertwined with their works of mercy a consistent, active campaign on behalf of peace and nonviolence. (They were well aware that spiritual works of mercy, like instructing the ignorant, counseling the doubtful, and admonishing the sinner, could be implemented in peace activism.) Articles in *The Catholic Worker* consistently preached nonviolence and opposed all wars, beginning with the Spanish Civil War of 1936. This was a courageous act for the fledgling movement, because almost all Catholics strongly supported Franco's forces, who were allied with the Spanish church.

It took even more courage for *The Catholic Worker* to oppose U.S. participation in World War II. Before Pearl Harbor, *The Catholic Worker* was one of the many voices urging the nation to stay out of war. After Pearl Harbor, it was one of the few voices that continued to condemn the war. Dorothy Day continued to see war as part of the larger picture of injustice and oppression in her own land: "We cannot keep silent. We have not kept silence in the face of the monstrous injustice of the class war, or the race war that goes on side by side with this world war." She wrote that she could understand why some of her fellow Catholic Workers supported the war cause; she asked for "mutual charity and forbearance among us all." Nevertheless, this issue divided the movement itself, sometimes bitterly. Subscriptions to the newspaper fell nearly 75 percent by 1945. The number of Houses of Hospitality dropped precipitously. Still, Day persisted in her commitment to nonviolence.[26]

When the United States instituted a military draft in 1940, it gave the Catholic Worker movement another front on which to work for nonviolence.

This issue became the focus for a theological debate, with a handful of Catholic theologians developing, for the first time, sophisticated arguments to justify Catholics in being conscientious objectors. These arguments reflected the personalism so basic to the Catholic Worker perspective. If the goal of society is to enhance the unique personal quality and destiny of each individual, no individual can or should be made subservient to the state. Yet when the state drafts people into military service, it turns them into mere cogs in its machine, ignoring their individual human dignity. Indeed, in an era of total war, the state at war tends to do this to all its citizens. The state claims absolute authority and demands absolute obedience from everyone, especially from its soldiers. This would put the state in place of God, Day argued, something that no Christian could dare accept. Catholic personalism means that the individual must retain ultimate power over the state, not vice versa. So it provides another powerful incentive for Catholics to oppose war and refuse to participate in it.

As in so many others issues, though, when Dorothy Day looked at conscientious objection she saw, above all, a way to take personal responsibility for showing love through self-sacrificial suffering: "The impulse to stand out against the state and go to jail rather than serve is an instinct for penance, to take on some of the suffering of the world, to share in it."[27]

By the 1950s, the personalism of Catholic Workers led Dorothy Day and others to feel that it was not enough to speak out against war and militarism. They must take personal responsibility to act. (By this time, the movement was clearly influenced by Gandhi.) Their first, and perhaps most important, action was refusing to take shelter during air raid drills in New York City in the mid 1950s. Day and others served short jail terms each year for this repeated offense. For Day, it was an act of conscience, refusing to participate in state-sponsored preparations for a global holocaust. It was a way of calling attention to the absurdity of "preparing" for a suicidal and genocidal war fought with nuclear bombs. Most important, though, going to jail was another opportunity to suffer, to do penance for the collective guilt of the nuclear arms race, and to sacrifice on behalf of the humanity that she loved.

In the long run, these seemingly tiny and irrelevant protests in New York had unexpectedly large results. They brought Catholics and non-Catholics together in a core of dedicated antinuclear activists. They became the mainspring of a growing protest against nuclear testing and nuclear weapons that became a prominent political force in the late 1950s and early 1960s. Among them were a number of veteran activists who had been conscientious objectors and had learned Gandhian civil-disobedience techniques during World War II. Their antinuclear activism kept the Gandhian tradition alive in the white community during the 1950s, just as that tradition was blossoming in the black community's civil rights movement. The lessons learned and structures created in the antinuclear movement, in turn, became the foundation of the largest peace movement in U.S. history: the movement to stop the Vietnam War.

When the Catholic Workers in New York publicly refused to take shelter, they could not know that they were planting one of the seeds that would blossom in the great peace movement of the late 1960s. However, they did not ask for assurance that their actions would have great results. Like Gandhi, Dorothy Day looked beyond results to the intrinsic rightness of her actions. Doing the right thing, day by day, was the only kind of success that mattered, she insisted. Jesus had seemed to be a failure in his lifetime, too. "But unless the seed fall into the earth and die, there is no harvest. And why must we see results? Our work is to sow. Another generation will be reaping the harvest."[28]

In 1965 she wrote prophetically: "The Christian revolution has scarcely begun in its pacifist-anarchist aspects."[29] That year marked the beginning of eight years of massive U.S. involvement in Vietnam. During those eight years of war, the Catholic peace movement grew rapidly, bringing the names of priests like Thomas Merton and the brothers Daniel and Phillip Berrigan to national prominence. By the end of the Vietnam War, there seemed no longer any question that nonviolence had a lasting (though always contested) place in the American Catholic scene. Indeed, when the peace movement began to fade in the late 1970s, it was largely Catholics who kept alive the tradition of civil disobedience against the state's preparations for nuclear war in what they called the Plowshares movement. When antinuclear activism faded again in the 1990s, the Plowshares movement continued its often lonely witness in that cause. All Catholic peace activists acknowledge a great debt to Dorothy Day as the founder of their movement.

There were certainly criticisms of Day, often from those who knew and loved her best. She could be irritable, impatient, and domineering. She sometimes seemed to act as if she were the entire Catholic Worker movement. During World War II, for example, she never took a poll of Catholic Workers about pacifism. She merely announced that the movement would resolutely oppose the war. Yet she usually retained the respect and loyalty even of those she offended.

Observers outside the Catholic Worker movement may ask other questions. Dorothy Day and the Catholic Workers are generally well respected in the larger nonviolence movement for their courageous devotion to principle and for their willingness to act consistently on their principles, even at tremendous personal cost. It is rarely noticed that their courage comes, in part, from their willingness to accept, and sometimes even seek out, opportunities for suffering. Day's nonviolence rested largely on the idea that it is better to suffer oneself than to inflict suffering on others. As she promoted the cause of peace, she also gave suffering a positive value. Perhaps this is a natural tendency in any movement based in Catholicism. But it is worth asking how this tendency affects the larger nonviolence movement. Does it impart to the whole movement a greater tendency to value suffering, and therefore perhaps to accept or even seek it? Does it pull the whole movement subtly in that direction?

As a Catholic, Day could develop a more consistent rationale than Gandhi for putting oneself into poverty while working hard to bring others out of poverty. But does the same rationale hold good for suffering? Does it make sense to put oneself voluntarily into suffering while working hard to take others out of their suffering? Does it make sense, for example, for an activist to go to jail for years, when that same activist out of jail could spend every day organizing for peace and justice? If one seeks out penitential suffering to alleviate the suffering of all humanity, do the means contradict the end? Is self-suffering necessarily the path to greater love? Or is the kind of love that requires sacrifice and self-suffering only one among many kinds of love—and perhaps not the kind that most people would choose?

Catholic Workers could respond to these questions in two ways. First, they could contend that voluntary suffering is right and proper, because we all share guilt for the ills of the world. Awareness of our guilt makes us feel responsible and therefore spurs us to act to undo the ills of the world. However, guilt does not work the same way for everyone. Many people find it a burdening emotion that depletes their energy and makes it harder to work for social change. If a commitment to nonviolence is made to depend on accepting guilt, that commitment may be less appealing for many people, probably for a majority of the population. Moreover, if the goal of nonviolence is a society of active love, some will question whether guilt should be encouraged by giving it a positive meaning on the path to that society. Again, there is the question of whether the means contradicts the end.

Catholic Workers could also respond to questions about suffering and love by pointing out that the love they aspire to is more than the ordinary love most people know. Dorothy Day often called it supernatural love and contrasted it explicitly with the natural love she had known before becoming Catholic. She never rejected natural love. But she always aimed to transform it into what she saw as a higher, supernatural kind of love. In her experience, she could love the created world more richly, and meet the needs of creatures more effectively, if she gave her fullest love to the Creator alone. No one can say that her experience was false. But one can ask how that experience affected others, as it was transformed into the Catholic Worker organization and tradition. No doubt some people found the same enhancement of love that Day found.

But others surely took it in a different, more conventional and familiar way. The familiar convention of Western civilization, rooted in Christianity, makes the natural and supernatural realms opposites and demands a choice between them. It says that the natural world is inferior to the supernatural and therefore less worthy of love. It pulls people away from their concern for creation and creatures. Day and the Catholic Workers are well aware of this danger and strive to avoid it. But does their quest for supernatural love, and for suffering as the path to that love, unwittingly perpetuate the old tradition and pull people away from love of this world? Yet again, this raises the question of means and ends. If guilt and suffering are prized as the way to move toward a new society, how much will that path shape the new society being created? Will it help people escape guilt and suffering, or will it perpetuate them? Do Catholic Workers look at the goal of a nonviolent, loving society through too narrow a lens? And does that make their whole vision too narrow to appeal to most people?[30]

These are all questions worth exploring. None of them diminishes the major contribution that Dorothy Day made to the nonviolence tradition. She was the first to offer U.S. Catholics a specifically Catholic way to participate fully in the idea and practice of nonviolence. By bringing Catholicism into the nonviolence movement, she broadened and enriched the movement in many ways. For those contributions, she has deservedly won enormous respect from all those who are committed to nonviolence.

11.

Martin Luther King, Jr.

Dr. Martin Luther King, Jr. (1929–68) was the greatest preacher and the greatest leader for social change of his generation. He had a unique way of putting together ideas and words to promote the most powerful nonviolent social change movement in U.S. history. His unique pattern was built predominantly out of his African American experience, filtered through predominantly white conceptual language. It has now become a valuable heritage for people of every color committed to, or thinking about, nonviolence.

King was neither a systematic theologian nor a great religious thinker. His ideas always arose not from theoretical reflection but from the specific demands of a concrete historical situation that required an active response. He himself said, "The experience in Montgomery [the bus boycott of 1955–56] did more to clarify my theology on the question of nonviolence than all of the books I had read."[1] But the concrete historical situation that shaped his thinking stretched back far earlier than Montgomery. He always acknowledged that he was, above all, a product of the South and the African American heritage of slavery, racism, and resistance. In the context of that heritage, any movement for social change had to be rooted in the religious life of the black community. Religion was the central focus of the community and the most basic foundation for all communal efforts.

As a graduate student in theology in the early 1950s, King absorbed a wide-ranging knowledge of white Christian theology and its philosophical underpinnings. But the way he used that knowledge showed that the black church was still his true home. He picked out the concepts that fit best into the black church tradition. He used those concepts to translate the basic principles of the black church into white theological language. He may have brought a few new ideas into the black Christian community, but they were not basic to his message. The fundamentals could all be found in the traditions he had learned as a child and a youth within the black community.

161

Above all was the most fundamental concept: Christianity is a religion of freedom and liberation. King certainly heard this from the white professors who taught him the theology of liberal Christianity. But he had heard it long before, and probably much more passionately, from his father and the other great preachers he heard every week as he was growing up.

The way King expressed his message also reflected the primacy of the black church tradition. That tradition sought truth primarily through personal experience, interpreted in light of the Bible and God's moral laws—not through rational arguments. It sought to persuade others of the truth primarily by testifying about personal experience and asserting the religious truths that gave meaning to that experience—not by proving truths logically. In his own speaking and writing, King tended to assert the basic principles and truths of his religious outlook rather than propose logical arguments for them. He used basic principles drawn from both black and white Christianity as building blocks for his sermons, speeches, and articles. They were primarily tools for exhortation and persuasion, not tools of systematic argumentation. In the tradition of black preaching, King placed no great value on original ideas; he felt free to take others' ideas and even their precise words (sometimes without acknowledging his sources).

So King could take many different concepts from difference sources, mixing and matching them to suit the specific occasion. He rarely offered any sustained linear exposition of ideas. He had no basic argument to make. He did have a distinctive array of concepts, out of which he built his distinctive discursive construction. But one can start anywhere in that construction and arrive logically at any other point. It is not a chain but rather a web of interwoven ideas. It is not meant to analyze ideas but to move people to action. In that sense King should not be regarded as a great thinker. Yet he was an intellectual, because he respected ideas and always wanted to be sure that his action was supported and interpreted by intelligent, reasonable ideas. To understand his commitment to nonviolence, and the central role he gave nonviolence in improving society, we must understand his web of ideas, acknowledging its complexity.

The Fundamental Ideas

At the very center of King's web of nonviolence thought is a central premise of all African American Christianity: religion is and must be a personal experience. This is because God is personal. King rejected the idea, popular in his day, that the image of a personal God is merely a symbol, a way for humans to imagine and relate to an ineffable spiritual abstraction. God really is personality, he affirmed. God is the infinite perfection of those qualities that make each one of us a person: self-consciousness and self-direction.[2] Therefore, the foundation of all being is infinite personality. Only personality is ultimately real. King could take literally the Bible's statement that God creates all humans in the divine image. This personalism (as theologians call it) provided a logical foundation for all of King's ethical and social teachings. Those teachings all center on two inherent qualities of all personality: freedom and equality.

Because God is perfectly free, every human being is innately free. "The essence of man is found in freedom," the freedom to deliberate, decide, and respond in any situation. The infinite value of each person means that each one of us should actualize our fullest potentials and the fullest possible range of values in our lives. To do that, we must have the fullest possible freedom. Freedom is "the opportunity to fulfill my total capacity untrammeled by any artificial barrier." Of course, life set limits to our freedom, and they must be respected. "Always freedom is within a predestined structure." Within that structure, though, every person deserves maximum freedom. When an artificial barrier is erected, someone else will be making choices for us. In that case, we lose our humanity and are "reduced to an animal." Freedom requires equal rights.[3]

King's notion of equality, like his notion of freedom, was grounded in his theology. Because each person is an image of God and partakes of the infinite values of personal being, each person is a "soul of infinite metaphysical value." Because God is the father of all people, no person can have more worth than another. But freedom and equality do not give us license to do whatever we please. Freedom is more than just the ability to act randomly. It is more than just acts of any kind. It is a condition of being. Freedom means having a clear sense of who we are, what we are determined to be, and why. It means that our acts come from choices made by "the centered totality of [our] being." That is why "freedom is one thing—you have it all, or you are not free."[4]

The root of equality, the fact that we are all created by the same God, means that we are all members of a single, infinitely valuable family. Just as God loves all of us equally, so we should love all members of the human family equally. Just as God is *agape* ("selfless love"), so we should treat all people with *agape* love. *Agape* is "understanding, redeeming good will for all men. It is an overflowing love which seeks nothing in return. It is the love of God working in the lives of men." "He who loves is a participant in the being of God." *Agape* does not mean that we should like all people; some people are indeed unlikable. But it means that we should respect every person's unique personality and help all individuals fulfill their highest potentials. Therefore, it means caring about what happens to every person and responding to each one's unique needs. *Agape* creates "true person-to-person relationships."[5]

Love of neighbor is the vital link between faith and action. There can be no individual spiritual development without a strong sense of social responsibility. King allowed no separation between spirit and matter or body and soul. He insisted that spiritual truths must be acted out in concrete social life. *Agape* acted out in society creates a sense of loving community. Because God is *agape*, God is always working to create community. Because our worth as individuals stems from being created in God's image, we too should always be creating community: "At the heart of all that civilization has meant and developed is 'community'—the mutually cooperative and voluntary venture of man to assume a semblance of responsibility for his brother."

King's stress on community reflected not only his theology but his life as an African American in the South, where the sense of family and community was a powerful reality. He may well have taken it for granted that the actions of groups were more meaningful and effective than the actions of individuals. In a sense, blacks and whites in the South formed a single community. Ironically, racism actually made them parts of a single community. The Jim Crow laws and the heritage of slavery that separated them also brought them together, by forming a single social system in which both races had to live. Few whites understood this, but it was painfully obvious to most blacks.

Intellectually, King grounded the need for community in his belief in God as creator. But he also offered an argument for community that needs no religious basis. He pointed out the obvious: "We are caught in an inescapable network of mutuality, tied in a single garment of destiny. Whatever affects one directly, affects all indirectly. This is the interrelated structure of all reality. You can never be what you ought to be until I become what I ought to be"—and vice versa. "The self cannot be a self without other selves. . . . All life is interrelated." "Creation is so designed that my personality can be fulfilled only in the context of community." All humans are one family because of this simple sociological and psychological fact.[6]

Therefore, I can create value only by cooperating with others. Those others must be free to fulfill their fullest potential in order to help me fulfill my potential. Since I am only free when fulfilling my own potential, I am only free when I am helping others to be free to fulfill their potential. So there is no conflict between freedom and responsibility to others in community. On the contrary, I can fulfill my freedom only by serving the needs of others, especially when their freedom is abridged. A threat to anyone's freedom is a threat to my own freedom. "Injustice anywhere is a threat to justice everywhere." These are objective moral laws imposed by the moral order of the universe. In order to fulfill myself, I must conform to that moral order; the first law of life is "other preservation," not self-preservation. To King, of course, these were God's laws; *agape* is the force that creates the divine moral order. And "the end of life is to do the will of God, come what may," which means always to act with love.[7]

Every person, whether religious or not, recognizes these laws, King claimed. All of us feel a need for justice, rooted in our inherent freedom, our intrinsic value, and our membership in an infinitely valuable community. This awareness is the source of our urge to freedom, dignity, and equal rights. Every person should be aware of their infinite value. Self-esteem is essential to a healthy identity formation. And a healthy sense of identity is essential to freedom. Since freedom must come from the center of our being, we are free only when we believe and feel ourselves to be free. Therefore King could say: "The Negro will only be truly free when he reaches down to the inner depths of his own being and signs with the pen and ink of assertive selfhood his own emancipation proclamation."[8]

Self-esteem and freedom are crucial for moral conscience. Because God, as person, is infinite moral conscience, every human being has a moral conscience and is always free to choose the good. Recognizing ourselves as the image of God is necessary for awakening our fullest powers of conscience. But if we do not love ourselves and affirm our dignity and rights, we cannot properly love others and affirm their dignity and rights. Nor can we take responsibility for our moral choices. One of the most tragic things about injustice and oppression is that it undermines self-esteem. Oppressed persons all too easily internalize the oppressor's image of them as less valuable than others. When self-esteem is low enough, it becomes self-hatred, which leads to hating others. Ultimately, the oppressed begin to cooperate with their oppressors and "become just as evil as the oppressors."[9]

Sin and the Beloved Community

The tragic paradox of life is that self-esteem, which we all need, is also the source of our human problems. We all want the affirmation and recognition and distinction that we deserve. We all want to stand out and be noticed, to be a somebody rather than a nobody. King called this (in one of his best-known sermons) "the drum major instinct." We resent it if someone else is playing the drum major role. Since everyone wants to be the drum major, conflict is unavoidable. "The great issue of life is to harness the drum major instinct."[10] Self-esteem must be nurtured yet held in check.

King's view of human nature was therefore ambivalent: "Man is neither innately good nor is he innately bad; he has potentialities for both." There is an absolute difference in principle between good and evil, but the two are always mixed together in every person. His thinking about human nature combined personalism with the thinking of Reinhold Niebuhr and another very influential theologian, Paul Tillich. Even in the worst person there is always a chance to choose the good, King said, because "the image of God is never totally gone." Therefore, human nature is essentially good. But our existential nature, the way we live from day to day, is estranged from our essence. Only in God is essence identical with actual existence. Because we are free and finite creatures, our free choices never measure up fully to the ideal of our essential goodness. Inevitably, we make some wrong choices. Inevitably, we transgress on the freedom and dignity of others and fail to respond fully to their needs. Inevitably, we sin. Sin is not merely caused by our separation from our essential nature. Sin *is* that state of separation. This is what traditional Christian theology means when it speaks of original sin.

King agreed with Niebuhr that sin is inevitable. He never gave up the idea that sin, selfishness, and the evil they cause are objective facts that must be acknowledged. Therefore, it is unreasonable to demand or hope for perfect selflessness and the elimination of all desire.[11] However, he did not agree with Niebuhr that society must depend on selfishly motivated, coercive actions. Although sin is inevitable in every one of us, we can nevertheless love others and work together in community to enrich the lives of all. King sometimes made this case by pointing to social-psychological facts. We need others to fulfill ourselves. We must live in whatever kind of community we create. The happier and healthier the community, the happier and healthier our own lives. And we can get great ego satisfaction from helping others and improving our community. We can satisfy the drum major instinct by being drum majors for justice and peace. For all these reasons, when we help others we are also serving ourselves: "We are in the fortunate position of having our deepest sense of morality coalesce with our self-interest."[12]

But for King, the problem of sin, like every other problem, is ultimately resolved by faith in God. His religion was deeply rooted in the Bible, particularly the Hebrew Bible's story of God rescuing the Israelite slaves out of Egypt and bringing them to the Promised Land. From Tillich, King took a subtle philosophical interpretation of that story of God's saving work in human history. In this interpretation, the slavery in Egypt (an exile from the Israelites' true home) is a symbol of our estrangement from our essential human nature. The Exodus, the return from exile in Egypt to the Promised Land, is a symbol of restoration to our essential nature, making existence match essence. Restoration and salvation are brought about by God's saving love. Divine love is the motive force of history. An infinitely loving God is always working to reconcile all that has been separated and to return humanity to its essential goodness. Divine love is a cosmic process that overcomes all alienation and fragmentation.

For King, the most crucial arena for God's saving work is human society. He never ignored the Christian hope for personal heavenly redemption. But he never separated it from the hope of societal earthly redemption. In true Christianity, as he saw it, the two are always dialectically related; each requires the other. To integrate oneself with God, a Christian must be fully integrated in social relationships with other people. The Christian church had started out as an effort to improve society, according to his reading of history, and it was obligated to stay true to those roots. In this, he was staying true to his own roots in African American Christianity, which always focused on the earthly liberation of God's people as well as the spiritual resurrection of the individual. King, like so many black preachers, easily merged the image of Jesus with the image of Moses, for both had overcome bitter trials in order to bring freedom. And every southern black could understand the complex experience of being rooted in a community yet still feeling like a stranger in that community. The Exodus story spoke directly to the hope of resolving that tension.

In King's reading of the Bible, social relationships are the way in which we express both our sin and the overcoming of sin. Humanity is, in its essence, a single community of interwoven destiny; we are always already bound together. But our society is driven by individualism and competition, because we are in sin, estranged from our essence. Competitive individualism leads to hierarchical social structures. Those above dominate those below, and the result is a society riddled with conflicts, separations, and injustice.

God is "love in action," overcoming political, economic, and social conflicts to return us to our communal essence. God's work of resolving historical conflict, harmonizing human relationships, and overcoming sin is the work of creating freedom and justice. "The universe is under the control of a loving purpose." "The moral arc of the universe bends toward justice." King did not claim that it was necessary to be religious to appreciate the force of his teaching. He said that the objective moral order, the fact of our interconnectedness, works to liberate all who are enslaved and corrects all injustices. Even those who do not believe in God must believe in "some creative force that works for togetherness, a creative force in this universe that works to bring the disconnected aspects of reality into a harmonious whole."[13]

For King himself, the only way to express this was the language of religion. In that language the goal of God's work in history is the kingdom of

God, which King called "the beloved community." This is the ideal of the Bible: a society of perfect freedom, justice, and harmony, where everyone follows the divine moral order. In the beloved community, everyone recognizes the truth that we all are, always have been, and always will be interdependent. And everyone acts upon that truth. The ideal is active interdependence and mutual service, not individual self-reliance and competition. Therefore, there are no hierarchies, no unresolvable conflicts, no oppression. The beloved community is one of perfect unity but not strict uniformity. Diversity is fully valued, because the distinctive qualities and potentials of every individual are fully valued. The unity comes from each one appreciating and enhancing the qualities that make every other one different and unique.

This vision of the beloved community is not an irrelevant utopian ideal, King insisted. God's moral order is constructed to reconcile all that is separated. God's love and power are infinite. Therefore, we have a guarantee that, despite all our sin, God can and will overcome all sin and reconcile every conflict, that some day humanity will live in the beloved community. This promise, in turn, guarantees the success of human efforts for justice, freedom, and community. But God does not do this alone. God calls humans to be co-workers in history. History is a dynamic theater of interacting forces; there are always new crises demanding human responses. King spoke of his own time of civil rights struggle as an era of especially acute historical tensions. But every crisis "can spell either salvation or doom." Every person must choose to act, to help history toward either chaos or community. Of course, chaos often precedes community: "When our days become dreary with low-hovering clouds and our nights become darker than a thousand midnights, we will know that we are living in the creative turmoil of a genuine civilization struggling to be born."[14]

This pattern had begun in biblical times, with the Exodus, which was "the opening chapter in a continuing story." The civil rights movement was another chapter, in King's view. Yet he did not teach that the beloved community will arrive in discrete stages. Now is always the time to participate fully in God's moral order, to follow God's lead and give special loving concern to those who suffer, who are outcast and helpless. For King, this meant plunging into the concrete struggle for justice, as a religiously meaningful act: "It's alright to talk about 'streets flowing with milk and honey,' but God has commanded us to be concerned about the slums down here, and his children who can't eat three square meals a day." In other words, Christianity must have an inescapably political dimension. It has a positive duty to work through the political system to secure equal rights and basic material needs for oneself and for all others.[15]

The effort must be political because it directly involves power: "Freedom is participation in power." The only way to get real reconciliation between groups is first to equalize their power, which requires a major shift in power relationships. And power is always political; it is "a social force any group can utilize by accumulating its elements in a planned, deliberate campaign to organize it under its own control." King saw nothing intrinsically bad about political power. His vision of the beloved community, as an ideal that can be realized in this world, implied the need for, and the possibility of, a moral and loving government. The beloved community would not eliminate power relationships, but it would set them right: "Power at its best is the right use of strength"; participation means sharing power so that no one dominates. In a society based on love, power would be used to obtain and maintain a just harmony, not for some to coerce others. So power would be exercised nonviolently.[16]

Drawing on Niebuhr's thought, King accepted the need for force and compulsion in order to achieve the beloved community. All people are sinners, he said, and political action in the present inevitably will be tainted by sin. But this is no reason to avoid politics, as long as the goal is freedom and justice: "We know through painful experience that freedom is never voluntarily given by the oppressor; it must be demanded by the oppressed."[17] The end of oppression may amount to a total revolution. Yet this revolution need not destroy social order. It is crucial to recognize that social order is good only when it promotes justice; order is a means to justice, not vice versa. When justice is lacking, revolution is necessary to make the social order follow the fit cosmic order. In the process, revolution will clearly reveal the social disorder that already exists yet has been hidden. This will appear to be a heightening of disorder. Rather than evoking chaos, however, revolution protects society against chaos if it promotes justice. The exercise of power, even revolutionary power, is moral, as long as it aims at the beloved community—and as long as it remains strictly nonviolent.

Nonviolence on the Practical Level

King argued for a strict, principled nonviolence on three levels: pragmatic, moral, and religious. He saw these three as interlocking and inseparable. But they can be distinguished for analytical purposes.

Pragmatically, he saw violence as self-defeating, because it is embedded in a network of harmful values. "Violence has been the inseparable twin of materialism, the hallmark of its grandeur and misery." "Violence grows to the degree that injustice prevails; the more injustice in a given community, the more violence, or potential violence, smolders in that community." When a society feels threatened by its own inadequacies, it uses violence to prop itself up. A militant mass movement that uses violence only increases the sense of threat and therefore provokes counter-violence. This increases conflict, "which in turn breeds anarchy." Out of anarchy comes more injustice and more violence.[18]

Nonviolence is the best antidote to violence and injustice, King affirmed. But it must be employed carefully. It must be preceded by careful investigation of the facts, to be sure that there is a real injustice being done. Then there must be a serious effort to negotiate a just solution. If negotiation fails, good people must purify themselves of fear and selfish motives and then take direct action. Action is even more important than the commitment to nonviolence: "There is one evil that is worse than violence, and that's cowardice." When King spoke of nonviolence, he always meant firm resistance: "the persistent and determined application of peaceable power to offenses against the community." There is nothing weak or passive in it. Far from backing away or easing tensions, nonviolence uses power to increase the tensions that already exist: "A community that has consistently refused to negotiate is forced to confront the issue. It seeks so to dramatize the issue that it can no longer be ignored."[19]

In King's analysis, nonviolence is practical because it offers a better chance of controlling the mounting tensions and avoiding mutual destruction. It is "an object lesson in power under discipline." It turns the tensions into a constructive energy that can move the conflict toward resolution. Everyone can see that the resisters are seeking reconciliation, not revenge for past oppression. Their tactics keep everyone focused on the evil being protested, without being distracted by personal animosities. Those who adhere to nonviolence always remember that their enemy is an evil social structure, not the people who support the structure. They accept the traditional American belief that everyone can make a new start, that all people can be redeemed. They even acknowledge that there may be some right on the opponents' side. Nonviolence "helps us to see the enemy's point of view, to hear his questions, to know his assessment of ourselves." Thus both sides can learn and grow from the conflict.[20]

Nonviolence also demonstrates the resisters' willingness to find moderate solutions and get the maximum justice for everyone. Therefore, it helps both sides avoid destructive extremes. Nonviolence eases the opponents' fears, though it does aim to evoke guilt and shame: "It weakens his morale and at the same time it works on his conscience. He just doesn't know how to handle it."[21] In the past, the opponent may have dealt with guilt feelings simply by repeating the familiar guilt-creating behavior. Resistance aims to make that impossible. What the resisters are seeking is a new situation, created by their opponents' free decision to act differently. But if they can awaken the sleeping conscience, they can induce changed behavior without humiliation. Then the hard work of reconciliation can begin.

King explained that he had seen this happen. For example, in the Birmingham, Alabama, protests of 1963, white policemen refused to obey the harsh orders of the racist police chief, "Bull" Connor: "Then slowly the Negroes stood up and advanced, and Connor's men fell back as though hypnotized. . . . I saw there, I felt there, for the first time, the pride and the *power* of nonviolence." That power was amplified by the television cameras showing the scene to the world. Because the blacks were strictly nonviolent, they stirred the conscience of most whites who watched; it was the turning point in public attitudes toward the civil rights movement. "The pressure of public opinion becomes an ally in your just cause," King knew, as long as you remain strictly nonviolent.[22]

All of these practical advantages of nonviolence were well understood before Martin Luther King, Jr., appeared on the scene. His analysis showed that he had carefully studied the tactics he learned from others. But he always insisted that genuine nonviolence had to be more than a pragmatic technique. It had to be a moral commitment. And it had to be more than just a collection of ideas. It had to be a way of life. His original contribution was to set nonviolence in the larger context of his moral and religious thought, to share that with the nation, and to embody it in the life of the political movement he led.

A Moral Argument for Nonviolence

King's moral argument for nonviolence was based on his belief in *agape*—selfless love—as the highest moral imperative. He assumed that nonviolent acts are, by definition, selfless acts of love aiming for the well-being of all. In the beloved community, all action would express *agape* love. A nonviolent act is one that makes the beloved community not only a distant goal, but a present reality.

King argued for nonviolence in terms of distant goal, present reality, and the inseparable link between the two. If the moral arc of the universe bends toward justice and the beloved community, then there is a universal moral order that binds all people and things together in mutual relationship. This means that the universe is a moral unity, with all its elements connected. Ends cannot be divorced from means. In fact, the ends preexist in the means; where one arrives depend on how one gets there. The future depends on the present.

Violence violates the universal moral order because violent means inevitably produce violent results. Thus violence creates conflict and separation, not only physically but psychologically. It may reflect the nature of our existence. But it directly contradicts our essence: the fact that "we are caught in an inescapable network of mutuality, tied in a single garment of destiny," that our individual freedom and fulfillment depends on the freedom and fulfillment of others. Only in acts of nonviolence do we embody this essential nature of the universe. Only nonviolence conforms to the fact of our present interconnectedness and dependence on others. And only nonviolent acts in the service of justice can move the universe toward its ultimate destination, in which our existence will fully embody our essence. Therefore, nonviolence is more than just a nice ideal. It is the only way to live and act in accord with how things really are, and are meant to be, in the world.

This explains why violent efforts to improve society are self-defeating. Every act of physical violence both reflects and increases an inner violence, which is hatred of an "other." Hatred leads us to depersonalize and dehumanize others, to treat them as objects rather than as people. Because violence always perpetuates this dehumanizing, it can only "intensify the cleavage in a broken community." In the end, it "leaves society in monologue rather than dialogue." To pursue the goal of community by means that drive people apart simply will not work. Even when violence is used to promote a just cause, it destroys the very community it seeks to create. So violence can never unify. It can never produce a social order that matches the moral order, the true nature of reality. It can only produce an endless cycle of meaningless chaos.[23]

The only way to follow the moral law of the universe is through reconciliation of what has been separated. Responding to hatred with love "is the only way to reestablish the broken community."[24] Principled nonviolence tries to bring people together at every step of the way in order to reach togetherness. It tries to harmonize people in order to create harmony. Its ends are fully present in its means. It makes the ultimate moral goal, the beloved community, a present reality. The beloved community is at peace. But this is not what King called "negative peace," which is just an absence of tension. Rather, it is the "positive peace" of *agape* actively grappling with and overcoming tensions to produce freedom and justice for all. Unless all are equally free to fulfill themselves in community, there will be and can be no genuine peace. Until all are equally free, society will be chaotic and distressed, because it will be contradicting the essential nature of reality.

Again, it must be stressed that this message of peace and love is not at all a counsel of passivity. It is the very opposite: "We adopt the means of nonviolence because our end is a community at peace with itself. We will try to persuade with our words, but if our words fail, we will try to persuade with our acts." That action may very well involve refusing to comply with, or actively breaking, an unjust law. King carefully analyzed the moral responsibility to break unjust laws: "A just law is a man-made code that squares with the moral law or the law of God. An unjust law is a code that is out of harmony with the moral law. . . . Any law that uplifts human personality is just. Any law that degrades human personality is unjust." Philosophically speaking, just laws treat persons as ends in themselves, while unjust laws treat persons as means to someone else's ends.[25]

Politically speaking, just laws treat everyone equally and are made by all the people affected by them. Unjust laws treat people unequally, making difference legal, so they must be imposed by others on those affected by them. Yet even when lawbreaking is justified, one must break the law openly and be willing to accept the penalty. This shows respect for the principle of a society based on legal order and a clear willingness to abide by just laws. (Pragmatically, it also reassures the wider society that resistance will not provoke disorder.)

Nonviolence and Christianity

King's pragmatic and moral arguments, voiced so eloquently, helped to give nonviolence a universal appeal. But he was always, first and foremost, a Christian preacher of the gospel. For him, the truest and most compelling arguments for nonviolence came from his religion. He set nonviolence at the center of the triangular relationship of self, others, and God. Nonviolence is the only way to create and preserve right relationships among all three. When those right relationships are acted out, especially in the midst of bitter conflict, it brings the beloved community a step closer. In the beloved community every person is neighbor to every other; no one can be an enemy. Nonviolence is the only means of social change that makes God's goal for the future visible in the present.

King preached against violence because to injure another person is to deny that person's sanctity. No matter how evil a person's acts may be, "the image of God is never totally gone." And violence injures the image of God. (King viewed violence against property differently from violence against people, because life, being personal, is sacred, while property has no personal being and thus cannot be sacred.) Since all people are our brothers and sisters, all deserve our empathy and solidarity, not our hatred or even our pity. So we must remain nonviolent for the same reason that we can demand justice: the inherent dignity and equality of all people as children of God. King also used this as an argument for the efficacy of nonviolence. Because the opponents remain at all times an image of God, they can always change their ways. Nonviolence aims to treat others as we would have them treat us, to show them "that mutually they confront the eternality of the basic worth of every member of the human family." There is no guarantee that this will evoke change, of course. But violence virtually guarantees that the opponent will not change.[26]

If the opponents do have a change of heart, it will probably be largely because they see nonviolent resisters being attacked and not fighting back. No doubt the impact of undeserved suffering can be explained psychologically. For a Christian, though, its meaning and power are ultimately theological. Redemptive suffering is the essence of the Christian story: "All who honor themselves with the claim of being Christians should compare themselves to Jesus. . . . [who] loved his enemies so fully that he died for them." Divine love is *agape* love, selfless and therefore self-sacrificing. Only *agape* redeems us from sin and broken community. Only in undeserved suffering can we be sure that our actions are selfless and therefore redemptive. That is the message of the cross and of Christianity: "The essence of the Epistle of Paul is that Christians should rejoice at being deemed worthy to suffer for what they believe." But suffering is redemptive only when it is for the sake of justice, part of a struggle to end the unjust suffering of others.[27]

King was sure that his African American audiences would readily understand this message because of their constant experience of persecution and pain. He aimed to give that pain meaning, as so many in his community before him had done. By making nonviolent resistance a moral and religious ideal, he could readily interpret it as Christlike suffering. So it helped to enhance self-esteem and lead away from bitterness. By leading a great movement, he could help others experience their suffering in a group, not alone, so that it became not only more meaningful but more endurable.

King's philosophical bent was always to harmonize opposites. As in his political life, this did not mean making compromises. It meant finding a way to take two extremes and bring them together without sacrificing the integrity of either. His thinking about nonviolence offers a good example. He brought together the natural desire to avoid the pain of violence and the equally natural desire to avoid the pain of injustice and moral evil. He was consciously trying to avoid the dangers he saw on both sides: "The nonviolent approach provides an answer to the long debated question of gradualism versus immediacy. On the one hand it prevents one from falling into the sort of patience which is an excuse for do-nothingism. . . . On the other hand it saves one from the irresponsible words which estrange without reconciling and the hasty judgment which is blind to the necessities of social process."[28]

King was also trying to bring together the seemingly irreconcilable views of the nonviolence tradition and its most famous critic, Reinhold Niebuhr. He certainly agreed with Niebuhr's argument that nonviolence was the only practical tactic for U.S. blacks to win their rights; armed uprising was a vain hope. He also agreed with Niebuhr that good and evil are mixed in every social situation and in every individual. King stated the logical implication: the nonviolent themselves are never sinless. Their lives and tactics are never pure. But they are choosing the less evil path, one that offers hope for goodness and justice overcoming the effects of sin.

Most important, perhaps, King shared Niebuhr's view that people will rarely, if ever, cease their unjust ways voluntarily. The only way to move society toward justice is by force, that is, by inflicting so much physical, economic, or psychological pain on the unjust that they change their ways because of their selfish desire to avoid the pain. King's greatest achievement in the theory of nonviolence was to reconcile Niebuhr's insistence on force with nonviolence's trust in human nature. Tactically, he did this by sanctioning coercive political moves (boycotts, sit-ins, and so forth), while gracing them with his gentle Christian oratory of love, forgiveness, and racial harmony. By publicly endorsing power politics and strict nonviolence simultaneously, he embodied the possibility of synthesizing the two.

Theologically, he did the same thing by adopting Tillich's idea of sin as estrangement from our essential nature. Though he never spelled this out explicitly, King assumed that Niebuhr was describing our existential nature (the way we live now), while the nonviolence movement deals with human nature in its eternal essence: just, loving, and good. Nonviolence can succeed because God's love is always working to overcome our existential estrangement and return us to our essence. Yet King cautioned that nonviolence cannot ignore the existential facts; it cannot be passive and simply wait for the unjust to mend their ways. He agreed with Niebuhr that some degree of coercion is always necessary. As long as that coercion is applied with *agape* love, in the service of a just cause, aiming to benefit all humanity, it helps move the world toward the beloved community. Therefore it is, by definition, nonviolent. This view made it possible for King to talk about nonviolent coercion. For Gandhi, this was an oxymoron; all coercion was by definition violence. King simply changed the definition of nonviolence and thus made nonviolent coercion possible.

King's effort to integrate Niebuhr's thought into nonviolence marked a subtle but profound shift in the nonviolence tradition. King's unchallenged prestige and the changing mood of the times combined to open the nonviolence movement to the idea of forceful compulsion as a legitimate means, though never as an end in itself. The successes of his movement (greater than any nonviolence movement in U.S. history, to most observers) made King's approach seem credible and appealing. Of course, those who took that view were judging by results, which is just what Niebuhr argued we must do and many earlier nonviolence thinkers had cautioned against. The willingness to judge by results was one more sign of a relative shift in the movement away from strict principles toward political efficacy—a shift that had been under way since World War I. It now received a tremendous practical and theoretical boost from the work and words of Martin Luther King, Jr.

Creating the Beloved Community in the United States

Among white people in the United States today, Martin Luther King, Jr., is widely regarded as the greatest African American, and perhaps the greatest American, of his generation. The immense respect he earned does not necessarily reflect widespread embracing of his thought. Certainly few of those who praise him, black or white, are familiar with the full range of his web of ideas. And few have committed themselves to the strict nonviolence that was so central to his message and life. It seems likely that his respect among whites comes largely from his unique ability to couch the message of black liberation in language that is meaningful and appealing to so many whites, especially Christian whites. By drawing on familiar language, he made nonviolent direct action and radical social change seem less threatening.

Most familiar of all were his words about "the American dream." Far from criticizing the values of white America, he praised them. He warmly endorsed the belief in democracy, progress, equal rights, and equal participation in the political community. He virtually equated his vision of the beloved community with the ensemble of American ideals. King was well served by the tradition of millennialism so basic to white culture in the United States. Although few whites had heard the exact words "the beloved community," most could easily understand what those words meant. Most were inclined (at least emotionally, if not intellectually) to believe that God is moving history toward some grand culmination and that the United States has a special role to play in God's plan. Most were inclined to believe that the United States is special because it provides more rights and more equal opportunity than other nations.

King played masterfully upon the rich rhetorical traditions of U.S. patriotism and millennialism. He made it clear that the civil rights movement asked only that whites live by their own stated ideals. He made it equally clear that the goal was integration and harmony. Desegregation without real integration would bring only "physical proximity without spiritual affinity . . . a stagnant equality of sameness rather than a constructive equality of oneness."[29]

He argued for integration not only on moral grounds but in very practical terms. Blacks and whites in the United States had to live together, whether they liked it or not, he pointed out. Blacks would never leave the United States en masse. Nor could they ever hope to become the dominant group in society. (Hearing this, whites could feel reassured that this powerful orator was not following the example of the anticolonial movements abroad. He was not rousing the oppressed to turn on and drive out the oppressors.) But blacks would no longer allow whites to dominate through segregation. So it was to everyone's advantage to integrate: "We have the duty to remove from political domination a small minority that cripples the economic and social institutions of our country and thereby degrades and impoverishes everyone."[30] By suggesting that only a "small minority" of whites supported racial discrimination, he implied that integration was a realistic goal. He made integration more possible simply by saying that it was possible.

Whites who followed King's words carefully knew that he wanted a beloved community that prized and enhanced diversity. But for most whites it was easy to assume that he was endorsing the familiar "melting pot" idea in which white, middle-class values were adopted by all. King also used the language of the Cold War, as the United States and the Soviet Union competed for the allegiance of people of color throughout the Third World. "The prestige of our nation is at stake," he warned; the civil rights issue could "determine the destiny of our civilization in the ideological struggle with communism."

Yet King did aim piercingly critical words at white America. He drew on the prophetic tradition of the Bible, which affirmed the essential goodness of God's chosen nation by criticizing its existential sins. He preached that the actuality of U.S. life failed to live up to the essence of America and the essence of Christianity. Above all, he denounced racism as the most bitter gap between the real and the ideal. Therefore, he presented the civil rights movement not as an attack on America, but as a call to white Americans to fulfill their own ideals and the American dream. And to Christians he presented the suffering of blacks as redemptive suffering; just as Christ had suffered to redeem all humanity, so blacks were suffering to redeem the entire nation. His Southern Christian Leadership Conference adopted as its motto, "To save the soul of America."

By depicting African Americans as a messianic group, akin to the biblical Israelites, King built on the U.S. millennial tradition of a chosen people with a special role in history. He proclaimed that U.S. blacks, in saving the United States, would be saving civilization. But in the context of his whole framework of thought, this idea took on a new meaning. The millennial mission was now to help God bring about the beloved community. In that community, everyone seeks to serve, not to dominate, others. Obviously, the only way to attain such a community is to begin now to serve others. And the place to begin is at home. King also applied his sociological theory of community on an international scale. Each nation can only preserve its own best values by helping others enhance theirs, he argued. Every nation should build and serve a humane world community for its own self-advantage. Each nation would flourish most if all showed "an overriding loyalty to mankind as a whole."[31]

Beyond Civil Rights

Until 1964, King's work and words focused almost entirely on gaining civil rights for African Americans in the South, where they were denied their rights by law. In 1964 and 1965, he began to look to the North. There he saw that there is more to justice than legal civil rights. He began to wonder whether the economic and social racism blacks suffered in the North might not be worse, because the racism was more hidden and the whites' conscience could not be so easily aroused.

Once he had broadened his view beyond legal rights and the South, King recognized that he was actually dealing with the entire range of injustices, and therefore the entire structure, of U.S. society. "Justice is indivisible," he declared; all political, economic, social issues are interrelated. So he began to consider a host of issues that he had not considered before. He looked at the role of technology and found that U.S. society tended to value technological means as ends in themselves, without asking what moral (or immoral) ends might be served by technological innovation: "The devices, techniques, mechanisms, and instrumentalities by means of which we live" had become more important in most people's lives than spiritual values.[32]

Looking at the machinery of production and consumption led to thinking about how products are distributed and consumed. King already believed that integration required equally shared political power and responsibility. Now he took full account of the links between political and economic power. He argued that integration required a major redistribution of wealth. To explain how this could be done, he had to become something of an economist: "We must make the nonproducer a consumer or we will find ourselves drowning in a sea of consumer goods." Why were so many people kept in poverty, as both nonproducers and nonconsumers? The basic answer he found was the nature of capitalism: "The profit motive, when it is the sole basis of an economic system, encourages a cutthroat competition and selfish ambition that inspire men to be more I-centered than thou-centered. . . . Capitalism fails to realize that life is social."[33]

Since King had started analyzing these issues out of his concern for integration, he was quick to see the links between capitalism and racism. He saw that private property, nearly all of which was owned by whites, supported and embodied the white power structure. On a more theoretical level, he saw that the institution of private property means valuing things that have no personal being and thus no genuine reality. A society built on such a dehumanizing basis will naturally dehumanize and exploit the "other." Property is the most basic symbol of exploitation. This, he said, was the meaning of the riots that began breaking out in northern black ghettos in 1964. The seemingly blind destruction of property was, above all, a protest against the institutionalized exploitation built into U.S. society.

King's focus on the North and the broader societal structures coincided with the escalation of the U.S. military effort in Vietnam, which began in 1965. The war soon became the most pervasive public issue in the nation. King could hardly avoid it. But he viewed it in the context of his new, broader vision. For him, as for all the more radical critics of the war, Vietnam was not an aberration from U.S. values, or an isolated case of excessive U.S. power. Rather, it was a logical and predictable outcome of U.S. values. It was a symptom of the deeper evils of capitalism, imperialism, and militarism.

As an advocate of nonviolence, King was naturally opposed to all war. As early as 1959 he had begun to preach against the dangers of war in the nuclear age. Calling nuclear weapons "the most colossal of all evils," he warned: "It is either nonviolence or nonexistence." By the mid 1960s, he saw links connecting nuclear weapons, conventional weapons, technology, and capitalism to racism. When a society makes machines and property more important than people, he said, it cannot stop "the giant triplets of racism, materialism, and militarism." He also saw this complex as the root of poverty. He explained that the exploitation of blacks in the United States is the paradigm for the exploitation of all poor Americans. Poverty here is directly related to the increase in U.S. capital investments abroad, which create more poverty and oppression in other nations. To sustain those oppressive structures, the United States must build up its military and be prepared to fight wars, like the war in Vietnam. Thus racism, poverty, materialism, and militarism are interwoven and "deeply rooted in the whole structure of our society." It was this whole structure that had led inexorably to the tragedy of Vietnam.[34]

In the last three years of his life King's words combined his increasingly sophisticated economic and political analysis with the moral and religious preaching that always remained his foundation. "We as a nation must undergo a radical revolution of values," he proclaimed. This call to revolution drew on the basic principle of nonviolence—attacking evil structures, not individual people. Since King had long supported this principle, it was natural for him to call for a total transformation of societal structures, a total change in "the system." It was equally natural for him to justify this in personalistic moral terms: "We must rapidly begin the shift from a 'thing-oriented' to a 'person-oriented' society."[35]

Here, too, nonviolence could make a crucial contribution. Through self-sacrificial suffering for others, people would learn that there are values more important than self. They would learn to separate themselves from the individualism, hedonism, and narcissism of our consumer society. They would act out their opposition to those values and encourage others to join in the nonviolent radical revolution. King admitted that he did not know what new structures would take the place of the unjust system we live under today. But he did not see that as a problem: "Structures will follow, if we keep our ears open to the spirit."[36]

Martin Luther King, Jr., did not live long enough to see new structures emerge or to lead any kind of revolution. There is no way to say what might have happened to the revolutionary fervor of the late 1960s had its greatest and most powerful leader survived. Perhaps he died because others feared that he might indeed be great and powerful enough to lead a revolution. There is no way to say what directions his life and thought might have taken had he survived. He was clearly learning and changing very rapidly in the last three years of his life.

In those three years he saw many African Americans turn away from his teaching of nonviolence to embrace a Black Power philosophy that urged blacks to take their rightful share of power and resources "by any means necessary." In the African American and radical white communities, King's commitment to nonviolence was criticized (sometimes quite harshly) as foolish obstinacy. His influence began to wane. Some said that his work was done, that the movement for social change had moved on to a new phase in which King's thought would be largely irrelevant. King was not deaf to these criticisms. He responded by voicing respect for the Black Power movement. He saw validity in its central argument: before power can be equalized between white and blacks, there must be some separate black structures, in order to build up black power. But, despite the immense pressures on him, he held firmly to his commitment to and arguments for nonviolence. So it seems likely that, no matter how long he might have lived and how radical he might have become, the revolution he worked for would always have remained a nonviolent revolution.

Would this have doomed him to the margins of the nation's political life? Or would he have moved the whole nation closer to nonviolence? The answer must remain forever unknown. As it is, his radical leanings in the last years of his life have been largely forgotten, their influence very marginal.

He is remembered and revered in both the black and white communities almost solely for his leadership of the civil rights movement in the South. Yet how much influence does that memory have upon the nation's life today? The success of the civil rights movement is widely debated because its ultimate results are so unclear. The lasting impact of King's nonviolence is even less clear. Did he make nonviolence a significant enduring force in the United States? Or did his nonviolence allow the white community to see him as harmless and therefore to ignore the radical challenge of his message? Is the creation of "Martin Luther King" as a national icon another way of avoiding that radical challenge? To what extent has the revered image permanently eclipsed the actual man and his message? Because the answers to all these questions remain uncertain, the true measure of King's influence remains uncertain as well. Perhaps it is simply too soon to tell.

12

Barbara Deming

B arbara Deming (1917–84) is probably the least known of all the great theorists of nonviolence in U.S. history. She certainly deserves to be better known, because she holds a very important place in the history of the idea of nonviolence. She is the most influential thinker who developed a systematic argument for nonviolence with no religious basis. More than anyone else, Deming made it intellectually plausible, and even respectable, for nonreligious people to commit themselves to nonviolence. She developed her ideas while participating in the peace and civil rights movements of the 1950s and 1960s. For the first time, large numbers of people with no Christian commitment embraced, or at least seriously explored, nonviolence. So she helped make a place in the nonviolence movement for many people who might otherwise have been unsure whether they could embrace nonviolence.

It was a rare moment in U.S. history, when it seemed that organized nonviolent movements could reshape society in substantial ways. This confidence was clearly evident in Barbara Deming's interpretation of nonviolence, and it was directly related to her strictly secular approach. With no religious belief as foundation or criterion, she was inclined to base nonviolence on its ability to achieve practical results. For Deming, the crucial question about nonviolence was not whether it brings us closer to God or improves our souls, but whether it could actually achieve concrete improvements in society, especially for the oppressed. In the years when she wrote her most influential statements, many people were willing to answer that question in the affirmative. And even Dr. Martin Luther King, Jr., the era's greatest voice for religious nonviolence, gave great weight to issues of practical success. So it seemed to make sense to base nonviolence on its potential for achieving results.

A Secular Basis for Nonviolence

Deming argued quite explicitly that nonviolence does not need a religious basis. There is no need to assume the existence of a spiritual higher power that will inevitably support nonviolent action and help it to succeed. In fact, religious belief can easily undermine efforts for social change. Religious people tend to assume that, as Dr. King often said, some cosmic force guarantees that the universe bends toward justice. They also tend to assume that everyone is somehow aware of this, that everyone has some degree of conscience, no matter how deeply buried it may be. Therefore, religious people too often view nonviolence as an appeal to the conscience of the oppressors. They expect too much from the oppressors. They use petition and prayer rather than force to achieve their goals: "The challenge to those who believe in nonviolent struggle is to learn to be aggressive enough."[1] Belief in God, or any religious belief, can make it harder to learn this vital lesson.

On this point and on others, Deming shared some basic ideas in common with Reinhold Niebuhr. They agreed that the fundamental goal is not to avoid violence but to bring justice to the victims of the profoundly unjust U.S. system. The value of any work for justice should be judged by its results. They saw justice as essentially a secular value, set apart from the realm of religion. Their fundamental question was how to get more justice. Their answers always involved some kind of compulsion or force. They assumed that unjust people will change their behavior, and the ideas they use to justify their behavior, only when they feel that their interests are threatened.

But Deming disagreed with Niebuhr on the most effective way to threaten the unjust. He assumed that some degree of violence (or at least a threat of violence) is most often necessary. She argued that nonviolence is always likely to be the most effective way to force social change. Thus she took ideas that Niebuhr used to criticize nonviolence and turned them into arguments in favor of nonviolence.

Deming understood Gandhi's term *satyagraha* to mean clinging to truth with one's entire weight, acting out the truth with one's body. That means relying on force to achieve one's goals. In fact, said Deming, all nonviolent activists assume this in practice, though they usually write as if they are appealing to moral factors in people and in the universe. Not that moral factors are irrelevant: "The most effective action *both* resorts to power *and* engages conscience. . . . It can in effect force [opponents] to consult their consciences—or to pretend to have them. . . . It can face the authorities with a new fact and say: accept this new situation which *we* have created."[2]

But if the only question that really matters is the tactical question—What works?—there is no reason to rule out violence in principle. Moreover, since no person is perfectly morally pure, there can be no absolute prohibition on violence.

Why, then, choose nonviolent tactics rather than violence? Barbara Deming's answer was based on her answer to a more basic question: Why fight for justice? Her answer to that question rested on the premise that every person deserves respect, simply by virtue of being a person. Respect means, above all, allowing each person to be fully himself or herself. That means respecting every person's right to make free choices and exercise free will. No matter what form injustice takes, it always consists of oppressors trying to deprive oppressed people of their freedom to be themselves by making free choices. Insofar as the oppressors succeed, they exercise illegitimate freedoms because they have taken away others' legitimate freedoms.

When we speak about social change, we mean creating or restoring a situation in which all people are equally respected, a society in which everyone can exercise legitimate freedoms because no one has illegitimate freedoms. That means creating new kinds of people out of both oppressors and oppressed. The oppressed must change both their own status as victims and the others' status as oppressors.

There is a direct link between justice and nonviolence, according to Deming, because injustice is always a form of violence. Violence is essentially the attempt to dominate another person and deprive that person of his or her own free will. This violence may be done through war or physical attack. But it can also be done by an economic system that denies people basic material needs, or by a political system that denies people full participation, or by a social system that denies them a sense of their own worth. These forms of structural violence are just as violent as any physical attack. Oppressed people who use violence to remove degrading conditions are using a lesser violence to end the greater violence of the system that degrades them and deprives them of their legitimate freedom.

A question naturally arises: If the goal is to put an end to people forcing their will upon others, why is it justified for the oppressed to use force, whether violent or not, to compel their oppressors to change? One of the advantages of nonviolence, in Deming's view, is precisely that it allows a justified use of force. Indeed, her definition of nonviolence is action that does not deprive any individuals of the freedom to do anything they are entitled to do. Nonviolence can and does deprive the opponent of the freedom to do some things. But those are things the opponents had no right to do in the first place, because they involve depriving others of their due freedom:

Some freedoms are basic freedoms, some are not. To impose upon another man's freedom to kill, or his freedom to help to kill, to recruit to kill, is not to violate his person in a fundamental way. . . . The man who acts nonviolently insists upon acting out his own will, refuses to act out another's—but in this way, only, exerts force upon the other, not tearing him away from himself but tearing from him only that which is not properly his own, the strength which has been loaned to him by all those who have been giving him obedience.[3]

In other words, nonviolence is a way of taking back one's own free will, which has been blocked by another. It may be necessary to coerce that other in order to achieve the goal, but it never involves depriving the other of his or her legitimate exercise of free will. So, it is morally justified to prevent people from making decisions, if those are decisions they have no right to make in the first place.

The question, for Deming, was not whether to force the unjust to change their ways, but how to do it most effectively. Her answer was that, in virtually every case, nonviolence is more effective than violence for ending, or at least reducing, the greater violence of injustice: "This is the heart of my argument: We can put *more* pressure on the antagonist for whom we show human concern."[4] She made her case by breaking down any nonviolent movement or action into the several steps it must follow in order to succeed. Nonviolent activists must gain control of the situation. They must make it clear that they have the power to force a lasting change in the injustice they oppose. They must, at the same time, compel the oppressors to at least consider accepting that change willingly, rather than merely under compulsion. They must also gain sympathy among the wider public audience. They must do all this while keeping violence to a minimum. Finally, they must change themselves so that they begin to act out the new kind of society they want to create for the future. Let us consider each of these steps in turn, to see why Deming believed each is best achieved by nonviolence.

Activists must gain control of the situation, as they confront their oppressors. The oppressors always have superior force, and they often try to retain control by using that force. A nonviolent response neutralizes that advantage, for it denies them the chance to win a contest of force versus force. But the advantage of nonviolence for control goes deeper than this. To get and keep control, the oppressed must be poised and balanced, like skilled martial arts warriors, ready to deal effectively with every unexpected change in the situation. Deming's principal argument against violence is that those who use it in the service of justice and social change undermine their own balance. They realize, whether consciously or not, that their means contradict their ends. They want to create a society based on justice, and most often on love, for all people. To do that, they must change people's consciousness as well as public institutions. If they try to create that change by killing people, they deny the inalienable rights to life and liberty they are trying to secure. That makes them feel confused, dizzy, off balance, and certainly not fully in control of themselves or the situation.

The way to acquire the balance needed for control is to make the means match the ends. The end is a society in which every person's worth and freedom are fully respected. So the means must never violate the inherent worth or freedom of any person. Few people can really feel love for their oppressors. But everyone can act on the essential assumption of nonviolence—"that all men's lives are of value, that there is something about any man to be loved, whether one can *feel* love for him or not. It happens that, if one does act on this assumption, it gives one much greater poise in the situation."[5]

When activists combine care and respect for their opponents' lives with a stubborn defiance of their opponents' actions, it gives the activists a uniquely effective control over the situation. Balancing self-assertion with love and concern for the other is the way to avoid dizziness: "The injunction that we should love our neighbors as ourselves means to us equally that we should love ourselves as we love our neighbors. We believe, in fact, that the one act of respect has little force unless matched by the other—in balance with it. . . . The acting out of that dual respect I would name as precisely the source of our power."[6] (Of course, it is important for activists to remember that loving an opponent does not necessarily mean—and usually should not mean—trusting that opponent.)

Just as nonviolence gives more balance to those who use it, it also throws their opponents off balance. "People who attack others need rationalizations for doing so. We undermine those rationalizations." The opponents expect a threat of losing everything, including their physical safety. When this ultimate threat is obviously taken away, they become confused; they hesitate in their response; they have to think before they act: "We undo their minds. And it is at this point that they become vulnerable to receiving a new idea."[7]

To use this advantage, nonviolent activists must always oppose unjust actions rather than the people who do the actions. They must separate the unjust person from his or her role in society: "Seek to destroy not the abusers of power but the sources of that power, which are certainly not their particular bodies."[8] By separating individuals from their roles, it is easier to establish communication with them. The more they are engaged in conversation, the more they can be influenced by nonviolent action. In all these ways, nonviolence makes the opponent the one who gets dizzy. And that gives the nonviolent activists more control of the situation.

Nonviolence also offers more control of a situation because it offers more control of the anger evoked in the situation. Both sets of antagonists will bring anger to any conflict, and their conflict will usually heighten the anger. But Deming distinguished between two kinds of anger. Unhealthy anger, or "affliction," is based on fear of the other. It despairs of making any meaningful change as long as the other exists. Since the other will probably continue to exist throughout the conflict situation, people motivated by unhealthy anger will continue to be afraid. Their fear will distort their perceptions, make them more dizzy, and prevent them from making the balanced rational decisions needed to gain control.

Balance and control come from healthy anger. This is just as aggressive as the unhealthy kind, but it is based on a belief and hope for change in social roles and institutions. Healthy anger demands change and creates the confrontations needed for change to occur. It also gives the other an opportunity to help make that change. "Our task, of course, is to transmute the anger that is affliction into the anger that is determination to bring about change. I think, in fact, that one could give that as a definition of revolution."[9] Deming recognized that at the beginning, when hope for change is just being born, people exercise their rights tentatively and feel unsure about them. Anger is bound to come out. It will be difficult to control at first, so it may be unhealthy.

The challenge for nonviolence is to transform unhealthy anger into healthy anger. The way to do that is to confront one's own unhealthy anger, to stop repressing it, and to recognize that anger at injustice and oppression is natural, especially for the victims of oppression. Admitting one's own unhealthy anger makes it easier to develop healthy anger and resist oppression nonviolently, which means more effectively: "If we are willing to confront our own most seemingly personal angers, in their raw state, and take upon ourselves the task of translating this raw anger into the disciplined anger of the search for change, we will find ourselves in a position to speak much more persuasively to comrades about the need to root out from all anger the spirit of murder."[10] Once anger is healthy and disciplined, it is no longer an obstacle to control. Rather, it becomes yet another useful vehicle for taking control of the situation.

Once control is demonstrated, activists must make it clear that they have the power to force a lasting change in the injustice they oppose. The fundamental goal is to make the opponents recognize that they must cease their injustice. But it is far better if the opponents can be brought to the point where they want to cease their injustice. By confronting the oppressor nonviolently, "one tries to shake him out of former attitudes and force him to appraise the situation now in a way that takes into consideration your needs as well as his."[11] The goal of nonviolent resistance is to force that new appraisal, to get everyone to see not just the immediate protest but the entire prevailing system in a new way. Resistance aims to show up the evil of the system. It aims to show that everyone living within an unjust system is actually a victim of that system, even those who seem to benefit most from it.

Nonviolence evokes this new perspective in several ways. Since the opponents cannot make violent protest the issue, they cannot easily shift the focus away from the main issue: their own injustice. The attack is clearly on their unjust actions rather than on their persons. This distinction urges the opponents to see themselves as whole persons, distinct from their roles in the social system. It creates a struggle between their minds and their bodies. So they are more likely to acknowledge the reality of what they have been doing. Then they can begin to think about changing their roles. They can begin to see the possibility of a society in which all people are respected and have full rights. Violence, on the other hand, makes it unlikely that the opponents will change their attitudes. It puts the focus on the immediate battle, not the long-term goals.

Violence also motivates people to react violently, out of fear. But if the opponents feel reassured about their safety and are no longer motivated by fear, they can assess their own best interests more objectively. They can see that their own long-term interests will be best served by changing the status quo: "They never can see it in their interest finally to accommodate themselves to the changes we are forcing unless we give them the liberty to do so. And they will only believe that we offer this liberty, only be able to imagine new lives for themselves, if we have refused to threaten them with any personal injury."[12] So all tactics should be ways of insisting on change while easing the immediate fears of the opponents.

Of course, the opponents have long-term fears of change too. It is usually the case that even oppressors fear the system of which they are a part. But they fear changing the system even more. Nonviolence is the only effective way to release them from that fear, to show them that what is really frightening is the status quo, not the activists who are demanding change. "It is not possible to affirm our own rights as inalienable simply by acting out: they are *mine*. We can affirm this only by acting out: they are *ours*— yours, and therefore mine; mine, and therefore yours—with a stress upon 'yours,' so that the minds of our antagonists and of their allies will attend."[13]

For all these reasons, nonviolent activists "have as it were two hands upon [the oppressor]—the one calming him, making him ask questions, as the other makes him move."[14] The hand that makes him move may even move him to switch sides and support the protestors' cause. If they treat their opponents as potential allies, explaining how all will benefit together from social change, there is a greater chance that some of the opponents will eventually become allies. This may not happen often. But it is far more likely if the protestors show genuine concern for all people, including their opponents.

Nonviolence also gives activists the best chance of gaining allies among the wider public, who are observers and bystanders: "Nonviolent tactics can move into action on our behalf men not naturally inclined to act for us." On the other hand, "violent tactics draw into actions that do us harm men for whom it is not at all natural to act against us." Violent protests frighten the public; they make the public more willing to accept repression in the name of law and order. That is why the oppressors often try to goad protestors into violence. Nonviolence prevents the opponents from gaining public sympathy, as they might if they were victims of violence. And the opponents' violence against unarmed people can eventually get their allies and supporters to stop giving support. Nonviolence is the best way to cultivate a positive public image.[15]

Another obvious advantage of nonviolence is that it breaks the cycle of violence and counter-violence. The oppressors may well escalate their violence at first, since they face no violence in return. The nonviolent activists will probably take more casualties than their opponents. But nonviolence does not count its victories in terms of who receives fewer casualties. It defines victory as a change in the opponents' policies and behaviors. And in the long run, nonviolence will decrease the violence, and there will be fewer casualties.

Finally, and very important, according to Barbara Deming, nonviolence is the only way that activists can change themselves, so that they begin to act out the new kind of society they want to create for the future: "The free man must be born before freedom can be won, and the brotherly man must be born before full brotherhood can be won. It will come into being only if we build it out of our very muscle and bone—by trying to act it out. And this cannot be put off." The goal is a society in which every person is accorded equal rights, in which every person respects and cares for every other person. One can claim the inalienable rights to life and the pursuit of happiness only if one grants this to all others, too. Nonviolence is "the only mode of battle that does, implicitly, respect this fact." It is the only mode of battle that makes its vision of the future a present reality. It is the only way to demand one's own rights and respect the rights of others at the same time: "We assert the respect due ourselves, when it is denied, through noncooperation; we assert the respect due all others, through our refusal to be violent."[16]

Nonviolent respect is a way of acting out human solidarity. It sends the message that the oppressed are not out to defeat their oppressors; they do not see the conflict as a zero-sum or win-lose contest. Rather, they understand that either everyone wins or everyone loses. This message is not totally disinterested. Treating others as fully human makes the most powerful demand that others treat us as fully human. Indeed, the best way to protect our own rights is to grant the same rights to even the most unjust opponent. So the best way to build a better future turns out to be, at the same time, the best way to protect our rights in the present.

Nonviolence works precisely because it combines practical pressure in the present with utopian visions of the future. It uses obstruction and non-cooperation to prevent the present system from functioning. It uses independent constructive activities to create an alternative system. Because economic pressures are often the most effective kind, nonviolent activists should be especially creative in devising an alternative economic system, so that the existing system and all its injustices can be shut down simply by being ignored. As a feminist, Deming added one more very important comment to her analysis. Nonviolence combines masculine self-assertion with feminine sympathy for all people. Thus it begins the journey to a more androgynous society in the future.

Beyond changing society, nonviolence also changes the individuals who employ it. Because they must separate individuals from their social roles, they see the social issues more clearly and create new attitudes in themselves as well as their opponents. They learn to set aside (or overcome) their learned desire for revenge. Instead, they learn to take satisfaction in a new kind of bold, heroic action. And they learn to feel in control of a situation without using violence. Nonviolence does require that people give up the seemingly "natural" desire to strike back, to seek revenge. It requires that this desire be subordinated to the overriding desire to improve society: "The point is to change one's life. The point is not to give some vent to the emotions that have been destroying one; the point is so to act that one can master them now."[17] The desire for revenge is one kind of unhealthy anger. The way to master it is to face one's own anger, accept it, and begin to get control over it. In this way, too, nonviolence in the present creates the kind of society that activists want to create for the future. It is not a society devoid of anger. It is a society where anger is healthy, a sign of hope, and a constructive step toward justice.

Can this kind of society ever exist in the future? Can nonviolence be put into practice on a large enough scale to overcome the massive injustices that the past has bequeathed to the present? Deming pointed out that we cannot know for sure, because nonviolence has never really been tried on a large scale. The movements led by Gandhi and King were only small beginnings. The actual practice of nonviolence is still being invented. It is like an experiment that has just begun; it is far too soon to say anything about the results. If people give up on nonviolence too soon, we will never discover its full potential. But Deming, for one, was convinced that if enough people join in the experiment, we will be surprised to discover just how enormous that potential is.

13

Thich Nhat Hanh

Thich Nhat Hanh (1926–) was born and raised in Vietnam. As a young man, he became a Buddhist monk. When Vietnam was gripped by civil war, he remained neutral. Although he did not support the North Vietnamese effort to reunify the nation by force, he was deeply involved in protests against the South Vietnamese government. In 1966, while he was touring the United States promoting peace, the South Vietnamese authorities told him he would not be allowed back into his native country. Since then, he has been a citizen of the world, teaching and modeling a distinctly modern Buddhist understanding of nonviolence. He has been the most influential leader of the movement called "engaged Buddhism," which has brought the influence of Buddhism into nonviolent activism in the United States. This influence is relatively recent; it is hard to say yet how much it may change the U.S. nonviolence tradition. But it is already important enough that it deserves to be studied as a contribution to the idea of nonviolence in the United States.

Interbeing

For Thich Nhat Hanh, nonviolence is a natural and necessary part of Buddhist religion. To understand his teachings, then, one must start with the most basic religious foundation: "In Buddhism the most important precept of all is to live in awareness, to know what is going on . . . to be aware of what we do, what we are, each minute." When we are totally mindful— in direct contact with reality, not just images of reality—we realize that "all phenomena are interdependent . . . endlessly interwoven." This is the foundation of Nhat Hanh's approach, not only to nonviolence but to all of life. He calls it the principle of interbeing. "In Buddhism there is no such thing as an individual." There is no such thing as a separate object, event, or

192

experience, because no part of the world can exist apart from all others. Rather, everything that looks like a separate entity is actually dependent on, and therefore interwoven with, something else. Everything (object, event, idea, experience, whatever) is made up of other things. Whatever appears to be an isolated "thing" is actually a combination of its constituent elements. These elements are the influences from the other things with which it is interwoven. And those elements, too, are made up of other combinations. The world is an endless web of combinations.[1]

But even this description of reality is misleading, because it is too static. The elements that make up the world are patterns of dependency and inter-weaving. In other words, they are relationships. When we are fully aware, we see that there are only relationships. All relationships are patterns of interaction. So they are, by definition, dynamic; they are patterns of change. There are no individual things, but only ongoing processes. These processes are made up of other, constantly changing processes. All of reality is combi-nations of patterns of relationships in process.

This is the basis of the traditional Buddhist teaching of emptiness: "Emp-tiness is a means of perceiving the nature of reality." When Buddhists say that everything is empty (at least in Nhat Hanh's interpretation), they mean that nothing has any independent permanent essence; nothing can exist by itself. Rather, every element is made up of other elements; paradoxically, each thing is made of what it is not. If all these other elements are removed, the thing is empty. But emptiness is not a negative concept. Since everything is dependent on and interrelated with something else, the chain of interbeing stretches out infinitely. Ultimately, everything is linked with everything else. "Empty, in this sense, means that it is full of everything, the entire cosmos." Philosophically speaking, the entire cosmos exists in every part of cosmos. The point of Buddhism is to transform this insight from an abstract philo-sophical idea into a lived reality that becomes the basis for everyday life.[2]

To achieve this transformation, we must transform ourselves. More pre-cisely, we must learn and then experience the truth that our ordinary notion of self is a fiction. If no thing has independent, self-subsistent being, then neither does what we call our self: "Life is one. We do not need to slice it into pieces and call this or that piece a self. What we call a self is made only of non-self elements. . . . We have to discard all distinctions between self and non-self." We have to experience everything, including what we call the self, as a manifestation of the sum total of all processes, a web of relation-ships woven into a much larger—indeed, infinite—web. That means over-coming our normal state of feeling like a subject experiencing objects. Bud-dhism teaches the "non-discrimination mind," which can see reality in its perfect state because it no longer sees as a subject looking at objects. Rather, at every moment it experiences the totality, of which the so-called self is an integral part. That totality is infinitely diverse yet fully unified: "Unity is diversity and diversity is unity."[3]

This is not as abstract as it may sound. Consider how we learn to recognize chairs, for example. No one teaches us the definition or "essence" of a chair. (In fact, it can be extremely frustrating to try to figure out the essential definition of *chair;* exactly what counts as a chair and what doesn't.) Instead, when we are small children people point at, or put us upon, various kinds of seats and say "chair." At first, that sound means nothing to us. We do not distinguish the chair from all the other visual and tactile stimuli bombarding our little brains. Gradually, we begin to make that distinction. We learn what a chair is by being able to separate out those relevant stimuli from the surrounding stimuli. As we are learning what a chair is, we are also learning what a table is, what a floor is, and so on. More precisely, we are learning where the table ends and the chair begins, where the floor ends and the chair begins. In other words, we learn what a chair is by learning to distinguish it from what is not a chair. We never actually learn the essential definition of *chair.* What we learn is the relationship between chair and not-chair. So the meaning of chair depends directly on the meaning of what is not-chair.

This is another way of understanding the teaching of emptiness: "All things rely on each other to be."[4] When we are fully aware and recognize emptiness, we see that the apparent boundaries between things, which we think are really there, are actually mental constructions. We realize that we can unlearn these boundaries; we can resist and overcome them. Again, though, to attain this awareness we must unlearn the most fundamental construction of all: the boundary we feel between the self and everything that is not-self. We must realize that, just as the chair depends on what is not-chair, so the self depends on what is not-self.

We can never define, or even know, our self. We can know only the infinite relationships between self and not-self. That is because what we call the self has no independent existence apart from those infinite relationships. The reality is not the self or the things we call other; the reality is only the constantly changing patterns of relationship between self and not-self. The reality is only the endless web of connections. As Nhat Hanh puts it, everything "inter-is" with everything else. Since everything depends on the totality of all, everything is already inside of everything else.

This is hard to understand, because we normally think of our self as some essential core of personal being, some intangible essence or "true self." We think that our perceptions, thoughts, feelings, desires, and so on are stuck onto that core and can be pulled off and replaced by others without changing the core. Buddhist teachers challenge their students to strip away all the perceptions, thoughts, feelings, and desires to reveal the "true self."

They are confident that the student will fail. The student will discover that we do not "have" perceptions, thoughts, feelings, and desires. Rather, we *are* all those processes, and nothing else. When we look carefully, we discover that those processes are all interactions between what we call self and what we call not-self. From this perspective, too, we are nothing but a constantly changing pattern of relationships. So everything that we call "out there" is already inside us.

The question for Buddhism is how to transform this philosophical theory into lived reality. The answer is to transcend the learned distinction between self and other, subject and object. The way to pursue this goal is to focus on our interbeing with the specific realities around us. "To understand something is to take that thing up and to be one with it." When we pay careful enough attention to that oneness, we discover that there is "no distinction between the contemplator and the contemplated."[5]

One way to do this is through meditation: "Meditation is to see into our own nature and wake up." Nhat Hanh teaches meditation through carefully focused breathing, mindful walking, and careful attention to trees and other natural objects. "To practice mindfulness and to look deeply into the nature of things is to discover the true nature of interbeing. There we find peace and develop the strength to be in touch with everything." We become fully present in the moment, not distracted by any concerns of past or future. This kind of meditation has always been an essential part of the Buddhist path to awakening.[6]

Engaged Buddhism

Nhat Hanh also brings into Buddhism a modern element of social consciousness. Most people may begin meditating to seek solutions for their problems. Eventually, though, meditation teaches that personal solutions must involve solutions to society's problems, and vice versa. The basis of this "engaged Buddhism" is the realization that every self is made up of all the elements that are not-self. All people in human society are within each one of us. All those who are victims of injustice, and perpetrators of injustice, are within each of us. So everyone shares responsibility for the social conditions that create every social evil. Each one of us, if we are fully aware, will identify with the criminal as well as the victim. As he put it in the poem "Call Me by My True Names":

> I am the twelve-year-old girl,
> refugee on a small boat,
> who throws herself into the ocean

after being raped by a sea pirate.
And I am the pirate,
my heart not yet capable
of seeing and loving.[7]

Engaged Buddhism teaches a cyclical process. By understanding the true nature of self, we better understand the true nature of society; we then use that enhanced understanding to gain an even deeper understanding of self, which leads to deeper understanding of society, and so on. Ultimately, we understand that self and society have no separate existence. They are just two ways of looking at the same unified reality. Our society makes it hard to realize this. Society teaches us to worry about the relationship between individual and society, as if the two were separate pieces of a puzzle that must somehow go together, yet cannot fit together. Society perpetuates this false problem because it wants us to be asleep, so that we will not do anything to change the status quo.

Awareness of interdependence makes it immediately evident that each of us shares responsibility for all that happens and will happen: "There is no phenomenon in the universe that does not immediately concern us." As soon as we recognize that responsibility, we are moved to act to improve the situation: "If we are very aware, we can do something to change the course of things." We are most motivated to work for change when we realize that our sense of being a separate self is illusory. We are all part of the same human process, all driven by the same human process. Changing that process means changing both situation and self: "Meditation is to see deeply into things, to see how we can change, how we can transform our situation. To transform our situation is also to transform our minds. To transform our minds is also to transform our situation, because the situation is mind, and mind is situation."[8]

Since the individual and society "inter-are," as Nhat Hanh says, each must nourish the other, or both will wither. The preservation of self is the same as the preservation of all; the improvement of self is the same as the improvement of all; the healing of one's own suffering is the same thing as the healing of all suffering. This is what Buddhists mean by compassion. It is (as the literal meaning of the word suggests) "feeling together with." Compassion means experiencing one's own fate and the fate of the other as identical. Therefore, it means experiencing the other's suffering as one's own suffering.

Compassion does not make any moral judgments about who is innocent and who is to blame. When we make such moral judgments, we take the stance of a subject observing objects. Thus we lose the sense of immediate interbeing that is the essence of compassion. But when we identify with everyone, we realize that our own being and society's good and evil aspects all share the same essential nature. "When we realize our nature of interbeing, we will stop blaming and killing, because we know that we inter-are."[9] So we cannot reject anyone or anything as fundamentally evil. We stop splitting the world into good versus evil. Instead, we will love and become friends with everyone.

This does not mean, however, that we stop acting on behalf of right and justice. On the contrary, it means that we have a new motivation to struggle for social change. Most people base their efforts at moral improvement on the belief that they are among the "good people," seeking to stop the "bad people." This can too easily become self-righteousness, which is a mask for selfishness. At bottom, self-righteous morality stems from a desire to control the world by creating fixed boundaries, like the boundary between good and evil. When these boundaries are used to control others, they lead to misunderstanding, narrow-mindedness, and even cruelty. The desire for control, in turn, grows out of a desire for security, having something unchanging to hold on to, to maintain the illusion of a permanent self.

When we are truly mindful, we recognize that nothing in life is any more permanent or secure than an ocean wave. We are always riding the crest of a wave. To try to hold on to anything is to pursue an impossible illusion of security. When we accept the truth of this impermanence, we realize that all boundaries are human constructs imposed on the unpredictable, and therefore uncontrollable, process of reality. So we make no effort to control or impose ourselves on others. We simply respond to the demand of the moment, without expecting to control the future.

Why respond? It is a natural impulse to ease our own suffering. If we accidentally put our finger in the fire, we do not think about what to do; we instinctively take our finger out of the fire. Compassion means having the same instinctive desire to ease all suffering, wherever and to whomever it occurs. This is the motive for engaged Buddhism and its efforts to create a more just world.

Compassion also allows us to be more objective, because we can see things more clearly and be more fully aware of the whole situation: "To love is to understand."[10] Most important, to love is to understand that, when suffering is humanly caused, the perpetrators actually suffer along with the victims. To love is to understand that the perpetrators are causing suffering because they themselves have suffered. The better we understand the causes of suffering, the more effectively we can work to relieve it. And when we offer others love and understanding, no matter how evil their deeds, we may be able to defuse the anger that is often the source of those deeds. Certainly we will be better models of the behavior we ask from others.

We cannot reach out to the world compassionately unless we become the compassion we want to offer others: "If you cannot be compassionate to yourself, you will not be able to be compassionate to others." "We can only be happy when we accept ourselves as we are. We must first be aware of all the elements within us, and then we must bring them into harmony." This is certainly not easy. We all have a desire for security, which makes it hard to accept the fact of impermanence. We all have emotions and ignorance, which create illusions that block accurate perception. Most difficult of all, usually, is our own unacknowledged anger. Once we recognize our own seeds of anger, we can stop nurturing them. We can convert them into constructive feelings of forgiveness and understanding, nurturing instead the seeds of compassion.[11]

Paradoxically, even knowledge can block accurate perception. We seek security from our sense of certainty—clinging to what we are sure we know. When we resist new ideas and refuse to change our views, we cannot see the truth clearly. Most important, we cannot see the truth that the world is always changing, that the next moment is inevitably unknown and unpredictable. Therefore, truth is always changing. No ideas are absolutely, permanently true. Ideas are only useful as means to reduce suffering. We should always be ready to give up our current ideas and knowledge when new circumstances call for new ones. Nhat Hanh says that even the Buddhist ideas he teaches, like the idea that there is no essential self, are only vehicles to heal suffering. Suffering is caused by attachment, even attachment to the idea of no-self. The way to compassion is nonattachment to all ideas, including both self and no-self.

In traditional Buddhism, the Buddha was most often presented as the one who knows how to heal suffering because he is "wide awake" (the literal meaning of the name Buddha). Engaged Buddhism teaches that each one of us can do this. Each of us has a Buddha nature, which is our innate capacity to wake up, to understand the truth of interbeing, and to love all reality. Everyone who wakes up embodies the Buddha and therefore becomes a Buddha body. In that sense, "You yourself are the Buddha."[12] We need not go to a monastery or a far-off mountaintop to become the Buddha. Anyone or anything can help us wake up. Everything teaches us Buddha's teachings, just by being what it is, a part of the endless web of interbeing.

Engaged Buddhism and Nonviolence

For Nhat Hanh, there is no question about being committed to nonviolence. Becoming a Buddha, or just setting out on the path to Buddhahood, means one must live nonviolently. Awareness of interbeing brings an obvious realization: "When you kill a living being, you kill yourself and everyone else as well."[13] The idea that I can better myself by doing violence to another is not so much morally wrong as logically mistaken. Since all others are already within me, whatever harm I do to them I do to myself as well. Awareness of interbeing naturally evokes a commitment to nonviolence. It evokes compassion and a desire to help all, which leaves no room and no motive for any kind of violence.

The real question is how to make life follow logic; how to overcome learned tendencies toward violence and sustain a life of nonviolence. The answer Nhat Hanh proposes is deceptively simple: "Our daily lives have the most to do with the situation of the world. If we can change our daily lives, we can change our governments and we can change the world. Our presidents and our governments are us. They reflect our lifestyle and our way of thinking. The way we hold a cup of tea, pick up a newspaper, and even use toilet paper have to do with peace."[14]

Nonviolence begins with changing the little habits of everyday life because so many of those habits now support the culture of violence. We are all part of that culture. Just as it is misguided to divide the world into "the good" and "the evil," so it is misleading to divide society into "the violent" and "the nonviolent," as if each person were all one or all the other. In fact, we are all on a continuum that blends the two. No one is ever perfectly nonviolent; everyone does some violence. And everyone practices, or has the potential to practice, some degree of nonviolence. So it is a mistake to begin by pointing an accusing finger at others. The place to begin is with oneself.

In meditation, as we learn to pay careful attention to our minds, we discover our own violence. We may not behave violently. But we all have seeds of anger and frustration, which cause the conflicts that are the source of violence. More precisely, Buddhist psychology tell us, we are anger and frustration, just as we are all the other thoughts and feelings flowing through us at any given moment. There is no real boundary between what we call our inner anger and what we call the external violence of society: "The bombs are us."[15] It is tempting to deny this, to imagine a boundary between self and world and to place all the violence on the other side of that boundary. That way, we do not have to deal with our own inner anger, which is the most frightening kind of violence. But resisting the anger inside us only increases the power those feelings have over us. Then it becomes more likely that those feelings will break out in external violence—perhaps aimed at the "bad" and "violent" people around us.

Mindfulness is the only way to escape the cycle of violence. By paying careful attention, we learn to see and accept the reality of who we are, anger and all. We learn to see, even more deeply, that our anger is caused by our own suffering. We can hold our anger and suffering tenderly, understand it, and have compassion for it. As we become aware of interbeing, however, we realize that what we call our suffering is actually the world's suffering. So, what we call our anger is actually the world's anger, the source of the world's conflict and violence. Recognizing that we are all entangled in the same web of violence does not make us feel guilty; it makes us feel liberated. We no longer have to choose sides and fight for "the good" against "the evil." Engaged Buddhists recognize the suffering that is always going on, on both sides of every boundary. So they can see that competing sides are equally victims of the unjust institutions, social systems, and ideas that perpetuate suffering. The anger and violence of the whole world needs to be understood just as compassionately as our own.

Engaged Buddhists oppose all violence, but especially the institutionalized violence embedded in everyday life. Virtually all economic, political, and social policies in any modern society are based on a dualism that ignores the truth of interbeing. So everyday life is bound to perpetuate suffering. But engaged Buddhists are careful to oppose the policies, not the people implementing them. They recognize that even the most powerful are victims of their own policies and suffer from them. To avoid increasing the dualism that leads to suffering, they generally avoid partisan politics. They make their contribution to society not as members of a party but as individual humans helping other humans.

When we see that the antagonists in any conflict are merely two sides of same the problem, we can stop fighting. We can become "non-fear, non-anger, and non-despair," and experience a new kind of calm, harmony, and peace. As Buddhist psychology would put it, we do not attain peace; we become peace. Nonviolence becomes more than an idea or a logical conclusion. It becomes a whole way of being. This is crucial, says Nhat Hanh, because ideas are never as important as relationships with people and things: "Breathing in and out, smiling together—that is real peace education." What we call outside is actually inside us. So each one of us is a whole environment, constantly interacting with other environments. A peaceful person is a peaceful environment and so creates peace just by his or her presence. This is the true meaning of "being peace."[16]

It is important to stress again that engaged Buddhism does not teach passivity, nor is it an excuse for passivity. On the contrary, it is an effort to create the most effective kind of activism. A Buddha does not want to win victories but only to ease suffering. So a Buddha wants everyone to have the same awareness of interbeing, of the fact that all share a common fate. Once we get beyond the idea of a zero-sum world, where every winner must create a loser, we can be free to work for the good of all. We can promote reconciliation between the two sides, rather than the victory of one over the other. Inner harmony gives the spiritual strength to face, directly and honestly, everyone's violence and suffering. With that full awareness, we can offer the most accurate analysis of a conflict situation and the suffering that has caused it. We can help each side tell of its own suffering and listen to the suffering of the other side.

And we can get the antagonists to listen to us, because they feel supported, not threatened. This is Thich Nhat Hanh's major point of criticism of current peace activists. They show righteous indignation, not the kind of universal love that is the only effective antidote to the violence that makes them indignant: "The peace movement can write very good protest letters, but they are not yet able to write a love letter."[17] The only way to make peace is to be peace, to set an example by showing love for all, no matter how wrong their behaviors may be.

Being peace and bringing full awareness is the way for activists to develop the most effective strategies for making peace. Paradoxically, these strategies are most effective precisely because a Buddha does not try to control their outcome. A Buddha understands that, because all reality is interconnected, there is no way to step outside of the situation in this moment in order to get control of it. Every effort to get that kind of illusory control only exacerbates conflict and violence. Rather, a Buddha lives fully in the present, doing what needs to be done in the immediate moment to ease suffering. "If we do our best, in full awareness and with a heart free from anger, we cannot worry about results."[18] Giving full awareness to the present moment, and being peace in that moment, is the best way to bring peace for the future. There can be no peace in the future if people are not peaceful in the present.

Finally, engaged Buddhism is also most effective because it protects the activist from burning out. When we are fully mindful, "we will know how to make small, steady steps" and take satisfaction from them. Those who act from non-anger and non-fear do not judge themselves by their victories and losses. They are happy when things improve, but they are not crushed when things don't improve. They can take the longest perspective because they are focused fully on the present moment. And they know that sometimes they should stop their political work for a while and turn back to introspective meditation, to "become oneself again in order to restore a point of stability."[19]

Nhat Hanh applies the same lesson to the newest phase of nonviolence: nonviolence against nature. He suggests that Buddhism offers the most powerful basis for environmentalism. Just as every person is within me, bound to me in interbeing, so is all of nature. Nature is our "larger self." All our environmental problems stem from the illusion that there is a basic difference between the human self and nature. Once we see through this illusion, we extend our compassion to every natural species. We respond immediately, in the present moment, to suffering anywhere in nature. We understand that suffering anywhere is our own suffering. So we must also take care of nature to ease our own suffering. We need the right kind of natural environment to maintain personal harmony, and we need personal harmony to have the right kind of natural environment. "The best way to take care of the environment is to take care of the environmentalist."[20] And the best way to take care of the environmentalist is to grow in nonviolence, in meditative mindfulness, in full awareness of the truth of interbeing.

Thich Nhat Hanh is the only figure studied in this book who was alive to see the dawn of the twenty-first century. At that time, his teachings were gaining an increasingly large following in the United States. His books were selling many copies and his personal appearances drawing huge audiences. Yet organized Buddhist action for specific changes in society seemed to be less successful. While such actions were not uncommon, they had not created a very large community of permanently committed, highly visible activists. In Asia, engaged Buddhist activism has succeeded in creating large and successful movements in the political and economic arena. Apparently, something different happens when Buddhism comes to the United States.

Nhat Hanh's writings may offer one clue to this difference. Insisting that good and evil are found in everyone, he gives many Americans the impression that value judgments of any kind should be avoided. This impression is an oversimplification of his thought, but it may appeal to people who do not want to take any definite stand for or against specific behaviors or policies. Although organized nonviolent activism avoids labeling anyone an enemy, it does require a certain sense of opposition to behaviors or policies. The people who promote those targeted behaviors or policies inevitably become opponents, those on the "other side." A certain kind of righteous indignation, or even anger, may also be a necessary ingredient in movements for social change. Nhat Hanh's words could easily be taken to mean that it is wrong to take sides, that no one should ever be seen as on the "other side" or an object of indignation, much less anger. This would mitigate against any kind of organized activism.

If evil is within all of us, then the best way to begin changing the world is to change ourselves. So Nhat Hanh would appeal most to people who want to be introspective and "work on themselves" rather than joining movements for political, economic, and social change. Following the slogan, "Peace begins with me," these individuals might rest content with their own spiritual development as their contribution to improving the world. Again, this would mitigate against their joining activist organizations working directly for specific changes in the world.

Critics of engaged Buddhism claim that too many of its adherents, trying to cultivate the Buddhist ideal of no-self, actually end up preoccupied with self. Their efforts to improve the world, though surely well intentioned, will have little impact on the world. This might reflect a distinctively American (particularly Protestant) tradition of religion as individual spiritual growth and self-development. It might also reflect a distinctively American contentment with the socioeconomic status quo, at least in the middle and upper-middle classes, where Buddhism tends to have the most appeal.

Critics might also suggest that Thich Nhat Hanh's American readers and audiences are drawn by the apparent simplicity of his teachings. Although Nhat Hanh's words are informed by a rich, complex Buddhist tradition, the words themselves tend to be simple and direct. He usually avoids or downplays the complexities that his words could entail. Often, he gives the impression that Buddhist theory and practice is quite easy. This could appeal to the American penchant for quick and easy solutions to difficult problems. Americans may also be drawn to Nhat Hanh's rather bright and sunny style. His words seem to have no shadow side. Although he acknowledges that he, like everyone, has seeds of anger, those seeds seem to have no effect upon his teaching. Readers and audiences are not likely to find their own anger and fear reflected in his words. Perhaps he appeals most to those who are trying to avoid their own anger and fear, even though he explicitly calls on people to face these feelings directly. People who want to avoid anger and fear may be precisely those who also want to avoid an adversarial stance and therefore stay away from organized activism.

For all these reasons, it may be difficult to build an American activist movement based on the teachings of Thich Nhat Hanh. However, it may be just a matter of time. Buddhism is gradually gaining more adherents in the United States. And within the Buddhist community, engaged Buddhism is gradually gaining more adherents. Whatever its practical outcome, the influence of Thich Nhat Hanh has already pushed the idea of nonviolence in new directions and enriched the nonviolence tradition. It is far too soon to predict what its lasting influence might be.

Conclusion

After surveying the wealth of ideas about nonviolence in U.S. history, it would seem audacious to make any definitive summary statement or draw any definite conclusions. This Conclusion, then, will only highlight a few of the most important trends in the past and raise a few questions to ponder for the future.

Through the end of the nineteenth century, the nonviolence tradition was motivated largely by issues of individual identity and authority. The tradition focused on the question, What kind of person do I want to be? It recognized that this question is always linked to another: What authority, if any, will I accept as binding upon me? In the twentieth century, the tradition continued to ask and answer these questions. But it enlarged its scope by putting increasing focus on the question, What kind of society do we want to live in? So it had to ask the inevitable corollary to that question: How can I help to create the kind of society I want to live in? Although the concern for individual identity and action was never lost, it was increasingly framed within a larger concern for group identity and action. Problems of individual morality were subsumed, more and more, in problems of social and economic institutions. The quest for personal spiritual growth was subsumed, more and more, into the quest for a society of genuine liberty and justice for all.

In the twentieth century, nonviolence came to be seen as the single path to both personal and societal ideals and as the bridge that could link the two. Despite their many differences, all the major theorists of the twentieth century agreed on some fundamental concepts that created this bridge. They generally started with the premise that all humanity (and, for many, all of cosmic reality) is interconnected. Everyone influences everyone else. Therefore, no one has the right to exercise authority over another against the other's will. Everyone has a right, and a responsibility, to make free choices. Only by exercising that right responsibly can an individual find his or her greatest fulfillment. Responsible freedom means respecting and promoting the freedom of all others; it means working for justice. It also means an attitude of universal love. Only a loving society can be just; only a just society can express love. No individual can attain the ideals of freedom,

204

justice, and love unless society is built upon, or at least moving toward, those ideals as shared values. Society will move toward those ideals only when they are realized in the lives of individuals. Society and the individual are interwoven. By the end of the twentieth century, these principles were generally accepted by nearly all groups and most individuals committed to nonviolent social change.

The growing focus on societal concerns in the twentieth century was connected to another momentous development: a growing focus on the results of nonviolent action. Through the late nineteenth century, nonviolence movements were still very much influenced by their roots in Christian nonresistance. Even when they organized for change, they concentrated on maintaining personal purity by avoiding violent resistance to evil. As the twentieth century went on, there was more and more desire to create a just society. Nonviolence could more readily be seen as a means to that end, rather than an end in itself that guarantees spiritual purity. Nonviolence was promoted as the best way to create, in the present, the kind of society people wanted for the future. This opened up the possibility that nonviolence could be used as a tool for coercion rather than a way to avoid any taint of coercive motives.

Many people now assume that nonviolence must meet the pragmatic test: Will it work? Will it create the social changes we want? If these questions seem so obviously the right ones to ask, that is testimony to the shift toward a focus on results. There is now a growing literature (inspired largely by the work of Gene Sharp) arguing for the efficacy of nonviolence. Though it offers theoretical arguments, it looks largely to the many examples in history of successful nonviolence. These examples can certainly offer encouragement. Nonviolent methods have indeed produced huge changes in some places and times. The U.S. civil rights movement and the independence struggle in India are only the best known of many dozens that could be cited. Anyone who lived through the end of the Cold War era remembers how stunning it was to see governments in the Soviet Union and throughout eastern Europe brought down by popular uprisings. This was a change of world-historical proportions, a change that few at the time had ever expected to see. And it all happened with scarcely a shot fired. Other movements around the world have followed a similar pattern.[1]

Before one hastens to judge by the pragmatic test, though, it may be worth noting the danger in this test. For every case in which nonviolence worked, it is easy to point to any number of cases in which it did not work. If people adopt the way of nonviolence because they believe that it will accomplish their goals, it is surely possible, and maybe probable, that they will be disappointed. Then they are likely to abandon their nonviolent stance. This kind of argument from history, though it may strengthen commitment to nonviolence in the short run, may end up weakening it in the long run.

Activists who have worked nonviolently for social change for many years often say that they do not judge the value of their work primarily by the results. They certainly try to achieve the best outcome they can. They do pay attention to results. However, they do not necessarily expect any results. They do what they do mainly because they think it is the right thing to do. They value the activism as an end in itself. In that sense, their efforts can never fail. That is why they do not "burn out." They can sustain their commitment and activities for so long precisely because they are not motivated primarily by results.

Religious and Secular Nonviolence

In the twentieth century, the trend toward more concern with social change and pragmatic results was linked to yet another change, perhaps the most significant of all. Nonviolence in the United States was gradually breaking free of its roots in Christianity. By the end of the twentieth century, although the movement was still hugely influenced by Christian faith and tradition, it also encompassed large numbers of people who adhered to some other religious faith or to none at all. This raises questions that may be, in theoretical terms, the most challenging questions for the nonviolence movement in years to come: How will the nonviolence movement respond to its increasingly ecumenical and secular character? Can it find a theory and language that can bring people together, allowing them to find common ground and embrace all points of view in their thinking and speaking?

The variety of religions has not posed a great problem, and very possibly it never will. Nonviolence is inherently tolerant; it attracts people who are and want to be tolerant. There is usually an easy acceptance of people of other faiths, as long as all share the same commitments to social change, spiritual values, and nonviolence. The question of secular nonviolence—without any religious basis at all—may prove more problematic. So far, that problem has also been held in check by goodwill and commitment to specific shared goals. In the long run, though, the movement may have to decide whether it can make theoretical room for a large component of people with no religious faith at all.

Intellectually, the crucial problem is to find a compelling basis for principled nonviolence that does not require any kind of religious, spiritual, or transcendent reality as its first premise. Thus far, Barbara Deming has provided perhaps the best example of a secular theory of nonviolence. Her premise is that every person deserves maximum freedom simply because he or she is human. But this begs the question, *Why* does every person have the right to make free choices and exercise free will? Most nonviolence thinkers find an answer by invoking some spiritual reality that is eternal, unchangeable, and therefore unchallengeable. But Deming can rely only on the human mind for an answer. She can offer only rational arguments, in the tradition of the eighteenth-century Enlightenment thinkers, who trusted reason to provide all truth.

The Enlightenment thinkers took this stand, in part, because they saw the many ways in which differences of religion could divide people and set them against each other. They also saw that religion seemed to be slowly but steadily losing its influence. Some other basis for truth was needed if people were going to learn to get along and to believe in the possibility of knowing the truth at all. Logical reasoning seemed to be the best foundation for truth and community. It is the same for everyone, at least in theory. So it should provide an indisputable basis for truth.

Because it is theoretically the same for everyone, reason also offers a more likely basis for overcoming human conflicts. Reason offers a language that all can share; it opens up channels of communication that religious foundations may cut off. Therefore, it is the best basis for tolerance, for avoiding the kind of fanaticism that religion can breed. Reason also provides the broadest possible foundation for the nonviolence movement, opening it up to the largest number of people. It can appeal to those who are primarily interested in pragmatic results as well as those who support nonviolence on principle. A purely rational theory like Deming's offers all these advantages.

It is noteworthy, though, that Deming did not argue logically for the primary value of individual freedom. Like most secular nonviolence adherents, she drew heavily on the Enlightenment tradition yet did not explicitly acknowledge it. Rather, like most with a secular stance, she took the inherent value, freedom, and rights of every person as an unquestioned starting point—a primary article of faith, held just as firmly, and with just as little proof, as any religious belief. Just as God is sacred in Christianity simply as God, the individual human being is sacred in secular nonviolence just because he or she is a human being. The secular stance can be, and most often is, just as much a leap of faith as the religious stance.

However, the nonviolence tradition can offer powerful logical arguments for a commitment to individual freedom and dignity. If reason is the ultimate source and test of truth, then everyone has equal access to the truth. No one can claim a special knowledge of truth based on a particular religion. Therefore, all people should be free to explore the truth for themselves and act upon the truth as they see it. No person should be allowed to coerce another. This premise of individual freedom lay at the heart of the

Protestant Reformation, particularly its more radical movements such as Anabaptism, a main source of all modern nonviolence movements. To install reason in the place of any transcendent reality is merely to move that tradition a step further in the same direction of radical individual freedom.

This link between reason and freedom has been spelled out most clearly in the anarchist tradition. Anarchists also see, however, that individual freedom is only meaningful—perhaps only possible—in a community where each person respects the freedom of all others. The insight that we are all interconnected needs no religious basis. It is readily obvious to anyone who thinks reasonably about the nature of human existence. Ironically, it was a devoutly religious man—Dr. Martin Luther King, Jr.—who made the most influential, and perhaps the most convincing, secular arguments for the link between individual freedom and community.

King also suggested another compelling secular argument for nonviolent social change. The best way to create the kind of world we want to have in the future is to act as if it were here now. As Gandhi put it, we should be the change we want to see in the world. Our lives are self-fulfilling prophecies; each choice we make turns the world in the direction of that choice. If we base our choices on a Niebuhrian premise that all people are inherently selfish, we make the world just a bit more selfish. If we assume that people can base their choices on selfless love, we bring the world just a bit closer to the society of selfless love that King called the beloved community. If we want to live, someday, in the beloved community—a world of genuine freedom, justice, love, mutuality, and nonviolence—we should stake our lives upon those values today. That leap of faith is bound to make those who take it better persons, regardless of the results of their particular actions for social change. Each individual's improvement, in turn, will make the entire society better. This argument for nonviolence can be compelling even to those who have no religious faith at all.

But there may be disadvantages in a rational foundation for nonviolence, too. Suppose that reason is the only basis for every person's inherent value and freedom. Then freedom, justice, and the worth of every individual are merely ideas in our minds. Where do those ideas come from? The Enlightenment tradition claimed that logical thinking gives us access to ideas that are universally and eternally true. The ideas are there, in some realm of cosmic objective truth, simply waiting to be discovered by clear, logical minds. But in the twentieth century that claim was radically challenged. It came to seem naive, simplistic, and in many quarters unsupportable. The notion of objective truth was besieged by evidence that all thinking is, to some extent, subjective, biased, and always liable to change. In the twenty-first century it is extremely difficult to maintain a belief in universal, eternal ideas that are self-evident to human reason. This means that any way of life based purely on reason now rests on a shaky foundation.

Religion is, in some ways, a much more firm foundation. That foundation is not illogical or opposed to reason. It can be understood in great logical detail (as many of the nonviolence thinkers have shown). Religion can, and often does, use reason as a buffer against fanaticism. But the deepest roots of religion transcend human reason. They are secured by a claim that they stem from some cosmic force or being. There is no way that logic can challenge this claim, since it is, by definition, beyond all logic. Once the initial claim is accepted as a basic premise, reason can go on to derive any number of other truth-claims from that premise. But as long as they are logically consistent with the basic premise, they too are immune from challenge.

The certainty that comes from religion provides powerful emotional support. Nonviolence needs this support, because it requires a willingness to endure suffering and perhaps even death. It is surely possible to endure suffering and face death for the sake of truths derived purely from human reason. But people often find stronger support in truths that they believe stem from some eternal force or being. Suffering for a religious truth may make a person feel more deeply embedded in the cosmic source of that truth. The cosmic source becomes more fully a part of the person. The suffering takes on cosmic meaning, and the suffering person expands, as it were, to a level of universal being. So does the cause for which the person is suffering. At least that is how it often feels to the religious nonviolent activist. The secular activist has the satisfaction of doing what seems to be indubitably right. But that satisfaction occurs on a more limited, mundane level of existence. With shallower roots, it may more easily be swept away by the threat of suffering and death.

The emotional support that comes from religion goes beyond the feeling of certainty it offers. Religious nonviolence is a tradition that is many centuries old. To be part of it is to be part of something deep and seemingly permanent in human culture, something shared with millions of other people. It has developed many symbolic words, images, and practices that evoke powerful nonrational responses. These can help make religious nonviolence a richly satisfying experience, not only intellectually but emotionally, socially, and even aesthetically. Secular nonviolence has a tradition of its own, rooted in the larger cultural environment of humanism. But it is too young to have developed anything so rich and powerful as the religious tradition offers. Since its roots do not transcend human reason, it may never be able to gain a richness and power equal to religious nonviolence. On the other hand, perhaps it simply has not had enough time.

Of course, there may be no need to choose between reason and religion as foundations for nonviolence. In the lived reality of the nonviolence community, both contribute greatly. The theoretical or potential conflicts between them are rarely evident in practice. There is no reason to assume that those conflicts will eventually intrude on the partnership between religion and reason. Moreover, both have shown their ability to engender love and compassion, which form the essential foundation of nonviolence. Whether that emotional foundation is framed in religious or secular terms may be a secondary question.

Nonviolence, Ideas, and the United States

For those of us who live in the United States, even the large majority who have no personal commitment to nonviolence, studying its ideas may have a special value. The United States is, and for the foreseeable future will be, the most powerful nation in the world. Its policies affect the life of every person in the world. All too often, that impact is not for the better. Indeed, all too often it brings some form of overt or covert violence. Simply because our impact and capacity for violence is so great, we who live in the United States have a special responsibility to think deeply about the question of violence.

Of course, most Americans feel quite sure that their nation uses violence only in self-defense. Since World War II, at least, our public life has been suffused by and structured around a fear of enemies. Whether the purported enemy has been fascism, communism, terrorism, or some other threat, the public has been called on to subordinate all other concerns to the overriding demand for national security. Yet the advent of the national security state has not succeeded in making the average person feel more secure. On the contrary, it has tended to reinforce the feeling that insecurity and threat now form the permanent condition of our national life. Far from a national security state, we actually live in a national insecurity state.

It may be that the only way to escape this dilemma is a radically new way of understanding relationships among nations, a new way drawn from the old tradition of nonviolence. That tradition is unique because it starts from the premise that we have no enemies, that the very idea of enemy is a profound misunderstanding of reality. The world cannot be simply divided into friends and enemies, good guys and bad guys. Everyone in the world is tied together to form what Martin Luther King, Jr., called "a single garment of destiny"; as the people discussed in this book observed, the actions of each affect all others. Harm to one is harm to all; security for one requires security for all. To be sure, we may try to influence others to change some of their behaviors. First, however, we must recognize how we help to create the problems we are trying to solve and the insecurity we are trying to alleviate. We must take a long, hard look at our own behaviors to see how they may engender and perpetuate the behaviors of others.

If U.S. national security policies are examined from the perspective of nonviolence, it will usually become clear that our own policies play a very large role in creating the very problems that they are supposed to solve. Rather than blaming and fighting an enemy, we may make ourselves most secure by correcting our own behaviors. That, in turn, requires us to change our attitudes. Above all, we must change some of our fundamental beliefs: that America is always the good guy; that we are beset by enemies who want to harm us without reasons; that our national life must be dedicated to fending off threats and overcoming foes. The nonviolence tradition may be our most valuable resource for finding a new way to think about the role of the United States in the world, a way that can bring more genuine security not only for ourselves, but for the whole world. We have a special responsibility to consider the alternative of nonviolence.

We also have a special opportunity to promote that alternative. It is an irony of our history that the nation deploying the most power around the globe has also enshrined one of the greatest teachers of nonviolence as a national hero. Martin Luther King, Jr., is widely revered by millions who have little understanding of the complexities of his idea of nonviolence. Most of those millions might have little sympathy for his idea if they did understand it. Yet the deep respect for Dr. King, and his eminent place in our national memory, afford a strong platform for promoting a sympathetic understanding of nonviolence and moving it to a more central place in our national life.

Dr. King is especially well suited to play this role because he encompassed so much of the nonviolence tradition in his own thought. He absorbed nearly all the main ideas of the white nonviolence community of the 1920s and 1930s, yet translated them into an idiom rooted in the black community. He recognized his intellectual debt to the historic peace churches and worked actively with them. He was profoundly influenced by Niebuhr as well as Gandhi. He joined Barbara Deming in seeing the links between the civil rights and peace movements. He was one of the first Americans to admire and support Thich Nhat Hanh.

Because his work synthesized so many influences, Dr. King was able to find a middle way among many of the alternatives offered by others' ideas. He showed how individual spiritual growth and social change are inextricably intertwined; how nonviolence could be both an end in itself and a means to improving society; how we could pursue practical results without letting results be the ultimate test of our actions; how Niebuhr's views of human nature could be incorporated into nonviolence thought; how coercion can be a legitimate practice of nonviolence; how religious and rational motives for nonviolence can reinforce each other; how religion, reason, and emotion can all work together to produce a life of love and compassion.

Many of the seeming contradictions that appear to be weaknesses in the thought of others became strengths in Dr. King's thought, because he showed how we can transcend the need to choose among these alternatives. Rather, we can draw upon all the resources of the tradition and bring all points of view together in a mutually strengthening harmony. That is certainly true to the spirit of nonviolence. It may be Martin Luther King, Jr., more than any other nonviolence thinker, who can point the way to a state of genuine national and global security in the future, one enriched by the idea of nonviolence.

Notes

1 The Anabaptists

1. For the Schleitheim Confession and many other early Anabaptist writings, see Daniel Liechty, ed., *Anabaptist Spirituality: Selected Writings* (New York: Paulist Press, 1994).

2 The Quakers

1. Hugh Barbour and J. William Frost, *The Quakers* (New York: Greenwood Press, 1988), 26.
2. Barbour and Frost, 40.
3. For a modern interpretation of this process, see Howard Haines Brinton, *Friends for 300 Years: The History and Beliefs of the Society of Friends since George Fox Started the Quaker Movement* (New York: Harper Bros., 1952), 106-9.
4. Brinton, 159.
5. Phillip P. Moulton, ed., *The Journal and Major Essays of John Woolman* (New York: Oxford University Press, 1971), 88.
6. Moulton, 60, 28, 29.
7. Moulton, 171, 250, 249, 92.
8. Edwin H. Cady, *John Woolman: The Mind of the Quaker Saint* (New York: Washington Square Press, 1966), 52.
9. Moulton, 30, 31, 128; Cady, 51-52.
10. Moulton, 241, 249.
11. Moulton, 240.
12. Moulton, 238.
13. Staughton Lynd and Alice Lynd, eds., *Nonviolence in America*, 2nd ed. (Maryknoll, N.Y.: Orbis Books, 1995), 10.
14. Lynd and Lynd, 5; Moulton, 60 n. 7, 72.
15. Moulton, 90.
16. Moulton, 91.
17. Cady, 52, 109.

3 William Lloyd Garrison and the Abolitionists

1. Truman Nelson, ed., *Documents of Upheaval: Selections from William Lloyd Garrison's The Liberator, 1831-1865* (New York: Hill and Wang, 1966), 141, 115.
2. Nelson, 73.

3. Aileen S. Kraditor, *Means and Ends in American Abolitionism: Garrison and His Critics on Strategy and Tactics, 1834-1850* (New York: Pantheon Books, 1969), 91.

4. Nelson, 73.

5. Kraditor, 88.

6. Nelson, 99, 123.

7. James Brewer Stewart, *Holy Warriors: The Abolitionists and American Slavery* (New York: Hill and Wang, 1976), 56; Nelson, 115.

8. Nelson, 143; Lewis Perry, *Radical Abolitionism: Anarchy and the Government of God in Antislavery Thought* (Ithaca, N.Y.: Cornell University Press, 1973), 53-56.

9. Staughton Lynd and Alice Lynd, eds., *Nonviolence in America*, 2nd ed. (Maryknoll, N.Y.: Orbis Books, 1995), 17; Nelson, 81.

10. Nelson, 142; Lynd and Lynd, 17.

11. Perry, *Radical Abolitionism*, 250.

12. Perry, *Radical Abolitionism*, 75.

13. Lynd and Lynd, 14.

14. Lynd and Lynd, 15; Nelson, 142.

15. Nelson, 142.

16. Nelson, 142.

17. Lynd and Lynd, 16.

18. Kraditor, 126.

19. Lynd and Lynd, 16.

20. Lewis Perry, "Adin Ballou's Hopedale Community and the Theology of Antislavery," *Church History* 39 (1970), 377–78.

21. Perry, "Adin Ballou's Hopedale Community," 378.

22. Adin Ballou, *Practical Christian Socialism: A Conversational Exposition of the True System of Human Society* (New York: AMS Press, 1974 [1854]), 150.

4 Henry David Thoreau

1. Henry David Thoreau, *Walden and Other Writings,* ed. Brooks Atkinson (New York: Modern Library, 1950), 256, 294.

2. Thoreau, *Walden*, 86, 88.

3. Thoreau, *Walden*, 121, 259, 295.

4. Thoreau, *Walden*, 87, 200, 81.

5. Thoreau, *Walden*, 292.

6. Thoreau, *Walden*, 196-97.

7. Thoreau, *Walden*, 64, 286.

8. Thoreau, *Walden*, 290.

9. Thoreau, *Walden*, 136.

10. Bob Pepperman Taylor, *America's Bachelor Uncle: Thoreau and the American Polity* (Lawrence, Kans.: University Press of Kansas, 1996), 80, 82.

11. Thoreau, *Walden*, 185.

12. Taylor, 79, 80.

13. Thoreau, *Walden*, 150.

14. Thoreau, *Walden*, 197-200.

15. Staughton Lynd and Alice Lynd, eds., *Nonviolence in America*, 2nd ed. (Maryknoll, N.Y.: Orbis Books, 1995), 22.

16. Lynd and Lynd, 38.

17. Thoreau, *Walden*, 287.

18. Henry David Thoreau, "Slavery in Massachusetts," in *Walden and Other Writings*, ed. Brooks Atkinson (New York: Modern Library, 1950), 673, 669.

19. Thoreau, "Slavery in Massachusetts," 675.

20. Lynd and Lynd, 28.

21. Jane Bennett, *Thoreau's Nature: Ethics, Politics, and the Wild* (Thousand Oaks, Calif.: Sage Publications, 1994), 13.

22. Thoreau, *Walden*, 68.

23. Thoreau, *Walden*, 65, 136.

24. Thoreau, "Slavery in Massachusetts," 676–77.

25. Thoreau, *Walden*, 150, 266.

26. Thoreau, "Slavery in Massachusetts," 676; Henry David Thoreau, "Plea for John Brown," in *Walden and Other Writings*, ed. Brooks Atkinson (New York: Modern Library, 1950), 693, 702.

5 The Anarchists

1. Alix Kates Shulman, ed., *Red Emma Speaks: An Emma Goldman Reader*, 3rd ed. (Atlantic Highlands, N.J.: Humanities Press, 1996), 68, 442.

2. Shulman, 68.

3. Shulman, 113, 442, 72.

4. Shulman, 435.

5. Shulman, 68, 75.

6. Shulman, 68.

7. Shulman, 167, 213.

8. Shulman, 161-62, 165, 166, 167.

9. Shulman, 211.

10. Shulman, 121, 76.

11. Shulman, 113.

12. Shulman, 45.

13. Shulman, 64, 391.

14. Shulman, 266, 259.

15. Shulman, 279.

16. Shulman, 253-54.

17. Staughton Lynd and Alice Lynd, eds., *Nonviolence in America*, 2nd ed. (Maryknoll, N.Y.: Orbis Books, 1995), 45.

18. Shulman, 401.

19. Janet Beihl, ed., *The Murray Bookchin Reader* (London and Washington: Cassell, 1997), 5, 6.

20. Biehl, 76.

21. Biehl, 105.

22. Biehl, 101.

23. Biehl, 7, 35.

24. Biehl, 8.

25. Biehl, 167.
26. Biehl, 167, 168.
27. Biehl, 170, 147.
28. Biehl, 152.

6 World War I

1. Leo Tolstoy, *Tolstoy's Writings on Civil Disobedience and Non-violence* (New York: Bergman Publishers, 1967), 14, 183, 284.
2. Tolstoy, 129, 79, 275.
3. Tolstoy, 207, 11.
4. Charles Chatfield, *For Peace and Justice: Pacificism in America, 1914-1941* (Knoxville, Tenn.: University of Tennessee Press, 1971), 31, 33.
5. Chatfield, 39.

7 Mahatma Gandhi

1. Rhagavan Iyer, ed., *The Essential Writings of Mahatma Gandhi* (Oxford: Oxford University Press, 1991), 227.
2. Iyer, 162, 156.
3. Iyer, 231-33.
4. Iyer, 236, 161.
5. Iyer 159.
6. Iyer, 232.
7. Iyer, 159.
8. Iyer, 174.
9. Iyer, 173-74.
10. Iyer, 227.
11. Iyer, 174, 242.
12. Iyer, 231, 415.
13. Iyer, 159; Dennis Dalton, ed., *Mahatma Gandhi: Selected Political Writings* (Indianapolis, Ind.: Hackett Publishing Co., 1996), 123.
14. Iyer, 175.
15. Iyer, 178.
16. Iyer, 289, 243, 235.
17. Iyer, 272; Dalton, 89; Iyer, 256.
18. Iyer, 246, 240, 257.
19. Iyer, 167.
20. Iyer, 285.
21. Iyer, 285.
22. Dalton, 116.
23. Dalton, 70.
24. Dalton, 53; Iyer, 233.
25. Iyer, 376.
26. Iyer, 236.
27. Iyer, 236.
28. Dalton, 62.

29. Iyer, 227; Dalton, 125; Iyer, 227.
30. Iyer, 376.
31. Iyer, 244.
32. Iyer, 273.
33. Iyer, 294.
34. Iyer, 392-93.
35. Dalton, 120.
36. Dalton, 20.
37. Dalton, 97-98, 100.
38. Dalton, 99.
39. Iyer, 328; Dalton, 14, 29.
40. Dalton, 91, 13.
41. Dalton, 46.
42. Dalton, 99.

8 Reinhold Niebuhr

1. Reinhold Niebuhr, *Moral Man and Immoral Society* (New York: Scribner, 1960 [1932]), 42.
2. Niebuhr, 42.
3. Niebuhr, 42.
4. Niebuhr, 44.
5. Niebuhr, 237.
6. Niebuhr, 44-45.
7. Niebuhr, 4.
8. Niebuhr, 6.
9. Niebuhr, 272, 19.
10. Niebuhr, 22.
11. Niebuhr, 70.
12. Niebuhr, 75.
13. Niebuhr, 78.
14. Niebuhr, 62, 63, 9.
15. Niebuhr, 170, 174, 171.
16. Niebuhr, 199.
17. Niebuhr, 235, 268.
18. Niebuhr, 172, 242.
19. Niebuhr, 240.
20. Niebuhr, 247, 248
21. Niebuhr, 251, 252.
22. Niebuhr, 273, 276.
23. Niebuhr, 271.
24. Niebuhr, 277.

9 A. J. Muste

1. Nat Hentoff, ed., *The Essays of A. J. Muste* (Indianapolis, Ind.: Bobbs-Merrill Co., 1967), 276.

2. A. J. Muste, *Non-Violence in an Aggressive World* (New York: Harper, 1972 [1940]), 179-80.

3. Hentoff, 201.

4. Muste, 5; Hentoff, 216; Muste, 5.

5. Hentoff, 202, 220, 208.

6. Hentoff, 201; Muste, 12.

7. Hentoff, 201.

8. Hentoff, 200, 310.

9. Muste, 177; Hentoff, 230.

10. Hentoff, 263, 270, 310.

11. Muste, 15; Hentoff, 225; Muste, 12-13; Hentoff, 294.

12. Muste, 175.

13. Hentoff, 200.

14. Muste, 13, 16, 17; Hentoff, 212.

15. Muste, 18; Hentoff, 231, 265, 226.

16. Muste, 176; Hentoff, 263, 265.

17. Hentoff, 208.

18. Hentoff, 220, 201.

19. Hentoff, 223; Muste, 143; Hentoff, 225.

20. Muste, 96, 88.

21. Hentoff, 221; Muste, 21, 27.

22. Muste, 18; Hentoff, 220.

23. Muste, 41; Muste, 24.

24. Muste, 5-6; Hentoff, 216.

25. Hentoff, 264, 261.

26. Hentoff, 264.

27. Muste, 154.

28. Muste, 38.

29. Muste, 162.

30. Hentoff, 244.

31. Muste, 149, 155.

32. Hentoff, 252.

33. Muste, 45.

34. Muste, 164.

35. Hentoff, 267, 218.

36. Muste, 157, 168.

37. Hentoff, 228.

38. Muste, 179-80; Hentoff, 264.

39. Muste, 178.

10 Dorothy Day and the Catholic Worker Movement

1. Robert Ellsberg, ed., *By Little and By Little: The Selected Writings of Dorothy Day* (New York: Alfred A. Knopf, 1983), 33, 39.

2. Ellsberg, 41.

3. Ellsberg, 87, 240.

4. Ellsberg, 343, 171.

5. Ellsberg, 140.

6. Ellsberg, 98.

7. Ellsberg, 91.

8. Ellsberg, 96, 323.

9. Ellsberg, 194.

10. Ellsberg, 124, 44.

11. Ellsberg, 313 , 126, 43, 103.

12. Ellsberg, 85, 98, 303, 111, 271.

13. Ellsberg, 85.

14. Ellsberg, 85.

15. Ellsberg, 235, 271, 330.

16. Ellsberg, 66.

17. Ellsberg, 307, 99, 109.

18. Ellsberg, 265, 343, 272.

19. Ellsberg, 243, 301, 354, 322.

20. Ellsberg, 339.

21. Ellsberg, 265, 317, 266.

22. Ellsberg, 105, 180.

23. Ellsberg, 280.

24. Ellsberg, 313.

25. Ellsberg, 111.

26. Ellsberg, 264, 262.

27. Ellsberg, 179.

28. Ellsberg, 92.

29. Ellsberg, 335.

30. For some interesting reflections on the question of asceticism in the nonviolence tradition, though not directed at Dorothy Day or the Catholic Workers (who are generally not ascetic in the strict sense), see David Dellinger, "Not Enough Love," in *Revolutionary Nonviolence: Essays by Dave Dellinger* (Garden City, N.Y.: Anchor Books, 1971), 263-69.

11 Martin Luther King, Jr.

1. James Melvin Washington, ed., *Testament of Hope: The Essential Writings of Martin Luther King, Jr.* (San Francisco: Harper & Row, 1986), 38.

2. Washington, 40.

3. Washington, 121, 120.

4. Washington, 626, 104.

5. Washington, 140, 11, 151.

6. Washington, 210, 122.

7. Washington, 10.

8. Washington, 582.

9. Washington, 482.

10. Washington, 262.

11. Washington, 48.

12. Washington, 626.

13. Washington, 88, 40.

14. Washington, 40, 226.
15. Washington, 619, 282.
16. Washington, 589, 312, 592.
17. Washington, 292.
18. Washington, 597, 362, 484.
19. Washington, 360, 628, 291.
20. Washington, 484, 237.
21. Washington, 334.
22. Washington, 347, 349.
23. Washington, 20, 482.
24. Washington, 103.
25. Washington, 485, 293.
26. Washington, 48, 125.
27. Washington, 234, 345.
28. Washington, 488.
29. Washington, 118.
30. Washington, 93.
31. Washington, 242.
32. Washington, 636, 620.
33. Washington, 615, 629, 630.
34. Washington, 39, 240, 315.
35. Washington, 640, 240.
36. Washington, 647.

12 Barbara Deming

1. Staughton Lynd and Alice Lynd, eds., *Nonviolence in America*, 2nd ed. (Maryknoll, N.Y.: Orbis Books, 1995), 425.
2. Lynd and Lynd, 413.
3. Lynd and Lynd, 414-15.
4. Lynd and Lynd, 415.
5. Lynd and Lynd, 413.
6. Barbara Deming, *Two Essays: On Anger; New Men, New Women: Some Thoughts on Nonviolence* (Philadelphia: New Society Publishers, 1982), 24.
7. Deming, 27.
8. Deming, 22.
9. Deming, 12.
10. Deming, 18.
11. Lynd and Lynd, 419.
12. Lynd and Lynd, 421.
13. Deming, 25.
14. Lynd and Lynd, 416.
15. Lynd and Lynd, 419.
16. Deming, 23; Lynd and Lynd, 193; Deming, 9.
17. Lynd and Lynd, 424.

13 Thich Nhat Hanh

1. Thich Nhat Hanh, *Being Peace* (Berkeley, Calif.: Parallax Press, 1988), 65-67; Thich Nhat Hanh, *Love in Action* (Berkeley, Calif.: Parallax Press, 1993), 129; Hanh, *Being Peace*, 45.

2. Daniel Berrigan and Thich Nhat Hanh, *The Raft Is Not the Shore: Conversations toward a Buddhist/Christian Awareness* (Maryknoll, N.Y.: Orbis Books, 2001), 6; Hanh, *Being Peace*, 46.

3. Hanh, *Love in Action*, 133, 129.

4. Berrigan and Hanh, *The Raft Is Not the Shore*, 120.

5. Hanh, *Being Peace*, 38-39.

6. Hanh, *Love in Action*, 110, 138.

7. Hanh, *Being Peace*, 64.

8. Hanh, *Love in Action*, 129; Hanh, *Being Peace*, 66, 74.

9. Hanh, *Love in Action*, 137.

10. Hanh, *Love in Action*, 86.

11. Hanh, *Being Peace*, 40; Hanh, *Love in Action*, 119.

12. Hanh, *Being Peace*, 12.

13. Hanh, *Love in Action*, 136.

14. Hanh, *Love in Action*, 109.

15. Hanh, *Love in Action*, 99.

16. Hanh, *Love in Action*, 135, 112.

17. Hanh, *Being Peace*, 79.

18. Hanh, *Love in Action*, 106.

19. Hanh, *Love in Action*, 135; Berrigan and Hanh, *The Raft Is Not the Shore*, 79.

20. Hanh, *Love in Action*, 132.

Conclusion

1. See Gene Sharp's pioneering work, *The Politics of Nonviolent Action*, 3 vols. (Boston: P. Sargent Publisher, 1973). For a convenient survey of nonviolent movements around the world in the late twentieth century, see Stephen Zunes, Lester R. Kurtz, and Sarah Beth Asher, eds., *Nonviolent Social Movements: A Geographical Perspective* (Malden, Mass.: Blackwell, 1999).

Bibliography

General History

Ackerman, Peter, and Jack DuVall. *A Force More Powerful: A Century of Nonviolent Conflict*. New York: St. Martin's Press, 2000.

Bainton, Roland H. *Christian Attitudes toward War and Peace*. New York: Abingdon Press, 1960.

Brock, Peter. *A Brief History of Pacifism from Jesus to Tolstoy*. 2nd ed. Syracuse: Syracuse University Press, 1992.

———. *Pacifism in Europe to 1914*. Princeton, N.J.: Princeton University Press, 1972.

Brock, Peter, and Nigel Young. *Pacifism in the Twentieth Century*. Syracuse, N.Y.: Syracuse University Press, 1999.

Cahill, Lisa Sowle. *Love Your Enemies: Discipleship, Pacifism, and Just War Theory*. Minneapolis: Fortress Press, 1994.

Dyck, Harvey L., ed. *The Pacifist Impulse in Historical Perspective*. Toronto: University of Toronto Press, 1996.

Johnson, James Turner. *The Quest for Peace: Three Moral Traditions in Western Cultural History*. Princeton, N.J.: Princeton University Press, 1987.

Schlabach, Theron F., and Richard T. Hughes, eds. *Proclaim Peace: Christian Pacifism from Unexpected Quarters*. Urbana, Ill.: University of Illinois Press, 1997.

Zunes, Stephen, Lester R. Kurtz, and Sarah Beth Asher, eds. *Nonviolent Social Movements: A Geographical Perspective*. Malden, Mass.: Blackwell, 1999.

Anabaptists

Brock, Peter. *Freedom from Violence: Sectarian Nonresistance from the Middle Ages to the Great War*. Toronto: University of Toronto Press, 1991.

Estep, William Roscoe. *The Anabaptist Story: An Introduction to Sixteenth-Century Anabaptism*. 3rd ed. Grand Rapids, Mich.: William B. Eerdmans Publishing Co., 1996.

Goertz, Hans-Jurgen. *The Anabaptists*. London: Routledge, 1996.

Liechty, Daniel, ed. *Early Anabaptist Spirituality: Selected Writings*. New York: Paulist Press, 1994.

Quakers

Bailey, Richard. *New Light on George Fox and Early Quakerism: The Making and Unmaking of a God.* San Francisco: Mellen Research University Press, 1992.

Barbour, Hugh, and J. William Frost. *The Quakers.* New York: Greenwood Press, 1988.

Brinton, Howard Haines. *Friends for 300 Years: The History and Beliefs of the Society of Friends since George Fox Started the Quaker Movement.* New York: Harper Bros., 1952.

Brock, Peter. *The Quaker Peace Testimony 1660 to 1914.* Syracuse, N.Y.: Syracuse University Press, 1990.

Cady, Edwin H. *John Woolman: The Mind of the Quaker Saint.* New York: Washington Square Press, 1966.

Dandelion, Pink. *A Sociological Analysis of the Theology of Quakers: The Silent Revolution.* Lewiston, N.Y.: Edward Mellen Press, 1996.

Endy, Melvin B., Jr. *William Penn and Early Quakerism.* Princeton, N.J.: Princeton University Press, 1973.

Gwyn, Douglas. *Apocalypse of the Word: The Life and Message of George Fox (1624-1691).* Richmond, Ind.: Friends United Press, 1986.

Hirst, Margaret Esther. *The Quakers in Peace and War: An Account of Their Peace Principles and Practice.* New York: J. S. Ozer, 1972 [1923].

Marietta, Jack D. *The Reformation of American Quakerism, 1748-1783.* Philadelphia: University of Pennsylvania Press, 1984.

Weddle, Meredith Baldwin. *Walking in the Way of Peace: Quaker Pacifism in the Seventeenth Century.* New York: Oxford University Press, 2001.

Woolman, John. *The Journal and Major Essays of John Woolman.* Edited by Phillip P. Moulton. New York: Oxford University Press, 1971.

General U.S. History

Brock, Peter. *Pacifism in the United States, From the Colonial Era to the First World War.* Princeton, N.J.: Princeton University Press, 1968.

Chatfield, Charles. *The American Peace Movement: Ideals and Activism.* New York: Twayne Publishers, 1992.

Cooney, Robert, and Helen Michalowski, eds. *The Power of the People: Active Nonviolence in the United States.* Philadelphia: New Society Publishers, 1987.

DeBenedetti, Charles. *The Peace Reform in American History.* Bloomington, Ind: Indiana University Press, 1980.

Lynd, Staughton, and Alice Lynd, eds. *Nonviolence in America.* 2nd ed. Maryknoll, N.Y.: Orbis Books, 1995.

O'Gorman, Angie, ed. *The Universe Bends toward Justice: A Reader on Christian Nonviolence in the U.S.* Philadelphia: New Society Publishers, 1990.

Peterson, Carl L. *Avoidance and Evasion of Military Service: An American History, 1626-1973.* San Francisco: International Scholars Publications, 1998.

Tracy, James. *Direct Action: Radical Pacifism from the Union Eight to the Chicago Seven.* Chicago: University of Chicago Press, 1996.

William Lloyd Garrison and the Abolitionists

Abzug, Robert H. *Cosmos Crumbling: American Reform and the Religious Imagination.* New York: Oxford University Press, 1994.

Ballou, Adin. *Practical Christian Socialism: A Conversational Exposition of the True System of Human Society.* New York: AMS Press, 1974 [1854].

Kraditor, Aileen S. *Means and Ends in American Abolitionism: Garrison and His Critics on Strategy and Tactics, 1834-1850.* New York: Pantheon Books, 1969.

Lowance, Mason, ed. *Against Slavery: An Abolitionist Reader.* New York: Penguin Books, 2000.

Mayer, Henry. *All on Fire: William Lloyd Garrison and the Abolition of Slavery.* New York: St. Martin's Press, 1998.

Nelson, Truman, ed. *Documents of Upheaval: Selections from William Lloyd Garrison's the Liberator, 1831-1865.* New York: Hill and Wang, 1966.

Newman, Richard S. *The Transformation of American Abolitionism: Fighting Slavery in the Early Republic.* Chapel Hill, N.C.: University of North Carolina Press, 2002.

Nye, Russel Blaine. *William Lloyd Garrison and the Humanitarian Reformers.* Boston: Little, Brown, 1955.

Perry, Lewis. "Adin Ballou's Hopedale Community and the Theology of Antislavery." *Church History* 39 (1970), 372-79.

———. *Radical Abolitionism: Anarchy and the Government of God in Antislavery Thought.* Ithaca, N.Y.: Cornell University Press, 1973.

Rogers, William B. *"We Are All Together Now": Frederick Douglass, William Lloyd Garrison, and the Prophetic Tradition.* New York: Garland Publishing, 1995.

Stewart, James Brewer. *Holy Warriors: The Abolitionists and American Slavery.* New York: Hill and Wang, 1976.

Strong, Douglas M. *Perfectionist Politics: Abolitionism and the Religious Tensions of American Democracy.* Syracuse, N.Y.: Syracuse University Press, 1999.

Ziegler, Valarie H. *The Advocates of Peace in Antebellum America.* Bloomington, Ind.: Indiana University Press, 1992.

Henry David Thoreau

Bennett, Jane. *Thoreau's Nature: Ethics, Politics, and the Wild.* Thousand Oaks, Calif.: Sage Publications, 1994.

Bickman, Martin. *Walden: Volatile Truths.* New York: Maxwell Macmillan International, 1992.

Botkin, Daniel B. *No Man's Garden: Thoreau and a New Vision for Civilization and Nature.* Washington, D.C.: Shearwater Books, 2001.

Hodder, Alan D. *Thoreau's Ecstatic Witness.* New Haven, Conn.: Yale University Press, 2001.

Taylor, Bob Pepperman. *America's Bachelor Uncle: Thoreau and the American Polity.* Lawrence, Kans.: University Press of Kansas, 1996.

Thoreau, Henry David. "Plea for John Brown." In *Walden and Other Writings,* edited by Brooks Atkinson. New York: Modern Library, 1950.

————. "Slavery in Massachusetts." In *Walden and Other Writings,* edited by Brooks Atkinson. New York: Modern Library, 1950.

————. *Walden and Other Writings.* Edited by Brooks Atkinson. New York: Modern Library, 1950.

Leo Tolstoy

Green, Martin Burgess. *Tolstoy and Gandhi, Men of Peace: A Biography.* New York: Basic Books, 1983.

Greenwood, Edward Baker. *Tolstoy: The Comprehensive Vision.* New York: St. Martin's Press, 1975.

Gustafson, Richard F. *Leo Tolstoy: Resident and Stranger.* Princeton, N.J.: Princeton University Press, 1986.

Redfearn, David. *Tolstoy: Principles for a New World Order.* London: Shepheard-Walwyn, 1992.

Sampson, Ronald Victor. *The Discovery of Peace.* New York: Pantheon Books, 1973.

Sokolow, Jayme A. *Leo Tolstoi's Christian Pacifism: The American Contribution.* Pittsburgh: University of Pittsburgh Center for Russian and East European Studies, 1987.

Tolstoy, Leo. *The Kingdom of God Is within You; Or, Christianity Not as a Mystical Teaching but as a New Concept of Life.* New York: Noonday Press, 1961.

————. *Tolstoy's Writings on Civil Disobedience and Non-Violence.* New York: Bergman Publishers, 1967.

Wilson, A. N. *Tolstoy.* New York: Norton, 1988.

Anarchists

Bookchin, Murray. *The Murray Bookchin Reader.* Edited by Janet Biehl. London and Washington: Cassell, 1997.

Goldman, Emma. *Red Emma Speaks: An Emma Goldman Reader.* Edited by Alix Kates Shulman. 3rd ed. Atlantic Highlands, N.J.: Humanities Press, 1996.

Miller, David. *Anarchism.* London: J. M. Dent, 1984.

Reichert, William O. *Partisans of Freedom: A Study in American Anarchism.* Bowling Green, Ohio: Bowling Green University Popular Press, 1976.

Sonn, Richard David. *Anarchism.* New York: Maxwell Macmillan International, 1992.

U.S. History from World War I to World War II

Chatfield, Charles. *For Peace and Justice: Pacificism in America, 1914-1941.* Knoxville, Tenn.: University of Tennessee Press, 1971.

DeBenedetti, Charles. *Origins of the Modern American Peace Movement, 1915-1929.* Millwood, N.Y.: KTO Press, 1978.

DeBenedetti, Charles, ed. *Peace Heroes in Twentieth-Century America.* Bloomington, Ind.: Indiana University Press, 1986.

Gregg, Richard Bartlett. *The Power of Non-violence*. Philadelphia: J. B. Lippincott Company, 1934.

Lamson, Peggy. *Roger Baldwin, Founder of the American Civil Liberties Union: A Portrait*. Boston: Houghton Mifflin, 1976.

Lunardini, Christine A. *The ABC-CLIO Companion to the American Peace Movement in the Twentieth Century*. Denver, Colo.: ABC-CLIO, 1994.

Patterson, David S. *Toward a Warless World: The Travail of the American Peace Movement, 1887-1914*. Bloomington, Ind.: Indiana University Press, 1976.

Wink, Walter, ed. *Peace Is the Way: Writings on Nonviolence from the Fellowship of Reconciliation*. Maryknoll, N.Y.: Orbis Books, 2000.

Niebuhr and Muste

Fox, Richard Wightman. *Reinhold Niebuhr: A Biography*. New York: Pantheon Books, 1985.

Kegley, Charles W., ed. *Reinhold Niebuhr, His Religious, Social, and Political Thought*. 2nd ed. New York: Pilgrim Press, 1984.

Kleinman, Mark L. *A World of Hope, a World of Fear: Henry A. Wallace, Reinhold Niebuhr, and American Liberalism*. Columbus, Ohio: Ohio State University Press, 2000.

Lovin, Robin W. *Reinhold Niebuhr and Christian Realism*. New York: Cambridge University Press, 1995.

McKeogh, Colm. *The Political Realism of Reinhold Niebuhr: A Pragmatic Approach to Just War*. New York: St. Martin's Press, 1997.

Meyer, Donald. *The Protestant Search for Political Realism, 1919-1941*. 2nd ed. Middletown, Conn.: Wesleyan University Press, 1988.

Muste, Abraham John. *The Essays of A. J. Muste*. Edited by Nat Hentoff. Indianapolis, Ind.: Bobbs-Merrill Co., 1967.

———. *Non-Violence in an Aggressive World*. New York: Harper, 1972 [1940].

Niebuhr, Reinhold. *Moral Man and Immoral Society*. New York: Scribner, 1960 [1932].

———. *The Nature and Destiny of Man: A Christian Interpretation*. 2 vols. New York: C. Scribner's Sons, 1941-43.

Robinson, Jo Ann. *Abraham Went Out: A Biography of A. J. Muste*. Philadelphia: Temple University Press, 1981.

Gandhi

Bondurant, Joan V. *Conquest of Violence: The Gandhian Philosophy of Conflict*. Berkeley and Los Angeles: University of California Press, 1965.

Brown, Judith M. *Gandhi: Prisoner of Hope*. New Haven, Conn.: Yale University Press, 1989.

Chapple, Christopher. *Nonviolence to Animals, Earth, and Self in Asian Traditions*. Albany, N.Y.: State University of New York Press, 1993.

Chatterjee, Margaret. *Gandhi's Religious Thought*. Notre Dame, Ind.: University of Notre Dame Press, 1983.

Clement, Catherine. *Gandhi: The Power of Pacifism*. New York: Harry N. Abrams, 1996.

Dalton, Dennis. *Mahatma Gandhi: Nonviolent Power in Action*. New York: Columbia University Press, 1993.

Easwaran, Eknath. *Gandhi, the Man: The Story of His Transformation*. 3rd ed. Tomales, Calif.: Nilgiri Press, 1997.

Gandhi, Mohandas K. *Essential Writings*. Edited by John Dear. Maryknoll, N.Y.: Orbis Books, 2002.

———. *The Essential Writings of Mahatma Gandhi*. Edited by Rhagavan Iyer. Oxford: Oxford University Press, 1991.

———. *Mahatma Gandhi: Selected Political Writings*. Edited by Dennis Dalton. Indianapolis, Ind.: Hackett Publishing Co., 1996.

Iyer, Raghavan N. *The Moral and Political Thought of Mahatma Gandhi*. New York: Oxford University Press, 1973.

Kapur, Sudarshan. *Raising up a Prophet: The African-American Encounter with Gandhi*. Boston: Beacon Press, 1992.

King, Mary. *Mahatma Gandhi and Martin Luther King, Jr.: The Power of Nonviolent Action*. Paris: UNESCO Publishing, 1999.

Mehta, Ved. *Mahatma Gandhi and His Apostles*. New York: Viking Press, 1977.

Nanda, Bal Ram. *Gandhi and His Critics*. Delhi: Oxford University Press, 1985.

Parekh, Bhikhu C. *Colonialism, Tradition, and Reform: An Analysis of Gandhi's Political Discourse*. Newbury Park, Calif.: Sage Publications, 1989.

———. *Gandhi*. Oxford: Oxford University Press, 1997.

———. *Gandhi's Political Philosophy: A Critical Examination*. Notre Dame, Ind.: University of Notre Dame Press, 1989.

Puri, Rashmi-Sudha. *Gandhi on War and Peace*. New York: Praeger, 1987.

Rothermund, Indira Nalin. *The Philosophy of Restraint: Mahatma Gandhi's Strategy and Indian Politics*. New York: Humanities Press, 1963.

Rudolph, Susanne Hoeber, and Lloyd I. Rudolph. *Gandhi: The Traditional Roots of Charisma*. Chicago: University of Chicago Press, 1983.

Sandhu, Swaran S. *Nonviolence in Indian Religious Thought and Political Action*. Philadelphia: Dorrance, 1977.

Tahtinen, Unto. *Indian Traditional Values*. Atlantic Highlands, N.J.: Humanities Press, 1983.

Wolpert, Stanley A. *Gandhi's Passion: The Life and Legacy of Mahatma Gandhi*. New York: Oxford University Press, 2001.

Martin Luther King, Jr., and the Civil Rights Movement

Baldwin, Lewis V. *To Make the Wounded Whole: The Cultural Legacy of Martin Luther King, Jr.* Minneapolis: Fortress Press, 1992.

Baldwin, Lewis V., et al., *The Legacy of Martin Luther King, Jr.: The Boundaries of Law, Politics, and Religion*. Notre Dame, Ind.: University of Notre Dame Press, 2002.

Branch, Taylor. *Parting the Waters: America in the King Years, 1954-1963*. New York: Simon & Schuster, 1988.

———. *Pillar of Fire: America in the King Years, 1963-1965.* New York: Simon & Schuster, 1998.

Burns, Stewart. *To The Mountaintop: Martin Luther King Jr.'s Sacred Mission to Save America, 1955-1968.* New York: Harper San Francisco, 2004.

Cone, James H. *Martin and Malcolm and America: A Dream or a Nightmare?* Maryknoll, N.Y.: Orbis Books, 1991.

Downing, Frederick L. *To See the Promised Land: The Faith Pilgrimage of Martin Luther King, Jr.* Macon, Ga.: Mercer University Press, 1986.

Dyson, Michael Eric. *I May Not Get There with You: The True Martin Luther King, Jr.* New York: Free Press, 2000.

Erskine, Noel Leo. *King among the Theologians.* Cleveland, Ohio: Pilgrim Press, 1994.

Frady, Marshall. *Martin Luther King, Jr.* New York: Penguin Group, 2002.

Harding, Vincent. *Martin Luther King, the Inconvenient Hero.* Maryknoll, N.Y.: Orbis Books, 1996.

Ivory, Luther D. *Toward a Theology of Radical Involvement: The Theological Legacy of Martin Luther King, Jr.* Nashville, Tenn.: Abingdon Press, 1997.

King, Martin Luther, Jr. *A Testament of Hope: The Essential Writings of Martin Luther King, Jr.* Edited by James Melvin Washington. San Francisco: Harper & Row, 1986.

———. *I Have a Dream: Writings and Speeches That Changed the World.* Edited by James Melvin Washington. San Francisco: Harper San Francisco, 1992.

———. *The Autobiography of Martin Luther King, Jr.* Edited by Clayborne Carson. New York: Intellectual Properties Management, Inc., in association with Warner Books, 1998.

Moses, Greg. *Revolution of Conscience: Martin Luther King, Jr., and the Philosophy of Nonviolence.* New York: Guilford Press, 1997.

Sunnemark, Fredrik. *Ring Out Freedom!: The Voice of Martin Luther King, Jr. and the Making of the Civil Rights Movement.* Bloomington, Ind.: Indiana University Press, 2004.

Dorothy Day and the Catholic Worker Movement

Coles, Robert. *Dorothy Day: A Radical Devotion.* Reading, Mass.: Addison-Wesley Publishing Co., 1987.

Day, Dorothy. *By Little and by Little: The Selected Writings of Dorothy Day.* Edited by Robert Ellsberg. New York: Alfred A. Knopf, 1983.

Klejment, Anne, and Nancy L. Roberts, eds. *American Catholic Pacifism: The Influence of Dorothy Day and the Catholic Worker Movement.* Westport, Conn.: Praeger, 1996.

McNeal, Patricia F. *Harder than War: Catholic Peacemaking in Twentieth-Century America.* New Brunswick, N.J.: Rutgers University Press, 1992.

O'Connor, June. *The Moral Vision of Dorothy Day: A Feminist Perspective.* New York: Crossroad, 1991.

Piehl, Mel. *Breaking Bread: The Catholic Worker and the Origin of Catholic Radicalism in America.* Philadelphia: Temple University Press, 1982.

Riegle, Rosalie G., ed. *Dorothy Day: Portraits by Those Who Knew Her.* Maryknoll, N.Y.: Orbis Books, 2003.

Troester, Rosalie Riegle, ed. *Voices from the Catholic Worker.* Philadelphia: Temple University Press, 1993.

White Nonviolence in the Cold War Era

DeBenedetti, Charles. *An American Ordeal: The Antiwar Movement of the Vietnam Era.* Syracuse, N.Y.: Syracuse University Press, 1990.

Dellinger, David T. *From Yale to Jail: The Life Story of a Moral Dissenter.* New York: Pantheon Books, 1993.

———. *Revolutionary Nonviolence: Essays by Dave Dellinger.* Garden City, N.Y.: Anchor Books, 1971.

Deming, Barbara. *Remembering Who We Are: Barbara Deming, in Dialogue with Gwenda Blair et al.* Tallahassee, Fla.: Naiad Press, 1981.

———. *Revolution and Equilibrium.* New York: Grossman Publishers, 1971.

———. *Two Essays: On Anger; New Men, New Women: Some Thoughts on Nonviolence.* Philadelphia: New Society Publishers, 1982.

———. *We Are All Part of One Another: A Barbara Deming Reader.* Edited by Jane Meyerding. Philadelphia: New Society Publishers, 1984.

Finn, James, ed. *Protest: Pacifism and Politics; Some Passionate Views on War and Nonviolence.* New York: Random House, 1968.

Jeffreys-Jones, Rhodri. *Peace Now!: American Society and the Ending of the Vietnam War.* New Haven, Conn.: Yale University Press, 1999.

Lieberman, Robbie. *The Strangest Dream: Communism, Anticommunism, and the U.S. Peace Movement, 1945-1963.* Syracuse, N.Y.: Syracuse University Press, 2000.

McCarthy, Ronald M., and Gene Sharp. *Nonviolent Action: A Research Guide.* New York: Garland Publishing Co., 1997.

Merton, Thomas. *Passion for Peace: The Social Essays.* Edited by William H. Shannon. New York: Crossroad Publishing, 1995.

———. *Thomas Merton on Peace.* New York: McCall Pub. Co., 1971.

Sharp, Gene. *The Politics of Nonviolent Action.* 3 vols. Boston: P. Sargent Publisher, 1973.

Small, Melvin. *Antiwarriors: The Vietnam War and the Battle for America's Hearts and Minds.* Wilmington, Del.: Scholarly Resources, 2002.

Smith, E. Timothy. *Opposition beyond the Water's Edge: Liberal Internationalists, Pacifists, and Containment, 1945-1953.* Westport, Conn.: Greenwood Press, 1999.

Wink, Walter, ed. *Peace Is the Way: Writings on Nonviolence from the Fellowship of Reconciliation.* Maryknoll, N.Y.: Orbis Books, 2000.

Thich Nhat Hanh and Engaged Buddhism

Aung San Suu Kyi. *The Voice of Hope: Conversations with Alan Clements.* New York: Seven Stories Press, 1997.

Berrigan, Daniel, and Thich Nhat Hanh. *The Raft Is Not the Shore: Conversations toward a Buddhist/Christian Awareness.* Maryknoll, N.Y.: Orbis Books, 2001.

Cartier, Jean-Pierre, and Rachel Cartier. *Thich Nhat Hanh: The Joy of Full Consciousness.* Berkeley, Calif.: North Atlantic Books, 2002.

Fu, Charles Wei-hsun, and Sandra A. Wawrytko, eds. *Buddhist Ethics and Modern Society: An International Symposium.* New York: Greenwood Press, 1991.

Jones, Ken. *The New Social Face of Buddhism: A Call to Action.* Boston: Wisdom Publications, 2003.

———. *The Social Face of Buddhism: An Approach to Political and Social Activism.* London: Wisdom Publications, 1989.

Kalupahana, David J. *Ethics in Early Buddhism.* Honolulu: University of Hawaii Press, 1995.

Keown, Damien V., Charles S. Prebish, and Wayne R. Husted, eds. *Buddhism and Human Rights.* Richmond, Surrey: Curzon, 1998.

King, Robert Harlen. *Thomas Merton and Thich Nhat Hanh: Engaged Spirituality in an Age of Globalization.* New York: Continuum, 2001.

Kraft, Kenneth, ed. *Inner Peace, World Peace: Essays on Buddhism and Nonviolence.* Albany, N.Y.: State University of New York Press, 1992.

Queen, Christopher S., ed. *Engaged Buddhism in the West.* Boston, Mass.: Wisdom Publications, 2000.

Queen, Christopher S., and Sallie B. King, eds. *Engaged Buddhism: Buddhist Liberation Movements in Asia.* Albany, N.Y.: State University of New York Press, 1996.

Sivaraksa, Sulak. *Seeds of Peace: A Buddhist Vision for Renewing Society.* Berkeley, Calif.: Parallax Press, 1991.

Thich Nhat Hanh. *Being Peace.* Berkeley, Calif.: Parallax Press, 1988.

———. *Essential Writings.* Edited by Robert Ellsberg. Maryknoll, N.Y.: Orbis Books, 2001.

———. *Love in Action.* Berkeley, Calif.: Parallax Press, 1993.

———. *The Miracle of Mindfulness!: A Manual of Meditation.* Boston: Beacon Press, 1976.

Index

231